GOD, GAYS & THE CHURCH

HUMAN SEXUALITY AND EXPERIENCE IN CHRISTIAN THINKING

'I found out that God had always loved me as I was, but that he loved me too much to leave me that way.'

Alan Chambers, Exodus International

'Truth, like surgery, may hurt, but it cures.'

Han Suyin, Chinese writer & physician

EDITED BY LISA NOLLAND, CHRIS SUGDEN & SARAH FINCH

The Latimer Trust

ISBN 978-0-946307-93-7

January 2008

Published by the Latimer Trust
PO Box 26685
London N14 4XQ

www.latimertrust.org

Contents

CULTURAL ANALYSIS AND SOCIAL ETHICS

See also:
Homophobia: An Unfinished Story and **The Seeker**
Professor J. Budziszewski
The Books, the Porn, the Truth *Dr Ronald G. Lee*
Civil Partnerships – Advice to Parishes and Clergy
The Revd Paul Perkin and Mrs Christine Perkin

Foreword

The Rt Revd Michael Scott-Joynt, Bishop of Winchester

This book has been planned by people who were profoundly concerned, for the sake of the integrity of the Church of England and of its teaching, about the overall character of the two Debates that took place in the Church of England's General Synod on February 28th 2007. I have agreed to write this Foreword because I share their fundamental concerns; and because I deeply regret that I did not, and as the day wore on, express these concerns much more distinctly when I had an opportunity to speak.

What took place that day, it seemed to me, was a public advocating and vaunting of behaviour contrary to the teaching of the Church of England, expressed most recently by the House of Bishops in its "teaching document", *Marriage,* published in September 1999: "Sexual intercourse, as an expression of faithful intimacy, properly belongs within marriage exclusively". The three or four individuals who spoke in this way received widespread support and encouragement from many other speakers, for what was an alternative, revisionist teaching, contrary not only to the teaching of the Church of England, but also to that of the Church as a whole.

Our integrity, as a Church that is properly serious about doctrine and discipline, was gravely undermined – and this, in the presence of both the group of ecumenical representatives and the Press, and only days after the Primates of the Anglican Communion had issued a Communiqué, written with great clarity, following their meeting in Dar-es-Salaam.

The following morning, what had been happening on the previous day was powerfully expressed, for me as for a number of others, in the Synod's opening Prayers when we heard the Lectionary Reading from Jeremiah (6:16):

"Thus says the Lord: Stand at the cross-roads and look, and ask for the ancient paths, where the good way lies; and walk in it, and find rest for your souls.

But they said, 'We will not walk in it.'"

Implicitly but clearly, many speakers also had in their sights the paragraphs of *Issues in Human Sexuality,* the 1991 Statement of the House of Bishops, which advised that although people who judged it appropriate as Christians to live in same-sex relationships should be made welcome in parish churches, the Church could not affirm their life-style, still less consider them for ordination into its sacramental and teaching ministries. I continue to judge that this is advice and teaching that the Church of England should advocate and defend – just as we know that there are people in many of our churches who are living together but are not married, but do not accept such people as candidates for Reader ministry or for training for ordination. *Issues* ... had, I believe, both ways of living in view in its paragraph 5.13: "the world will assume that all ways of living which an ordained person is allowed to adopt are in Christian eyes equally valid".

And on February 28th, 2007 it was as if a fourth element, Experience, had been added to what is, for Anglicans, the classic trio of "authorities" (though these authorities always have differing claims upon our consent): Scripture, the Church down the centuries, and Intelligent Reflection. Often, in the course of the day, speakers not only appealed to Christians' "experience" and told their own or others' stories, but also did so as if these "trumped" the classic trio! With Christians in every century including our own, and in every part of the world, I should want to continue to say that every Christian is called to have her or his "experience" conformed to the teachings of Scripture, and then to those of the "great tradition" of the Church down the centuries as it has reflected upon Scripture intelligently and in the Spirit. So some of the essays that follow offer experience of the transforming power of the Gospel.

+Michael Winton:

Christ the King, 2007.

The Stage is Set

Dr Lisa Severine Nolland, Canon Dr Christopher Sugden and Sarah Finch

The debates on human sexuality have dominated the affairs of the Anglican Communion during the last few years. The subject has also been a matter of great concern within every major Christian denomination in the West. The orthodox Christian understanding of the purpose and proper enjoyment of human sexuality has now been challenged in unmistakeable ways, not only in the Western media and society at large, but also within the churches. And this is a radically new development: in the past, the questions that are now being raised, and the answers that are now being given, had not even been thought of or considered.

The Anglican Church has had to wrestle with this subject, whether it has liked it or not. The official Anglican policy has been that clergy with a homosexual orientation could only be ministers if they remained celibate. But some now say that new insights from the scientific and psychological worlds should bring about a radical re-evaluation. Now we are being told that being gay is like being heterosexual – that people are born this way – and that it is cruel and unjust to forbid them to enter into faithful, loving, committed same-sex partnerships.

The impact of this thinking on the Church of England has been immense. The Revd Colin Coward, the Director of Changing Attitude, the premier Anglican LGBT organization, insists that a thousand LGBT clergy are already officiating in the Church of England. How can there be such a dramatic discrepancy between the official policy and the claimed evidence? It is difficult to avoid the conclusion that, at least at certain levels, there has been a fairly significant collusion on the part of some leading figures. Moreover, others who have held the accepted historic line have done so with a defensive posture, wishing all the while that the problem would go away. Some have taken a more pragmatic view, arguing that it appears that the horse has already bolted, and thus there is no need to lock the stable. A very few leaders have been courageous enough to address this challenge in public. It is not surprising, therefore, that in the Church of England's House of Bishops there is a wide range of opinion.

It was on account of this diversity of opinion among the bishops that events transpired as they did at General Synod in February 2007. Often described as the Parliament of the Church of England, the General

Synod, consisting of all forty-four diocesan bishops, nine suffragan (i.e. local) bishops, and over 400 elected clergy and lay people, meets two or sometimes three times a year. The Agenda for February's meeting contained two Private Member's Motions which were coming up for debate because, in both cases, more than a hundred members had signed them. It is important to realize that, according to Standing Orders, nothing can stop a Private Member's Motion from being debated, once it has gained the necessary support. The House of Bishops may not be in favour, but nothing can be done.

The degree of support that has been obtained, by a Private Member's Motion that is going to be debated, is a matter of public knowledge; the number of signatures appears in the Agenda. But since it is impossible to tell *why* members of Synod have given their support, it is unwise to attempt to draw a conclusion as to the meaning of the strength of support. Some people may have wanted to see the topic of homosexuality properly debated once and for all; some may have been sympathetic in a general way towards the proposer of the motion, and others, of course, were determined to change the mind, and the teaching, of the Church of England. This determination was very clearly evident in many of the speeches in the debate. The fact is that, for the first Private Member's Motion, which called for the welcome and affirmation of lesbian and gay Christians, the number of signatures was **124**. The total membership of General Synod is 467, so this number of signatures represents **26.5%** of that total membership.

An outline of the ensuing debate, and also of the second Private Member's Motion debate, on Civil Partnerships, may be found at the Annex on page 247. The full transcripts of the debates may be found at www.cofe.anglican.org/about/gensynod/proceedings.

Because, in the debates, there were more pro-gay people called to speak than others, we were keenly aware that the other side of the argument never had a chance. This book is designed to put forward a number of the compelling arguments in support of traditional Biblical morality, many of which were not heard in the debates. The material is relevant for everyone interested in these issues, wherever they are and whatever they believe.

Prologue

Dr Lisa Nolland and Canon Dr Christopher Sugden

The public debates that are prompted by the activist gay lobby are currently set in the context of 'This is my experience', whether in the General Synod of the Church of England (February 2007) or the Oxford Union (October 2007). Christians are encouraged to give their witness and testimony, and are used to doing so, but this has always been on the basis of witness to the faith once delivered to the saints, and the truth of the gospel as revealed in Jesus Christ and the Bible. A new strand is being developed by the activist gay lobby. Their arguments start from a privileged concept of 'experience' as ultimate and unquestionable interpreter and arbitrator: 'This is my experience. On it I base *my* understanding of truth, and you gravely offend me if you suggest that this is anything other than what I describe, an experience of the love and compassion of God.'

It is very hard, in public debate, to contradict this line of argument successfully. The reason is that listeners are normally ready with sympathy, and do not like seeing people being victimized or embarrassed in public. And it is especially hard to contradict this line of argument when there is no one present whose experience of homosexual practice and lifestyle is the opposite of this. In such debates, people with the opposite experience are usually absent; they may even have been excluded.

In the interests of enabling people to have the whole picture, we have brought into the discussion, in this book, the testimony and experience of people who would contradict the claims of the activist gay lobby, and who also seek to make their testimony a witness to the power of the love of God in the gospel, as revealed in the scriptures, as opposed to making their experience a reason for rewriting the gospel or discarding the scriptures.

While this book was prompted by the challenge of the Church of England's debate, the issues it addresses are not limited to that debate. That debate, and the points that were raised within it, are cited in order to give specificity to what is nowadays being encountered as a regular line of argument.

In the debate in the General Synod of the Church of England, on the morning of Wednesday 28 February 2007, concerning Gay and Lesbian Christians, the Archbishop of Canterbury focused on the heart of the matter in his intervention. He argued that Synod did not want 'to be rejecting outright any statement of this Synod's commitment to listening, to compassion, to creating a safe space.' Therefore he proposed the acceptance of an amendment that welcomed Gay and Lesbian Christians as full members of the Church. (The amendment was to insert the wording that this Synod 'welcome the opportunities offered by these Lambeth resolutions, including for the Church of England to engage in an open, full and godly dialogue about human sexuality', and 'and acknowledge the importance of lesbian and gay members of the Church of England participating in the Listening Process as full members of the Church of England.') But what is the nature and ultimate purpose of listening? What are we actually to do, once we have listened? And what is the definition of 'safety'?

I.   *A safe place*

The Church, whether the word refers to the community of God's people or to a building, should be a safe place. But what is the definition of safety here? We are indeed safe in the love, mercy and protection of God; and we must be able to be safe with each other, as well. The American therapist, Janelle Hallman, describes 'safety' in psychotherapeutic terms which should resonate – but often do not – with what we experience in the company of fellow Christians in the context of the local church:

> A safe place provides emotional and physical protection. A safe place has a sense of fullness, not emptiness. A safe place offers care and containment. A safe place is constant, without shocking surprises. A safe place promotes respect. A safe place is warm and relaxing. A safe place is where you are known and accepted. A safe place creates trust. A safe place may become home to the homeless. A safe place allows you to feel and talk. A safe place allows you to be yourself. A safe place is where you can grow and develop.[1]

But safety on its own is just the start. Safety provides the much-needed environment in which our journey to God, to wholeness and holiness, can occur. Within this context, then, we are able to do what we must do: take stock, be psychologically and spiritually honest, and attend willingly to our own 'issues' – our sins of omission and commission, and our weaknesses,

---

[1] Janelle M. Hallman, 'Helping Women with Same-Sex Attraction'; http://narth.com/docs/hallman.pdf

failings and blind-spots. We are not shielded from the requirements of God's holiness and the results of his judgement: we are enabled to meet them. Lest we should forget these requirements, there is a visual reminder of them in many Anglican churches, where the Ten Commandments are inscribed on the wall behind the communion table. Holiness is requisite for living in God's presence and by his power.

In the Church, those with same-sex attraction (SSA) should be completely free from fear of violence or rejection, as should everyone, regardless of his or her struggles and regardless of the nature of those struggles. Jesus offered people safety from those who would publicly attack them – 'Neither do I condemn you,' he said to the woman caught in adultery. But he also said to her, 'Go, and from now on sin no more.' (John 8:11). The church is radically inclusive: everyone is wanted, everyone is welcomed, but no one is allowed to remain the same. God loves us too much to leave us as we are. As John Newton, the former slave trader, put it so well: 'I am not what I ought to be, I am not what I want to be, I am not what I hope to be in another world; but still I am not what I once used to be, and by the grace of God I am what I am.'

2.   *Who they are*

Much of the argumentation of Wednesday's debate was based on the need, on the part of those who have embraced a gay identity and lifestyle, because that is integral to who they are as people, to be authentic and transparent, and to be publicly known, accepted and affirmed as gay, or partnered gay, Christian sisters and brothers.[2]

This call must be taken seriously – and those who have brought this

---

[2] In this context and for the purposes of this article we deploy their language of self-identification and designation; moreover, we will use 'gay' as shorthand for all gay, lesbian, bi-sexual and trans-gender (GLBT) folk. The traditional Christian belief is that the expression 'gay Christianity' is a radical contradiction in terms. According to Professor Robert Gagnon, 'A "gay man" or "lesbian woman" who calls him- or herself a Christian while engaging in serial, unrepentant, and self-affirmed homosexual activity could be "considered" a Christian who is at risk of not inheriting eternal life. There is an elementary distinction here between being and behavior, where a Christian engages in behavior that is not Christian.' From 'Can One Be a "Gay Evangelical"? My answer to a *New York Times* reporter and how she reported it', 16 December 2006;
http://www.robgagnon.net/GayEvangelicalNewYorkTimes.htm

book to birth endeavour to take it seriously. We have invested in attending to and engaging with the actual life experiences of gay Christians. However, we realise that often we are told only part of the story, and only part of *their* story. We believe that all of us – gay, straight, bi-sexual, or whatever – need to have a full briefing and access to all the pertinent facts, not just those to do with sexuality, but also the ones to do with a person's well-being, health and life-expectancy. This, too, is part of being honest.

The question of what constitutes personhood comes to the fore here. Is it constituted by a person's sexuality, a sexuality which is innate and immutable? For many speakers in the debate, the presupposition which determined the outcome was that gay people's sexuality was a 'given', a part of their being, over which they had no control. Mary Gilbert said as much: 'The fact that someone has a homosexual orientation, about which they have as much choice as I do about my gender ....' This is a fundamental assumption on which much of the case is built, and for which there is no scientific evidence. Dr Neil Whitehead engages with this issue in his article, *Same Sex Attraction (SSA): Is it innate, and immutable?* In *How Might Homosexuality Develop? Putting the Pieces Together*, Dr Jeffrey Satinover describes a SSA trajectory, aspects of which are commonly shared, and which he has encountered over years of working with SSA strugglers.

3.   *The timing is not right*

In the Synod debate, much was made of the argument this was neither the time nor the place for such a debate, or for such decisions. According to the Bishop of Gloucester, 'There are better moments and worse moments to face an issue where we have no consensus. In the light of the Primates' meeting, I believe this to be one of those worse moments. Does the Synod want an outcome that will be perceived, perhaps misperceived, in the Anglican Communion as the Church of England shifting its ground in one direction or another?'

Whenever it is presented, this argument is vulnerable to the question: 'When then *is* the right time? Justice delayed is justice denied.' It is a pragmatic argument – made at a safe distance and with apparently little at stake. And as such it fails to acknowledge that this is a pressing matter which cuts to the quick for many gay Christians and their allies. For them, it is a deep issue of social and moral justice and one which must be faced now. Not to do so simply perpetuates bigotry, pain and oppression, and is indefensible. We concur, though for very different reasons. Ignoring this 'elephant in the room' simply puts off the inevitable; it is actually unhelpful and irresponsible, continuing a 'lose-lose' situation for all, if not in the short term, then certainly in the long.

4. Listening and dialogue

There were calls for listening and open-minded, open-ended, transparent dialogue. Such listening and dialogue was claimed by the Revd Mary Gilbert to be 'only worthwhile if we allow the possibility of change. We need to acknowledge that an open and honest dialogue, that listening to the voices and experiences of gay and lesbian members of our church, may lead to change ... without a sense that the outcome is already decided.'

In the debate we were asked to be willing to listen to and empathize with gay voices and narrative; we were also asked *not* to evaluate whether homosexuality was morally right, wrong or indeterminate. In fact, however, these two requests are intimately correlated and they were deployed in a brilliantly psychological way. The former softened us up and conditioned us to accept the latter – or, at least, to find it very difficult not to accept it, publicly. The terminus was one of gay domination of the high moral ground, with undecided people in the middle simply getting tired of all the bickering and wanting to move on. Perhaps it should not have surprised us, therefore, that in the ensuing dialogue on this issue, options that had hitherto been thought of as illegitimate or unacceptable were now being seen as available, permissible and even laudable: this was Blue Sky Thinking at its best.[3]

Of course it was a set-up. It had already been determined for us that gay sex was morally unproblematic, hence the possibility of this debate occurring in the first place. No one 'debates' in an open-minded, open-ended manner issues which are truly considered beyond the pale or utterly, irredeemably unacceptable by the collective (e.g. 'This house affirms consensual cannibalism', say – and as this phenomenon occurred recently in Germany the topic is not irrelevant). Or if they do, it is solely upon the basis of correcting the fallacy, righting the wrong. Were gay Christians and their allies willing to change their lifestyles, their behaviour or their views in the light of the biblical and Christian witness? We think not – in fact, it was

---

[3] The two Wednesday debates were placed on the agenda through the means of a Private Member's Motion. Each member of Synod has the right to suggest a motion for debate. Such motions are set out on paper and Synod members are invited to sign up to those they wish to see debated. If a motion receives 100 signatures, it is then debated by the whole Synod.

quite the opposite. Those whose fallacies seemed to stand in greatest need of correction were the erring orthodox. 'Not Listening' (in this particular way to this particular side of the debate) raised serious questions as to whether we were following the gospel values of love, compassion and grace.

What was odd, however, was how only certain voices, representing certain moral and theological positions, received the lion's share of the Listening Time. Why the narrow, non-inclusive selection? We were encouraged to believe that engaging in the Listening Process would mean connecting with a local Changing Attitude group! What about all those other Christian organizations which help SSA people? In one speech reference was made to the testimony of a man who, through the power of Christ and Christian fellowship, had moved beyond SSA to heterosexual marriage. And, the evening before the debate, a fringe meeting had been held in Church House at which two people, who had been caught up in the gay world, one for many years, gave their testimonies. They told how they had been changed and empowered by Jesus Christ to live new and better lives. Their narratives and others like them are part of this book. But these testimonies were not the experiences that we were being urged to listen to, or were even being allowed to hear! Those calling for an 'open' dialogue were in fact calling for a one-sided dialogue, and a censored one at that (see below).

There are many sources for post-gay testimonies on the websites of Living Waters, Redeemed Lives, Exodus International, Zacchaeus Trust and NARTH.

In the debate Dr Philip Giddings spoke of his concern that, in the amended amendment, 'Listening' was actually a one-way journey to a pre-determined, non-negotiable destination. There was never any *real* doubt about 'outcome' now, was there?

One final comment on the Listening Process, concerning those we were allowed to listen to – and those who were given a miss: why did we hear no voices representing the Christian bisexual and transgender communities? What happened to them? Changing Attitude is unequivocal in its public support for, and inclusion of, folk with these self-identities and lifestyles. And yet they were hidden from view, silent – or silenced.

Perhaps it has to do with Synodical readiness. Though the presently-emerging transgender community can appear more 'traditional' in a certain sense, their peers in the bisexual community actually give the game away. Though some 'bis' have sequential relationships with people of one sex and then the other, others need, want and publicly embrace relationships with both sexes simultaneously. They are *not* mono-sexual, i.e. relating to either the same sex or the other sex in a full-orbed emotional, psychological and sexual way. The assumptions undergirding a Noah's Ark (two-by-two) relational paradigm are unhelpful, irrelevant and possibly offensive. But these assumptions also are too radical for consideration for many at this stage – hence their elision.

A comparison of sorts might make things clearer. Adultery is still considered immoral, wrong or sinful (by most), but it would be possible for us to engage in a proper Listening Process in relation to it. However, it would operate with a completely different inner dynamic, and potential outcome too. A Christian dialogue on this traumatic subject could be very profitable in terms of listening to people who have committed adultery or who have suffered from its effects. We could better understand and empathize with what leads people to make such choices and engage in such behaviour, and understand also the impact that adultery has had, subsequently, upon themselves, their spouses and their families. However, an open, frank dialogue in Christian terms would not be undermined if it were framed by the conviction that adultery is essentially, categorically, always wrong. This framing was completely absent from Gay Wednesday's debate.

5.   *The lifestyle being commended*

'The motion is asking for an acceptance that lesbian and gay Christians seek to follow patterns of holy living: lives which exhibit fidelity, commitment, self-sacrifice and which are mutually life-giving.'

But what is the precise nature of this fidelity and commitment? Members of Synod spoke of same-sex partnerships of 30 years and 11 years. In common parlance 'fidelity' can actually be understood and interpreted in different ways: the word, like many others, has changed. In the gay community, 'monogamy' currently means being in an emotionally committed relationship with one partner, but not automatically, necessarily, a sexually exclusive relationship. When terms like 'committed', 'faithful', 'loving', 'stable' and so on are deployed in gay apologetic, heterosexuals assume that what they keep 'hearing' about must mean sexual exclusivity. It is a natural enough assumption but it is a falsely-based one, nevertheless, and possibly quite inaccurate.

Research by Drs Paul and Kirk Cameron describes other aspects of alternative sexual lifestyles which are mostly ignored or evaded. In the following paragraphs from their report, 'Federal Distortion of the Homosexual Footprint', figures are given which, we realize, are hotly contested. However, we feel that this research needs to be included as part of the discussion.

Non-reporting, or Exaggeration, of Homosexual Prevalence. By ignoring the paucity of older homosexuals, Federal bureaucracies in three countries have exaggerated the size of the homosexual footprint. In 2003, Statistics Canada reported on a random sample of 121,300 adults, reporting that 1.7% were bi/homosexual. [It should be noted that the adults reported on were all under the age of 60.] Because of a decline in incidence from about 2% of adults aged in their 20s and 30s to a third of one percent among the old, the inclusion of respondents aged 60+ yields a revised estimate of 1.4%. [These findings come from the authors' previous research.] In 2005, the U.S. National Center for Health Statistics interviewed a random sample of 11,571 younger adults, but misreported the findings to indicate more frequent same-sex sexual experience. In 2005, the British Department of Trade and Industry said "a wide range of research" indicated "lesbian, gay and bisexual people constitute 5-7% of the total adult population." Yet surveys which included adults of all ages put the prevalence closer to 1-2%. Curious mistakes and omissions for well-funded bureaucracies charged with 'reporting the truth.'

Link to Early Death. Exclusion of older adults increases the reported size of the homosexual footprint, and also tends to obscure the apparent early death of those engaging in homosexuality. Median ages of death in 'gay marriage' for 561 gays and 91 lesbians in Denmark (1990–2002) and 31 gays and 6 lesbians in Norway (1997–2002) were similar to U.S. gay obituaries during the same period: 52 yr. for 710 gays who ostensibly did not die of AIDS, 42 yr. for those 1,476 who supposedly did; and 55 yr. for 143 lesbians. [It should be noted that the U.S. statistics are based on obituaries where a gay lifestyle is reported. The incidence is probably higher.] On average, ever-married men outlived the ever-homosexually-partnered by 23 years in Denmark (74 yr. v. 51 yr.), and 25 years in Norway (77 yr. v. 52 yr.); ever-married women outlived the ever-homosexually-partnered in Denmark by 22 years (78 yr. v. 56 yr.), and in Norway by almost 25 years (81 yr. v. 56 yr.).

Implications. By not sampling (U.S., Britain) or reporting on (Canada) those aged 60+, the objectivity of central bureaucracies is called into question. That the ~2% of adults who engage in homosexuality have life spans at least 20 years shorter than the general adult population, in countries contributing relevant data has implications for social policy: e.g., 'gay rights' (the decrement in the gay lifespan appears similar in societies that legally protect homosexuals or don't, suggesting that 'discrimination' does not cause their earlier death); gay marriage (which unlike man-woman marriage appears not to increase longevity); adoption (children of homosexuals are more frequently orphaned); favorable depiction of the homosexual lifestyle in schools (which is inconsistent with condemning the lesser harm of smoking); special protections for those who engage in homosexuality (why not also protect others whose sexual choices — such as polygamy or adultery — cause disruption and extra costs?); and equitable allocation of social resources (why spend excessively on HIV when cancer, heart disease, etc. afflict many more citizens?).[4]

Interesting corroboration for the above comes from the Vancouver research of Robert Hogg *et al*, 'HIV infection and risk behaviours among young gay and bisexual men in Vancouver', published in the *Canadian Medical Association Journal* in January 2000.

Concerning the incidence of homosexuality, it is often argued that homosexuality is a normal facet of human behaviour, since it is so widespread and prevalent amongst both men and women. However, research over the last two decades has very clearly shown that the ten percent figure initially proposed by Kinsey for the incidence of homosexuality among the adult population is a gross over-exaggeration. The best research is a rate of between 2 and 3 per cent, varying not just by country, but also by region.[5]

These figures of 2 to 3% disguise a further subtlety in sexual indentification. Often the research will include all those who report any form of homosexual activity in the past five years, rather than those who deliberately self-identify as gay. A significant number of men and women would tick the box on homosexual activity without necessarily counting themselves as homosexual. Furthermore, large numbers of men and women who may have in the past engaged in homosexual activity no longer do so and, conversely, some adults take up homosexual activity later in life.

---

[4] http://www.anglican-mainstream.net/wp-content/uploads/2007/04/EPA_2007_Homo_Footprint_032107.pdf
[5] See further here: http://www.catholiceducation.org/articles/homosexuality/h00095.html.

Therefore, the use of the 10% figure by some activists, together with idea of 'once gay always gay', is a form of identity politics that is challenged by the reality of much lower figures for the incidence of homosexuality, and the evidence that large numbers of men and women express different sexual preferences over their lifetime. The 10% figure is a form of mis-information which should be gently but firmly questioned in order for the debate around homosexuality to be carried out on the basis of truth about prevalence.

Dr Ronald Lee's *The Books, The Porn, The Truth* describes his two-decade search for the man of his dreams and, in the process, brings to light some of the (mostly invisible) aspects of dominant gay culture. Dr Lisa Nolland's *Gay Wednesday's Gay Pain* and *Unexpected Consequences: The Sexualization of Youth* argue for uncensored truth-telling about the physical realities of same-sex lifestyles and also the terminus for this sexual revolution. The appendix *Gay health, sex and culture* is also relevant here. More information is available on www.narth.com

6.   Poisoning the wells

The Rev Mary Bide referred to two spinster teachers who had been formative in her early years at school. They shared the same house. The speaker suggested that it may well have been that these two teachers were lesbians.

> Many years ago, when I was at primary school, the school was run by Miss Bell and Miss Lemon, two wonderful ladies who shared the administration of the school and also shared their home together. Nobody enquired into the nature of their relationship; it was not deemed relevant to their ability to run the school. They were fantastic teachers and they nurtured me in my Christian faith. I wonder what would happen today? Would we be questioning whether they were appropriate people to have the care of small children? What if either of them had actually wanted to become ordained? Would we be delving into what they did in the bedroom?

It is tragic that neither Miss Bell nor Miss Lemon was alive and present to defend herself. Ms Bide is in a rigid, radically-defined time warp – a contemporary one – which assumes that because two single women shared a house they probably also shared a bed and a sex life and, more to the point, that this shared sex life was morally neutral or positive. We would argue that this is public defamation of character: to suggest that these women – who gave their lives to the work of educating children and were, in all probability, exemplary in their personal lives – were lesbians simply because they lived together, is totally unjust. Moreover, given the cultural domination of the gay agenda today, if a currently-alive heterosexual Miss Bell wished to live with her dear also-heterosexual friend, Miss Lemon, she may well choose not to, given the sexualized nature of many 'domestic relationships' in public perception now. Single heterosexual friends tell me that this is their present experience (and are we listening to them, we wonder?). The new public freedom to couple domestically for gays has meant a significant curtailment in the freedom of unmarried heterosexual women and men to share a home and a life with a same-sex friend. What is even more disconcerting, however, is Ms Bide's utter inability to see that if her lesbian scenario *is* correct, it is morally problematic. The same applies to the frank admission by another Synod member, a female, that she had lived with her boyfriend for six years before marriage. Lovely lesbian schoolteachers and a cohabiting heterosexual couple were portrayed as mere variations on the theme of 'normal'.

7. The silence of the bishops

Seven bishops contributed to the debates: the Archbishop of Canterbury, and the Bishops of Worcester, Guildford, Liverpool, Gloucester, Lincoln and Winchester. Apart from the Bishop of Winchester, who ran out of time, not one bishop stood to commend the health and wholesomeness of the traditional Christian and Anglican teaching on marriage which was being publicly disavowed in many of the Synod speeches. It was later argued by some bishops that the amendments spoke for them. However, in the debate three bishops had pushed a revisionist agenda in terms of these motions. Given such a development, why the ominous silence from the rest of the bishops? As the gay advocates, Marshall Kirk and Hunter Madsen, rightly (though in a very different context) remind us, 'what you don't condemn, you condone, and for what you condone, you're responsible'.[6]

8. Welcome, inclusion and affirmation

The language of the motion speaks of the welcome of gays and lesbians as full members of the Church. This welcome is being taken to include

---

[6] Marshall Kirk and Hunter Madsen, *After the Ball: How America Will Conquer Its Fear and Hatred of Gays in the 90s* (Doubleday, 1989), p. 358.

welcome to all the sacraments (including marriage for those who regard it as a sacrament) and offices. In his Foreword to this book, the Bishop of Winchester writes on the difference between welcome, which is given to all who come to hear the Gospel – which is good news for all of us as sinners – and affirmation.

The point is often made that there are numerous daily examples of sin among church members. Even if homosexual practice *is* regarded as a sin, why decide that this one sinful behaviour is a reason for parting company, breaking fellowship, splitting the Church? The difference is that openly-embraced and -affirmed homosexual practice is being publicly presented as compatible with a relationship blessed by God, and with a vocation to serve in the ordained ministry. While Christians may engage in countless other sinful practices – and no doubt do! – those practices are not being claimed as being honoured and blessed by God, or as being examples of holy living. As an instance of this public presentation of compatibility, we are thinking of the claim, made by Mary Bide, that people in persistent homosexual practice could be models and examples, helping others into a full, open and honest relationship with God:

> 'We need to ask ourselves what it is we need in the Church. Surely we need people, both lay and ordained, who can help others into a full, open and honest relationship with God. Who better to do that than those people, gay and lesbian Christians, who have struggled with their own sense of identity, often in the face of a hostile society and a hostile Church, and yet who have found their lives and their relationships blessed by God.'

9.   The testimony of Scripture

Professor Anthony Thiselton stressed that homosexuality, in the sense of same-sex erotic relationships, was indeed known to the scriptural writers: 'There is plenty of evidence that male-to-male relationships defined identity in some writings in the ancient world; that they involve affection and not exploitation.' A number of speakers shared his concern that the background paper on the scriptures (circulated to all members of Synod) was not only woefully inadequate, but also that it actually exposed clearly the assumptions beneath the ambiguous wording of the motion. However, the criticism was shrugged off. Instead, we were informed that 'many of us are travelling the same biblical journeys: we are arriving at different destinations. We need to be talking robustly to each other, and we have started that this morning.' It seemed to be quite acceptable to some, therefore, to live in complete disagreement with what the scriptures, by all tenets of scholarship and study over centuries, have been united on. As Lord (Richard) Harries, a passionate advocate of the full inclusion of lesbians and gays in the life of the Church, has acknowledged, if the Church of England is to change its view on homosexuality it will first have to change its view of scripture. This is the first step in the process.

In *A Faithful Church: The Bible and Same-Sex Sex*, Professor Robert A. J. Gagnon handles hermeneutic issues arising from the biblical materials, and Professor Edith M. Humphrey argues that women's ordination is not in the same theological or biblical category as gay rights, in *'One of These Things is Not Like the Others': Women's Ordination, Homoeroticism and Faithfulness.*

10. Horror stories and false alternatives

A number of horror stories, about the physical and verbal mistreatment that some lesbians and gays have suffered, were brought together in the debate. These events are indeed deplorable, and we stand fully against such treatment of any individual, for whatever reason! But, in connection with these stories, the case is then made that the only alternative is a full welcome and affirmation for lesbians and gays on their terms: the assumption is made that anyone who opposes the full inclusion of lesbians and gays in the Church, on *their* terms, must be identified in some way with the perpetrators of this outrageous behaviour, or be validating it. 'Where your words are equivocal you do pander to this behaviour,' said John Ward, one of the speakers in the debate who also moved an amendment. This is not just. There are numerous Christian ministries, fully and actively supported by orthodox Christians, which provide specialist help and counsel for those struggling with SSA.

In Church House that morning, the only options being offered in the Listening Process were, either to accept lesbians and gays on their terms or, if one was unable or unwilling to do so, to be recognized as actively aiding and abetting their oppressors.

11. The missionary strategy

The Revd Simon Butler argued: 'Lesbian and gay people find it very hard to hear the good news, because that message is drowned out by moral questions concerning sex. As a missionary strategy, I believe this is full of shortcomings. It is, theologically, the saving experience of God's love that precedes sanctification. It is not sanctification that qualifies you to receive the love of Jesus.'

However, there is no such thing as a general, generic Gospel. In the scripture the Gospel is defined as Good News to the Poor, and applied with specific requirements for specific people groups and individuals. What might a universal Gospel look like? And whose criteria of universality would define it?

The gay person wants the Gospel to relate to her or him as a gay person, with her or his gayness being accepted. Simon Butler appears to believe that a universal Gospel will be so powerful that it will be transformative. But the gay person wants to be addressed in her or his identity as a gay person, as if being gay were first and foremost in their identity, and as though their sexual practices – i.e. gay sex – were irrelevant.

What makes this a first order issue is that in this the gay person is redefining for herself or himself what the Bible unequivocally declares to be 'sin', by saying that in this respect the Bible does not apply to her or him. And yet the sin which damages and destroys, the sin which must be repented of and for which Christ died, and the nature, therefore, of what he redeems gay people from, and for – these are all, *sine qua non*, first order issues.

Would Paul have said to the Jew that there is no need to repent of her or his Jewish pride and disdain of Gentiles? Or that she or he may enter into the Christian community with all those aspects of Jewish identity intact?

The call of the Gospel is to repent, to believe and to allow God into one's life – to dissolve, rebuild, renew, and transform.

12.   *These opinions are held in faith, with honesty and integrity*

This sort of claim was made by a number of speakers. But opinions held in faith, with honesty and integrity, remain personal opinions, however honestly and sincerely they may be held. And just because something is sincerely held, it does not mean that it is true! People have been sincerely wrong about all sorts of issues in the past. The Christian faith is based upon the revelation of God, as it has been received and understood by the Church down the ages.

Moreover, many of these opinions seem to be held upon the basis of knowing a lovely, obviously-good-for-each-other lesbian or gay couple – or perhaps more than one. This, then, leads to questioning the traditional biblical view – 'How can it be wrong when it seems so right?' – and moves on into a grey, 'no-easy-answers' ambiguity. So much dust has been thrown into the air, now, that seeing anything clearly can be difficult, especially when it is so much easier not to. For most of us, of course, the crux of the issue is that we want to be seen as Mr or Mrs Nice. Who wants to disapprove of another's (perhaps) hard-won happiness? In the final analysis, this positive experience determines the moral, theological and cultural outcome of the argument. This experience, of course, is only a very partial exposure to the issue in its entirety, but it does the trick. It convinces.

We are reminded of a rather exasperated comment from the marriage advocate, David Blankenhorn, about the well-intentioned *gay* marriage advocate, Jonathan Rauch, who honestly believes that gay marriage will be good for gays, straights, society and even for the institution of marriage, and argues the case at length and with passion.

> [Jonathan Rauch] can create and sustain his dream for the future only by writing as if he lived today in a dream world where the only thing that matters is his own logic, his own personal vision of the future. He gets around huge bodies of disconfirming evidence simply by ignoring them.[7]

Included in this volume, therefore, is evidence which the committed lesbian or gay couple will probably *not* be sharing with their sympathetic heterosexual friends. Indeed, they might not even be aware of it. See Professor J Budziszewski's articles, *Homophobia: An Unfinished Story* and *The Seeker*. See also, in this connection, Dr Lee's previously mentioned article, and the appendices, *Why children need mothers and fathers*, *Culture war casualties* and, perhaps most importantly, *Winning through the media: A strategy that has worked*.

13. People who have tried to change

Reference was made by the Revd Hugh Lee to 'those many gay and lesbian people who have tried to change their sexuality because the Church has told them that they should do, and who have been really hurt and have found that that was not God's will for them.'

There are two problems with this statement. The first is the notion that in this matter God's will is person-and-context specific, allowing for

---

[7] David Blankenhorn, *The Future of Marriage* (Encounter, 2007), p. 130.

diametrically-opposite moral terminations. Does the Almighty say to this married man that his will for him allows for sexual straying and betrayal, but to that married man that it does not? God's will does not operate in this mode. The second problem relates to the 'walking wounded'. Most of us – if we are honest – must deal with compulsions, addictions and various sorts of psychological brokenness. We may have tried valiantly to 'mend' them, but in vain. SSA is just one of many burdens that people carry. It may well be the case that, in some people's lives, issues were not addressed at the right time, or in the right way, or with the necessary expertise. However, simply citing failed cases of 'cure' is no proof that the diagnosis is wrong! The Revd Peter Ould and James Parker, who spoke in the Synod fringe meeting mentioned above, and others, give testimony to their very real experience of change. For a psychiatric assessment of 'failed cures', see Dr Joseph Nicolosi's *What If I Don't Change?* and compare his *Post-Gay: Understanding SSA As A 'Signal'*.

Some of us will know well the complaints made by 'ex-ex-gays' who are disillusioned, embittered and even deeply angered by the lack of success of their 'treatment'. These are profoundly painful issues and there are no easy answers. However, some appallingly naïve and home-grown forms of treatment have been circulated and promoted, and these, after their inevitable failure, have caused the individuals involved to rubbish the whole concept of Reparative Therapy. This is completely understandable, but also, completely unfair: the real thing had never been given a chance.

There is another important aspect that should be considered as well. Many resources are presently expended on assisting those addicted to drugs and alcohol and those contemplating suicide. Recently the government admitted that its drug rehabilitation programme had enabled only a tiny fraction of drug users to kick their habit entirely in the last year.[8] The National Treatment Agency's apparent 'success' rates are modest indeed, while those of, say, Alcoholics Anonymous or the Samaritans, might be somewhat higher, but by no means 100%. Do we then assert that all these programmes are worthless and should be

---

[8] According to a recent article in *The Independent*, 'The Big Question: Are drug treatment programmes a waste of taxpayers' money?', only 3% of participants are 'completely drug free' after treatment. Given the apparently intractable nature of 'addiction' for so many, some claim that drugs should be legalized. Others, of course, disagree and argue for even tougher policies to be taken by the state, congruent with providing help for those desirous of change. What is indisputable is that all this costs the British taxpayer literally millions of pounds; for many people drug dependency remains a life-long issue.
http://news.independent.co.uk/health/article3112796.ece

curtailed? No, we don't. We seek to improve the operation of the programmes, so that they can help more people reach greater levels of wholeness and well-being, and we also encourage those who struggle to have another 'go', to get a different mode of help, perhaps – but not to abandon the quest.

To enable people to understand what is exactly involved with Reparative Therapy, we are including Dr Nicolosi's technical, but psychologically illuminating, *'The Primacy of Affect': A Psychotherapeutic Approach.* To enable people to understand what is involved in the journey to inner healing, we are also including the Revd Mario Bergner's *Pastoral Considerations For Homosexuality.* This article was submitted as a contribution to the Listening Process in August 2007.

14. The secular setting of religious belief and practice in the Church of England

Secularity changes the conditions for belief. Belief in God is challenged, viewed with suspicion or derision, or regarded as only one option among many.

What is actually under attack is any order imposed on the world by rationality or by an external authority. Such an imposition is seen as stifling human creativity and action, and limiting our 'fun'. So what is posited is an immanent order, arising out of the world, rather than a transcendent order to which the world aspires and for which it is destined. Instead of having a heavenly order, which could be expressed in creation, we have simply a human order produced by human reason. This began when grace and nature were separated. If creation plays by its own rules, why do we need God? So the world got 'disenchanted', spiritually disinherited. Science now provides the tools to discover the self-sufficient immanent order. I do not need God to intervene for me – even if he could manage it. The universe is emptied of his presence. What counts is nature. What counts is now.

What is the condition of human life? Jesus said he had come to enable people to have fullness of life, not in the next world but in this one. But is this plausible? Can we, do we, actually believe it? This is the crux of the issue: the possibility of transformation. It is at the heart of the struggle with secularity. Can the world, can people, can even we as Christians, be changed, transformed, in radical, fundamental, essential ways? Secularity thinks not.

Secularity encourages us to discover authentic human life and to locate our real fulfilment within ourselves. It's the best we can do, after all! The Christian calling is to find and fulfil something higher: God's will – and by so doing, we lose our old diseased self and find our real true self.

In this secular context religions compose and express themselves in different ways. The focus is on our experience, authenticity and 'process', not on what is viewed in terms of archaic religious institutions, fixed doctrinal formulations and moral abstractions. Quest and submission are the two drives. The focus of religion is passionate, personal and on the inside and must be expressed out – this is the result of secularity.

So, in the Synod debate we were seeing the way in which secularity was determining the conditions for the articulation and communication of religious belief. The religious focus was on experience, authenticity and transparency: it was alive, fluid, spontaneous, on the cusp. The drive was to express an inner religious journey as opposed to an aspiration to find and fulfil God's will. Since, supposedly, nature cannot be transformed, our best efforts must be 'damage containment' and management of the inevitable expression of what it is claimed people have no choice over – namely their sexual orientation. This, it was argued, must be provided in civil partnerships and also in equality at every level of national and church life.

15. *Civil Partnerships*

The need for clearer guidelines presses at all levels of the church.

The Revd Roderick Thomas asked for guidelines about what to tell an unmarried couple who came to him to enquire about baptism. He told them it would be a good idea for them to explore the possibilities of marriage first and get matters in the right order, and thereby give a primary demonstration, in their case, of Christian living. He also asked about the situation in which a couple, who recently came to him asking for their child to be baptised, told him that one of the godparents was living in a gay and committed relationship. Was he wrong to suggest that that godparent should be encouraged to explore the Bible's teaching on human sexuality, before the parents went ahead with including him among those who were to be godparents?

For this reason we include in this book the pastoral guidelines written by the Revd Paul Perkin and Mrs Christine Perkin, *Civil Partnerships – Advice to UK Parishes and Clergy*, for such situations. These guidelines, we believe, represent more faithfully than the House of Bishops' *Guidelines* God's loving best for all people.

The wider cultural dimensions of civil partnerships, and in particular, the often-repeated question as to how marriage is damaged by them, is addressed in the appendix, *How can my civil partnership possibly damage marriage, yours or anyone else's?*

16. The existence of other sexual minorities, which are now beginning to emerge from their closets

Decades ago the most socially 'advanced' began to hear of the pain and exclusion of the lesbian and gay contingent. Of course, these are not the only sexual minorities out there, a fact that the most 'progressive' LG groups have long since acknowledged in their policies. Now, the most current terminology is LGBT – inclusive of bisexual and transgendered sexual minorities. However, few seem aware of what the bisexual element entails – the sexual and emotional relating to both genders, either sequentially or simultaneously. Lisa had a close friendship with a married bisexual female – who for a time was in love with her (love passed but the friendship remained) – but knows other bisexuals who have had sequential relationships with first one gender and then the other. Bisexuality is one of the key elements for the newest sexual minority on the cusp, standing now at the edge of the closet – the polys, or polamourists (literally 'plural loves' or committed non-monogamy). Polys are now marching in the gay pride parades – they even organize their own – and are trying to get the attention and approval of a we-don't-want-to-know, binary-obsessive society. Reading poly narrative today is like reading the gay and lesbian narrative of the 70s and 80s. For polys the Noah's Ark principle (two-by-two) is archaic.

But polys are not the only organized sexual minority groups to demand equal recognition for their way of 'being' and 'doing' sex, love and family. Polygamists – actually polygynists (think Mormon, with one alpha heterosexual male and plural heterosexual females) – are not far behind, nor are 'zoos' (those whose orientation is towards intimate relationships with animals), 'boylover' and 'girllovers' (those whose orientation is to the young; the pejorative terms for such folk is paedophile, according to their now-out spokespeople), etc. See *Gay Wednesday's 'Gay Pain'*, the Glossary and Appendix 6, *Finally*, for more.

The key point is that many people are now thinking – and living – outside the box of traditional Christian morality and behaviour: it is truly a Brave New World. These people want exactly what those in the LGBT communities have now achieved. Their narrative sounds just like that of the now-familiar LGBT. What is our response to them?

17. Conclusion

It is the hope of the editors and the contributors that people on all sides of this current discussion will find the material we have gathered both stimulating and helpful. The motto of the Anglican Communion is 'The truth will set you free', drawing from Jesus' words in John 8.32. The truth *is* out there. Jesus promises that it is knowable, available and accessible, and that it can set *all* of us free.

Lisa Severine Nolland's doctoral dissertation (University of Bristol) has recently been published as *A Victorian Feminist Christian: Josephine Butler, the Prostitutes and God* (Paternoster) and she currently works as a lay chaplain. She has taught in North America and the UK at primary, secondary and tertiary levels and is website consultant for Anglican Mainstream.net. She lives in Bristol with her husband, John, their teenage daughter, Elisabeth and, until his death, a beautiful Golden Retriever, Shem – and is stepmother to David, whose mother died when he was seven. For more than twenty years she and John have been connected with Trinity College, Bristol, where John is Vice Principal. To help her cope with 2008, she regularly escapes into the realms of the English historical and literary past, *Just William*, architecture and botany. Her claim to fame is that of being related to a *Titanic* steerage survivor, Oscar Hedman, her irascible great-uncle, ironically known as Uncle Happy.

Canon Dr Christopher Sugden is married to Elaine, a consultant in cancer. They have three adult children, two of whom are married, and two granddaughters. After a curacy at St George's Leeds and a part-time post at Radio Leeds, Chris and Elaine went to India for six years. Chris worked as an assistant presbyter in a Church of South India congregation (St John's Bangalore) and in non-formal theological education. Elaine worked in community health. On return to England Chris was invited to be part of the international team that founded the Oxford Centre for Mission Studies, a study and research centre for church leaders from Africa, Asia and Latin America. Over seventy doctoral students have graduated from it in the last twenty years. His own research work has been in Liberation Theology (1974) and in Christian Social Ministry in India and Indonesia (1988). Chris is a statutory canon of St Luke's Cathedral, Jos, in Northern Nigeria and commissary for the Bishop of North East Caribbean and Aruba in the West Indies. With Elaine he runs an allotment in North Hinksey where they live. They like Saabs and Morris Minors. Chris is Executive Secretary of Anglican Mainstream (www.anglican-mainstream.net).

1.   Post-Gay: The Transforming Power of God

In the General Synod debates on Wednesday, 28 February 2007, there were several stories from people in same-sex relations, clergy as well as lay people, who were asking for inclusion as they were. The evening before, Anglican Mainstream had hosted a General Synod 'fringe meeting' in Church House, in which two people spoke of the transformation they had experienced, in their sexual preferences, through the power of God.

The Revd Peter Ould and James Parker, both of whom have worked with people who have unwanted same-sex attraction, spoke from their own experience of moving out of homosexual attraction and practice into a fuller identity in Christ. They also answered questions. Such voices are seldom heard in the current debates.

The meeting, which was a contribution to the Anglican Communion Listening Process, was chaired by the Venerable Michael Lawson, Archdeacon of Hampstead. Thirty-five people attended.

The following accounts, based on notes taken at the time, have been adapted for publication.

1.   *The Revd Peter Ould*

I will tell you a bit of my story, and also tell you why I made the lifestyle choices that I did. Now in my thirties, I grew up in Sheffield. My father was an international contract lawyer, and my mother was Austrian. I had meningitis when I was 15, went to university at 19, and moved to London at the age of 23. It was at the time of the move to London that issues around my sexuality first emerged. Up till then I had thought that I was just waiting for the right girl to come along. But one evening I was in my flat, watching MTV, and I saw a man on the screen. 'I could snog him,' I thought.

People talk about 'feeling Gay'. For me, it was a sudden realization that this was my sexual attraction. I went to speak to people in my church, and ended up talking to a man from an ex-gay ministry. I remember being asked if I *wanted* to change. Here was I, aged 23, realizing that I was attracted to my own sex. It was very real, and I was interested in simply coping with it, rather than thinking about whether I could change. I did, however, realize that there was a clear conflict between my feelings and my theology.

Now in my twenties, and an evangelical Christian, two things made me realize God's plans for me. The first was my academic training as a statistician. At the time when I 'came out' to myself, there was a lot of scientific stuff about homosexuality in the media. I was reading all I could get. But one thing struck me: none of this stood up to hard analysis. Either the sample groups were too small, or the repeat studies refuted the claims. I was therefore convinced that there was no firm evidence that my same-sex attraction was hard-wired. It was this conviction that first made me move to where I am today – and where I now want to live every day.

Secondly, I began to understand the power of signifiers and symbols as, coming from an Evangelical background, I explored in greater depth the Catholic heritage of my faith. I was looking at Genesis chapter 1 and also at Ephesians chapter 5, which describes the relationship between Christ and the Church. Could I justify a same-sex relationship *theologically?* I used to hang discussions on the meaning of certain Greek words. And yet, I discovered that there was an overarching theme in the Bible about the Christian man being called to signify Christ in his marriage, and that this theme applied to me. In the same way, Ephesians chapter 5 showed that a Christian wife in her marriage signifies the Church. But if you have a husband and a husband, where is the Church? And if you have a wife and a wife, where is Christ?

My theology seemed to be right, but after eighteen months of praying to God, and not changing, I heard God asking me, 'If you take seriously the truth that your choices about sexual behaviour ultimately speak about Me, will you let me do with your life whatever I want? Will you be celibate if I call you to that?' This was a real challenge to me. It suddenly seemed as if God wasn't offering me what I wanted, namely change, but rather was calling me to let His will be done, whatever that was.

So one very tearful night I finally said to God, 'If that's how it's going to be, I will remain celibate.'

Four weeks later, I went on a prayer ministry team weekend with my church. We were in the garden of one of the members of the church, and a girl asked what we should do if someone came for prayer and said they were gay. The vicar replied, 'Well, of course, no one is really gay.' It was as if someone had thrown a switch! Up to that point, even though I realized that the Bible never makes the distinction of gay or straight, and simply calls us to be the man or woman that God created us to be, I still felt identified internally as gay. It was what defined me, because I didn't know anything else. But suddenly I thought, 'That's not my real identity! I'm called to be a man, not gay or straight. God doesn't make that distinction, and therefore neither should I.'

It was as though a weight had lifted off me. By the time I had driven back to London and joined in the evening worship service at church, I suddenly realized I was no longer thinking of myself as homosexual. I realized I was the same as all the men next to me. There was nothing different about me, either in what I was capable of, or how God viewed me. God had begun the work of healing the wounds of my past.

As I was growing up, I failed to make close emotional ties, both with my same-sex peers and with adult role models. I was small, unsporty and annoyingly intelligent and precocious. I was a geek! I didn't know how to relate to boys or men, and though I wanted to be a man, I had no idea how to do it. When you grow up not feeling like other guys, you can grow up feeling as though you do not belong. Being gay, however, finally told me who I actually was and where 'I belonged'. Finally understanding who you are gives you some form of security and identity, so taking a step away from that is almost like stepping into nothingness. It was really scary.

Despite this, from the time of that prayer ministry weekend, God began to do an amazing thing in my life. As I brought to Him the brokenness of my past, His Spirit began a deep work of healing those wounds. If you get measles, you don't put calamine lotion on the skin to heal it, rather you tuck yourself up in bed and let your white blood cells fight deep within you to rid the body of the harmful presence. In the same way, God healed the wounds in my past. The wound of having no same-sex peers or adult role models, the symptoms of same-sex attraction and the need for affirmation from a man – these things disappeared. It was not that the 'rash' had been healed but that the 'virus' had been dealt with.

Today, I am a completely different man from the person I was in my teen years and early twenties. Far from being afraid of men who were different from me, I began to discover that I was the same as they were. I no longer think of myself as heterosexual or homosexual, I'm simply Peter, whom God created to glorify Him in His creation. I've seen God heal my past and change the desires and emotions that were trapped by it. He's called me not only to help others walk in freedom, but also to enable the

Church to respond with compassion and care to those whose sexuality is broken, as mine was.

Peter Ould, serving in the Diocese of St Albans, pastors people with same-sex attraction. He was involved in setting up Redeemed Lives UK. He is married to Gayle, and they are expecting their first child in May 2008. He is the curate at Christ Church, Ware.

2. James Parker

This evening I want to give you my testimony about being in relationship with Jesus Christ. It is on account of Him that I have come to know the truth of these verses from the book of the prophet Joel, which have pursued me through my adult years:

> 'And I will restore to you the years that the locusts have eaten ... I will pour out my spirit upon all flesh' (Joel 2, v25 and v28)

The homosexuality debate has – not by choice, I must add – been woven into the fabric of my being. The term 'homosexuality' has only been in circulation for around 150 years. We would rather call it same-sex attraction. Up to my mid-teens I saw my identity as homosexual, but from 16 onwards I saw myself as gay. 'Homosexual' signified that I was erotically attracted to my own gender but had never acted upon this. 'Gay', on the other hand, meant that I was ready and available to engage in sexual activity with a member of the same sex, and to take my place among the gay community.

I now have the honour to meet with many men and women who

deal with same-sex attraction. Each of their stories is unique and therefore different, and yet there are always certain strands that appear in every story once it has been fully heard and understood. Allow me to begin by telling you something of my own story.

I was born, with a twin sister, outside of marriage and we were abandoned at birth. After being fostered and eventually adopted into a practising Anglican family, we joined three other older children and were raised in a Christian home by a loving, married father and mother.

I only ever recall being strongly attracted to men in my formative years. The first sexual experience I can recall was with a teacher in my school. (Though only 16, I was already drinking heavily.) I was disturbed by some aspects of this experience and so I spoke to another man some months later about what had happened. He told me that I needed to have 'a good experience of love', and so he in turn took me to bed. At the age of 17 I 'came out' to my parents. Their response was one of unconditional love and acceptance. 'We love you,' they said. However, they also added with great wisdom, 'The rules your siblings live under, you live under. There's no sexual expression in the family home except between those who are married.'

Unbeknown to anyone else, I was spending most of my money on hardcore gay pornography at this time. I 'came out' to a number of friends at secondary school. Interestingly, I never experienced any homophobic response at all. In fact, I seemed to gain respect from others as a result of my honesty. It was liberating to be known and accepted for what I had always felt and believed myself to be.

I then moved to London to further my studies. A whole new world opened up for me. I began to explore my sexuality in a way I had never been able to and took my place among the capital's gay community. Because of my Christian upbringing and my desire to know more about God, I went along to the Lesbian and Gay Christian Movement. I regularly attended the meetings of the LGCM. I learnt a lot about safe sex at that time – but not a lot about the Gospel!

I had always believed, certainly up to this point, that my calling was to shake up the church, to persuade church people to accept gay people, and to recognize that 'God made us this way'. I found myself having a number of unfulfilling relationships. Eventually I settled down with a long-term boyfriend, called Steve. I was at university, and I was helping to set up a lesbian and gay group there.

One man, however, stood out to me among all the other students.

He witnessed to me by the fact that he prayed fervently. What was even more noticeable is that he seemed to reach out to take an interest in me, and actually to love me. He would hold my gaze as we talked. He would speak to me in an affirming way. He even gave me a hug at times. This was quite a challenge, both for him and for me, because I was known by some behind my back as the 'college queer'. This man's witness to the truth of the gospel was robust and deeply attractive. He put himself on the line for me and, I began to realize slowly, was giving me something that no one else was giving me.

My boyfriend, Steve, seemed to be looking for a sense of fulfilment from me, for affirmation of his very personhood and manhood, even though externally he was a very masculine man and gave off an air of confidence. I too was unwittingly looking for the same from him, something which neither of us could give to the other. This other man, on the other hand, had already been affirmed at the core of his person from birth upwards and so was able to bestow a sense of the 'true masculine' upon me in a way that someone homosexually orientated appears unable to do.

This man spoke to me about what it was to be a Christian. He told me I needed to have a relationship with Jesus. He spoke with me about the need to lay my past before the Cross of Christ, to repent of any outstanding sin and to receive the Holy Spirit of God. I did this to the best of my ability. Steve started to see a difference in my life. He, a lapsed Christian, came and gave his life to Jesus. We would pray together daily, and read Scripture regularly. We became the 'gay couple' invited to 'straight' dinner parties. I honestly believed that God had answered my prayers in sending me such a good man. Life could not be better, or so it seemed, and we bore witness to God's presence in a committed gay relationship.

But as the Spirit began to work in me, I saw that there were deeper needs within me that were not being satisfied. What looked wonderful, healthy and normal on the outside was not all it appeared to be on the inside. God was asking me to give myself *totally* to Him. I slowly began to realize that God was telling me to stop this relationship. I struggled and squirmed with this for a time. Eventually, I told Steve our relationship had to stop. I burnt everything to do with homosexuality. I was able to join other Christians who were willing to love me in a healthy way. Attention, affection and affirmation – the core emotional needs I was seeking after – were suddenly poured into the centre of my being and I found a whole new level of self-acceptance that I had never known before, or even knew existed.

My vicar heard about my decision to end my relationship with

Steve. He told me that I was crazy and should go back to him. But I knew God was calling me in a different direction. I chose to leave behind my place in the gay community and took my place among non-gay friendships. I still went before God believing myself to have been born gay and thinking that gay was OK, but God began to reveal to me some areas of my life which I needed painfully to face, and where further repentance was often needed. He also began to show me things that were real rubbish in my past. For instance, there were many consequences from my having been sexually abused between the ages of 8 and 11. The majority of same-sex strugglers, I have since come to learn, have been sexually abused. It is widespread now throughout our society, achieved surreptitiously today by means of deliberate sexual imagery and language in advertising and the media. Even before being abused I had a deep-seated hunger for a father's love, and an awareness that other masculine needs had not been met during my earliest developmental years. With this father-hunger now eroticised it was not surprising that I should find myself addicted to gay pornography by my late teens, and desiring more and more to act this out in early adulthood.

One of the key idols I had to renounce and reject was the intertwining of my sexuality with my Christian identity. I could no longer authentically stand before God and call myself a gay Christian. The two were a paradox. Everything sexual about me had to come into submission before Christ, along with the other factors of my life, so that anything broken could be revealed, redeemed and restored.

As the Spirit of God began to stir in me, it was as though my soul was being led by Jesus to God the Father. As I got in touch with His powerful presence – the presence I had previously been lacking, and been closed off to – aspects about me began to change. My voice gradually became deeper. My walk became more masculine. The incessant erotic pull I had towards men began to lessen, and somehow it felt controllable for the first time in my life. As I learnt to listen daily to God in prayer and to submit to His Word, true masculinity – the very essence of God Himself – began to be instilled into me and in turn rise within me. I came to love being a man. This was nothing short of miraculous for me, because there had been times in the past when I had felt like a woman trapped in a man's body. For a time I then moved into feeling strongly asexual, but now, with every day, I realize more and more that I *love* being a man.

There were different degrees of brokenness that needed to be healed. Without taking the time to listen daily to the voice of the Holy Spirit in prayer, I was unable to recognize and deal with the many underlying emotional issues within me that needed resolution. On the outside I seemed like an ordinary, gifted, young man. I saw nothing wrong with me. But God showed me that I was fallen and in need of His healing touch, as is true for every human being, irrespective of their sexual feelings or what they believe to be their 'orientation'.

I came to understand clearly that behind my sexual attraction and arousal towards men was a need for meaningful masculine affirmation and connection, which at first looked very much like the gay relationships I had previously been involved in. However, the difference, I soon learned, was that I needed to fulfill the *true, deeper* need which could only be met legitimately through non-erotic connection with members of my own sex, rather than through the false, or surface, desire of lust.

I began to reflect upon the many men I had come to know while in the gay community. We had all been led to believe that homosexuality was a normal variant of human sexuality and that homosexuals were as psychologically healthy as the rest of the population. And yet I had met with a significantly higher rate of psychological disorders, substance abuse problems and suicidal ideation than exists in the general public. Contemporary research, I later discovered, endorsed these realizations. I could now see that we had all been conned.

We must not dilute the truth, even though this can be very hard to hear and live out at times. I was fortunate enough to be offered this by my parents, by the man who reached out to me at university, and by others within a Holy Spirit-filled community of believers. I needed people – both men and women – who would engage in non-sexual, intimate contact with my soul, my emotional world and, yes, with my body in an appropriate, pure way.

What I thought was my homosexuality was in fact my brokenness. Ultimately, gay affirmation did not answer my deepest needs and 'springboard' me into a fulfilled life, even though it kept promising this to me en route. Gender affirmation, on the hand, does. I only wish that every young man and woman, none of whom chooses to be same-sex attracted, could be *fully* informed about the scientific studies that have been done, proving that people are not born gay, and pointing to the truth that change really is possible.

I have had the honour of meeting hundreds of men and women who are at different stages on the journey of rejecting an identity based solely or predominantly on sexuality. These women and men are now living healthier, happier and more fulfilled lives as they embrace their true identity based on their God-given gender. These are the new minority whose voices are rarely heard or welcomed in the public arena. In fact, their stories are usually dismissed or scorned by gay activists who are quick to see them as bigoted and intolerant. Yet these men and women struggle in the same ways and have walked the same paths as many of those now active in promoting the gay lifestyle.

The years during which I was not affirmed as a man are slowly being restored to me. Like everyone else, I am a work in progress and in need of more change. Yet God continues to pour out His Spirit upon my flesh and upon all those who earnestly desire to walk in His ways of truth. The challenge is this: will we surrender and be open to what He has promised us?

James Parker has worked alongside internationally renowned sports people and classical artists, has helped to spread the gospel across Africa and the Middle East and, until recently, has worked for organizations whose role partially involves ministering to men and women struggling with unwanted same-sex attraction. He is married, and his enthusiasms include eating chocolate and working with young people.

3.   Questions and Discussion

Question: You were with the LGCM, but you distanced yourself from that. How was your reaction to this distancing?

Answer: When I made the decision to leave behind homosexuality, I had to make a brand new start. I have not been back to LCGM since then, although I do pray for those who are in LGCM. They are always my brothers and sisters.

Question: You said that the change came when God spoke to you. I would like to know how that happened. Was there a voice in your head? Were you reading the Bible?

Answer: It was a theological conviction. You can know your theology in your head, but until it shifts down here ... [to the heart]. Also in terms of who I was, it was a theological thing. I was convinced that I was not born to be gay. It was as though the chains that were keeping me gripped just fell off. Also, it was the affirmation of male friends who said, 'You are as good a bloke as we are.' If you are sufficiently exposed to the light, the dark has to flee. It is a realization that the darkness has to flee. If people aren't taught sufficiently about every aspect of homosexuality, their consciences cannot be illuminated. I came into the realization that Jesus is Lord over all my life. I had to let Jesus be king. All the ex-gay literature had this notion of purgation.

Question: When you are working with people, would you refuse to allow them to remain in the orientation in which they are?

Answer 1: I never prayed to be made heterosexual, and I would not ask anyone else to do the same. My prayer was, 'Lord, make me into the man you created me to be' and has never been, 'Lord, heal me from homosexuality'. If God is the designer, then He knows the blueprints of my life better than anyone else could ever know! Everybody whose heart truly meets with Jesus Christ has to make a decision. No one can meet with Christ and not be changed. I also admit that change looks different for every individual. But we must all be careful not to dictate in advance what change may look like. My prayer changed from being, 'Lord, I want You to give me a man' to 'Lord, I want *You.*' Our calling is to meet with God and to allow Him to deal with us as He best sees fit.

Answer 2: Most of the men in our groups were struggling with all sorts of sexual issues, but the central issue is about God dealing with the wounds in one's life. The question is, 'Am I going to let God have control in my life?' I have not worked with a single person in the pursuit of holiness who has not been transformed by God. (I have also met people who have given God six months – this sounds like giving God your terms!) When you give your life to God, things happen.

Question: I want to ask about the language you have used and the language you have not used. How do you characterize the behaviour and attraction in your own life? I also hear from another quarter that many people, who are ex-gay, relapse.

Answer 1: If you give your life to Christ, you cannot have things your own way. If you go back to wanting things your own way then you have a relapse. The same happens with alcoholism etc.

Answer 2: We use the expression 'same-sex attraction'. 'Gay' carries with it the assumption that being gay is hard-wired. Therefore, one's gay actions become part of being gay. We construct a language that allows us to explore these things. If I say 'same-sex attraction', the understanding is different.

Question: I struggled with sexuality till my mid-20s. My Civil Partnership gives me strength to do God's work. I am pleased you have found a place of conviction.

Answer: Thank you. One thing has very much struck me in this debate. At the foot of the cross of Christ, I still find men deeply attractive but there is no sexual dimension to this. This allows me to serve God more, to be obedient to His Word and to see other men as brothers, not as potential lovers or idols.

See also

'Tug of War' by Fr Mario Bergner; http://74.1.174.242/RedeemedLives/products/articles/
    Autumn05TugOfWar.asp?from=ARTICLE
Strength in Weakness: Overcoming Sexual and Relational Brokenness by Andrew Comiskey
    (InterVarsity Press, 2003).
The Broken Image: Restoring Personal Wholeness through Healing Prayer by Leanne Payne
    (Hamewith/Baker Books, 1981).
Setting Love in Order: Hope and Healing for the Homosexual by Mario Bergner
    (Hamewith/Baker Books, 1995).

2.   Post-Lesbian: My Testimony

I went to an all-girls school. It's not that uncommon for girls, at a certain stage, to be attracted to girls, but then they go on to become attracted to boys. I found, though, that while my peers were starting to think about boys, my thoughts were towards girls. I fell in love with three or four girls during school years. Each one was an unrequited love. I never told a soul how I felt, nor about the 'parallel universe' that went on in my mind, in which I conjured up a whole story about being a boy and developing a relationship with the particular girl I was in love with. I thought I was a kind of 'freak'. I didn't know that anyone else had attractions for the same sex. I never heard people or the media discuss this phenomenon. I thought it was like a disease that I just had to put up with. I was highly embarrassed that this was going on in me and felt terribly ashamed.

During my first year of college I became a Christian. I fell in love with Jesus and almost immediately wanted to spend my life telling others about Him. I later worked with a Christian mission organisation and devoted my life to 'knowing God and making Him known'. I forgot my same sex attraction problem and for a few years at least it wasn't an issue. However, it came back when I found myself in love with a friend of mine. I fantasised about her, but again shared this with no-one and was somewhat in denial myself. Fast forward a few more years and I felt called to go and work in Asia. In preparation for this I went through a cross-cultural training programme. This, though, did not prepare me for the level of culture shock I felt when I arrived in the country. I was thrust into the national culture at the deep end, living and working with nationals. I hardly ever met up with any British people or Europeans and was immersed in local culture. I felt very alone with no-one to discuss the feelings of culture shock with.

One girl in the house I shared took particular interest in me, asking me at the end of the day how my day had gone. I started to open my heart to her. We increasingly spent time off together. A few months later we went to stay a weekend with her grandparents who lived in a primitive wooden house surrounded by banana trees. As is common there, we shared a bed. All of a sudden we became physical in our relationship. It seemed to happen out of the blue. We were both stunned. I sat for hours on the window ledge looking out at the banana trees, unable to take in what had happened. I hadn't had any feelings of attraction for her before this physical encounter. I hadn't thought about her sexually at all. Rather, I was attracted to her godliness.

Back at home, the problem was that we were sharing a bedroom. We found that the physical encounter had been so powerful that it felt like sleeping in a room with a magnet the size of a skyscraper. We tried to resist but the pull was so powerful. Our relationship became sexual and continued like this for about two years. Both in full-time Christian ministry we knew this was wrong. We should have told the leadership. Two things stopped us. One was that the relationship we were in felt so powerful and, if I'm honest, so good, that I didn't want to give it up. It felt like the best thing that had ever happened to me in terms of relationship with another person. It was the deepest level of intimacy I had ever known, probably including God. I didn't know it then, but my Christian life had to date been about 'commitment' and 'activism', rather than a deep intimacy with a loving God. Secondly, others on the staff had been discovered to have had affairs, and had then been interrogated and suspended for months (the Asian culture being shame-based). I found I couldn't face such an ordeal. Basically I was in love, and it was the first time in my life that this was reciprocated and I could touch and be with the one I loved.

Susie (I'll call her) had been dating a guy on the staff before I'd arrived and they had broken up. He started making overtures towards her once more, and spending time with her whenever in town. Eventually he asked her to marry him. Both of us wanted a healthy relationship between us and I encouraged her in her relationship with him. They decided to get married. I remember one evening, while away helping to run a conference, I cried out to the Lord, "I'll give her up to you Lord, but please let me sit by her in heaven." It was heart-wrenching but I believed that the Lord would strengthen me to go through the separation.

She asked me if I would be their wedding co-ordinator. I felt I couldn't refuse this request but it made it all the more painful. At the wedding itself I wanted to scream out, "Please don't leave me!", but I couldn't, of course, and the marriage went ahead. I don't know how I made it through the reception. My heart felt broken in a million pieces. They went off on their honeymoon and I struggled with every fibre of my being to stay together. I couldn't express the grief I felt because everyone would realise what an unhealthy relationship this had been. A few months down the road I started to feel panicky. A deep sense of abandonment pervaded my being. When I met up with a friend I would find that on saying goodbye to that person, I felt like a little three-year-old who had just lost her mother. I felt like that all the time. I found it almost unbearable that Susie was nearby but not accessible. I had lost her. I found it increasingly hard to function and felt myself slipping into despair.

Another staff member was friendly towards me and we became friends. One day she 'came on' to me sexually and I couldn't believe that this was happening again. Although not in love with this person, it was again so powerful that I got into a second relationship. This was a relationship 'on the rebound', but I had to acknowledge that same sex attraction was a serious problem in my life and that I ought to resign from the staff. This was a very difficult decision because I wanted to spend my life with this organisation. I was very reluctant to leave, but integrity finally won and when I'd returned to England I finally gave in my notice. Back home, though, I still told no-one at all what had happened. I knew I needed help but didn't know where to get it. On my resignation, my supporting church told me that I was no longer 'missionary status,' and that the last cheque I'd received was the last one I was going to get. I'm sure they didn't mean it this way, but it felt like the 'straw that broke the camel's back'. Up until then I had been hanging on to the edge of the cliff with my fingertips. It felt as though the missions elder had come along and stamped on my fingers, and I then went hurtling down into the abyss. I felt in the grip of death; despair and anxiety were constant companions.

Mary Queen of Scots had an affair. Her lover was sent to Denmark and put in prison, where he went mad. I felt like that man. I felt I couldn't live without Susie. I cried as soon as I woke up, I cried at work, and I cried going to sleep. I felt fearful all the time. The world had become an unsafe and scary place. I felt acutely alone. I didn't know where to turn. I was desperate. Every day was a struggle to keep alive. Death seemed the only way to stop the pain, but I knew I couldn't do that to my parents.

And where was God in all this? It felt as though He had disappeared off to planet Pluto and left me entirely on my own. He had gone. I couldn't understand it: I had taken what I thought was a step of obedience, in giving up Susie, and yet God *hadn't* given me the strength to go through the separation. Even my nights were filled with terror. I found it hard to read the Bible or pray. I found faith slipping away, even though I didn't want that. I desperately wanted and needed God and His presence.

I went to a 'healing meeting' at a local Anglican church and at the end the speaker prayed for me. I had, until that moment, been quite sceptical of 'memories.' But after the speaker's very short, gentle, and in no way suggestive prayer for me, it was like going back in time to when I was two months old. For the first two months of my life I was with my mother but I was then taken away from her and given to another couple. I was adopted. The memory was like reliving the moment when she left me. It felt devastating. Emotions such as abandonment and despair flooded through me. In the 'memory' I kept looking for her to come back to get me but she didn't come. I cried and cried in that church long after everyone else had gone home.

This experience was a light bulb moment. Although I lived in that sense of abandonment every day, I now understood that there was a cause for those feelings, an origin. Something had happened many, many years ago, long since 'forgotten', but something that had actually had a devastating effect on me – my mother had left me. I couldn't rationally remember that event, but I believe the effects of it had stayed in my spirit. So, when I experienced a deep level of intimacy in the present day with Susie, which was then lost, it was like reliving the loss of my mother. This helped me understand why the level of grief I felt over Susie was a pathological type of grief. I began to read about mother-child attachment, and I discovered that a baby feels like one entity with its mother, not a separate being. So if a baby is removed from its mother it feels despair, even a sense of being in the grip of death, because mother equals life.

I also began reading books about same sex attraction and I read that women who are attracted to women are sometimes looking for connection with their mother. This made perfect sense to me. It also gave me hope. Whereas up until that point I had always seen my condition as a lifelong 'disorder', which I just had to put up with and live with as best I could, now I began to think that perhaps, if there is a cause to the condition, there is also hope that it could change. Here, I think, is the great shame about the prevailing belief within our society, including among Christians, that homosexuality is genetic or inherited, rather than environmentally caused. If it *is* genetic there is not much hope for change. In actual fact, to date there have been no convincing arguments to show that it is genetic. Arguments such as Simon LeVay's study on the brain structure of homosexuals have been discredited. But that is a discussion for another time.

Having said that, I believe that the environmental causes often happen so early that the homosexual person feels that he or she has 'always been this way'. And for the Christian this is problematic indeed. It does indeed feel as though you've been born with brown eyes, and yet the Bible says it is a sin to have brown eyes, you should have blue eyes. But what can you do? Your eyes are brown and that's all there is to it. A huge struggle ensues between faith and the condition you find yourself in. You feel you're in an impossible place.

At last I had a little inkling of hope that healing might be possible. Also, at this time, I opened up to a lady from church with whom I was meeting for weekly counselling. I gradually began to tell a few others about my story. I was very cautious, knowing that I could so easily be judged. I was deeply afraid of rejection and felt very ashamed of what I had done, of what I was. Each time I thought of telling a person, I prayed and sought confirmation from the Lord. I told only those I felt He was impressing on me to tell. In each instance I was not rejected, as I had feared; each person was supportive. This was amazing to me. However, the message from some quarters of the church was very negative. I heard homosexuality being condemned from the pulpit and in the media, and I thought, 'No wonder we do not open up about our struggle. We're afraid of being kicked out.' Indeed, some have said that the Church either kicks out homosexuals or ordains them! There seems to be no in-between. As a struggler, one feels caught up in the middle of the politics. So much energy is put into debating whether homosexuality is right or wrong, but I think too little energy is put into helping those who struggle, who would rather not be homosexual if they could choose.

I got in touch with the two ministries in England that are part of Exodus International Ministries: Courage Trust[1] and True Freedom Trust. I went to meet with Jeremy Marks and found out that Courage helped men but did not have the resources or the staff to help women. True Freedom Trust put me in touch with a counsellor in London. I met with her for three months, but to be honest that seemed a waste of time. She had no understanding, as far as I could tell, about homosexuality. I rang Living Waters in London, but after a few calls with no-one replying I tried another option. I rang Exodus International in the States and asked them if they knew of any ministry that helped women, preferably one that had a residential programme. They told me they knew of one ministry – in the States. I immediately rang them and spoke to a staff member there. She had come out of a same sex attraction background herself and it was wonderful for me, for the first time in my life, to be able to talk with someone who had 'been there' herself. As she said, she had 'been there, done that, and bought the T shirt'. After a few phone calls with the ministry I decided to apply for their live-in programme. I was accepted and flew to the States in February 1997. I thought, "I will give this a year and then, if it doesn't 'work', I will leave, go and live the life I want, and give up trying to follow God's ways." What He was calling me to do – to be heterosexual when I was homosexual – still seemed completely incongruous.

---

[1] Courage Trust is no longer with Exodus International Ministries. Jeremy Marks liberalized his views and now encourages his lesbian and gay contacts to settle down in same-sex partnerships. (Eds.)

My time there was what you might call 'bumpy', but I'll leave out the details of that. They told me to get a 'no brainer' job so that I could concentrate on healing. I worked for several months on a farm and drove a tractor for a living! I thought this was not a great way to become more feminine (!), but the Ministry Director reminded me that femininity was a matter of the heart, not appearance. I felt lower (if that's possible) having to do such a menial job, but God met me on that tractor. I was surrounded by His beautiful creation, and I listened to teaching tapes while driving. And the Lord did some healing as I went around the farm, mowing along the 80 miles of fences. I had individual counselling and a once-a-week group meeting as well.

Getting to know others who struggled with homosexuality, I discovered that there seemed to be a theme in our lives. In childhood we had experienced a rupture in the relationship with our same sex parent. This was true for both the women and the men involved in the ministry. We had each felt a distance, in some way, from our same sex parent; I sensed that homosexuals were always trying to repair the relationship with their same sex parent. This instinct of mine was confirmed by the belief of the writer, Elizabeth Moberly,[2] who suggests that it is more accurate to call us homo-emotional than homosexual. This is because what we experience is fundamentally an *emotional* drive to reconnect with the parent.

At the end of my first year in the States, I had another very brief sexual encounter with another woman in the ministry – it was a weekend thing. After this I felt so discouraged that I began to ask questions: "Is it really possible to be healed?" and "What does the Bible really say about it?" I went through a period of reading more widely – the 'liberal' arguments as well as the 'conservative' ones. I had now started studying for a Masters in Counselling and a Masters in Theology, and I talked to my New Testament professor, Joel Green, about the issue and my struggle. He was exceedingly helpful – helpful in that he gave me time to dialogue about it and didn't immediately come down on one side or the other. As a good academic and thinking person he listens and tries to understand all sides. However, he had to conclude that wherever the Bible speaks of homosexuality it speaks of it in a negative way. He was also full of grace for the homosexual, saying that we are all on a level playing field when we stand before God. For

---

[2] Elizabeth Moberly, *Homosexuality: A New Christian Ethic* (Cambridge: James Clark & Co., 1983).

[4] Joel Green, 'Homosexual Relations: Some Biblical and Theological Co-ordinates', *ABE Journal* 2 (1,1994) pp. 3-12.

example, all of us have probably gossiped or been jealous (stated by the apostle Paul to be sins worthy of eternal damnation, along with other sins including homosexuality). So, Dr. Green says, who among us can say that we have not also sinned, and are not equal with the homosexual? "This ought to remind us of our common need for the grace of God ... that we are all implicated in the Fall ... and that, not only is the grace of God manifest most profoundly in the cross for us all, it is also needed by everyone of us."[4] Who then is in the position of being able to throw stones?

I discovered a new Jesus, who was full of compassion. He went so often to those whom the religious establishment of the day thought unacceptable, those who wouldn't have been allowed near the Temple, never mind in it. I loved this Jesus.

I studied the arguments of the pro-homosexual Christians. I really wanted to believe their arguments that homosexuality was not sin. That would make everything so very much easier in my life. If only God said it was all right, I would be free not to take the path of pain. But however much I desired it I could not be convinced by their arguments.

In this period of searching I found that psychoanalysts had worked with homosexuals in the early 20th century, when the condition was still classified as a disorder. And they had had success in seeing a change in sexual orientation. This again gave me hope. I thought, "If they can see change, perhaps we in the Church can too, because we have not only the insights of psychology but the Holy Spirit too." Albert Ellis, a leading psychoanalyst of the day, thought that homosexuals in therapy who didn't see change had quit the healing process too early, being unwilling to push through all the pain that the process brings up, and opting out prematurely.[5] (Pain, after all, is exceedingly unpleasant). I do believe that Christians who go through various types of healing programme often fall back into the 'lifestyle' because they do not see the process through to the end. Added to this should be the fact that the programmes they engage in tend to use only a cognitive approach, instead of inviting the help of the Holy Spirit, who is called our counselor and who is so good at healing. At the ministry I was involved in, we used to say that in order to achieve lasting healing one had to get to the roots of the condition, not focus on the 'fruit' i.e. the behaviour. I believe that's why we saw more 'success', in terms of people feeling a change of orientation, than some of the other Exodus ministries.

---

[5] Albert Ellis, *Homosexuality: Its Causes and Cure* (New York: Lyle Stuart, 1965).

So I went back to the healing process with renewed strength, reassured that I was after all on the right path. As much as I wanted a different path, I had to stay on this one. This healing path included looking at my beliefs and feelings towards men, as well as my beliefs and feelings towards women. Men, I had felt, were not capable of nurturing. I didn't want to entrust my life to a man. God showed me how the very thing I had longed for – someone to care and provide for me – was indeed what He had 'wired' men to do. I had wanted to care and provide for Susie, but I began to see that actually care and provision were the very things I had wanted for myself. I had been very independent and self-sufficient, but this was only because, basically, I had thought I was on my own, and had to survive on my own. Actually my heart had longed for someone to protect me. I started to pray that God would enable me to see men as He wanted me to see them.

This is just one example of the things I began to see and understand about myself. I also realised that my longing for the affection of a woman was actually a legitimate need. It hadn't been my fault that I had been separated from my mother and left with a deep hunger. But it was my choice what I did with that desire. So I began to turn to the Lord to fill that hunger, instead of looking towards women to do so. I learned how to sit before the Lord and 'receive' from Him. (A big change after a life of 'doing' for God!) I learned that He took delight in me, was excited about me and just enjoyed being with me, instead of looking for what I could do for Him (which is such a ridiculous thought, anyway). Whereas before I had a need to be needed, I suddenly 'got it' that it is so much better to be wanted rather than needed, just wanted for who I was, not for what I did. Contemplative prayer, imagining myself with God, has probably been the main source of any healing I have had so far. To receive love and a sense of belonging and security from Him rather than through a person – this is true healing, whatever one's condition in life.

On my return to England after nearly six years in the States, I reconnected with an old male friend from London days. We began to spend time together and I found myself strangely attracted to him, so much so that as we started 'dating' it became difficult to restrain ourselves physically. It felt like the right time in my journey to begin to make the step of relating with the opposite sex in a new kind of way. It had now been four or five years since I had felt any attraction towards any woman. I recognised that I still had a way to go in relating with the opposite sex, but I felt the Lord nudging me to step into a relationship with this man, assuring me that He would work things out as we went along. We got married in 2004. In a sense it felt like an arranged marriage, but one arranged by the Lord, I believe. I sensed that the Lord would lead me into deeper love for my husband as time went on. The first year was very rocky. I realised how I still had a lot of fears about entrusting my life to a man. There were times when I just didn't want to return home to him.

I feel it is an absolute miracle that I am married. (I wish I had been brave enough to seek help earlier in life.) I know that lots of homosexuals marry, some believing that marriage will act as a 'cure'. I didn't want to do that. It had to be at the right time in my own journey of healing. I am still on that journey, and so I don't talk of healing in black and white terms. On my bad days doubts can sneak in, and I wonder whether change is ever really possible. But thankfully those days are now few and far between. People often remark how happy I seem. I do feel very contented with life, and I feel happy in my relationship with my husband. The contentment comes from finding in God my sense of belonging, security and rest – those feelings that a mother gives to her child. As a result, I no longer have in me a hunger for the affection of a woman, which I used to think would give me that sense of belonging, security and rest. I feel deeply content in a way I've perhaps never known before, and if that's what it means to be healed, I like it.

We are grateful to our author for sharing her story, her journey into wholeness, with us. As it is often painful for people to revisit their past, we appreciate her willingness to do so. She has asked to remain anonymous and we respect her wishes.

(Detail from Rembrandt's *Return of the Prodigal Son* © Hermitage Museum)

See also

'Helping Women with Same-Sex Attraction' by Janelle M. Hallman, MA, LPC;
    http://www.narth.com/docs/hallman.pdf
'Leaving Lesbianism and Confronting LGBT Activism—My Story by Siena de la Croix';
    http://www.narth.com/docs/leaving2.html

'Ministry to Lesbian Women', by Melissa Fryrear, in *God's Grace and the Homosexual Next Door* by Alan Chambers and the Exodus International Leadership Team (Harvest House, 2006), pp. 173-203.

Restoring Sexual Identity: Hope for Women Who Struggle with Same-Sex Attraction by Anne Paulk (Harvest House, 2003).

'Going Straight' by Lauren Quaintance;
http://catholiceducation.org/articles/homosexuality/h00076.html

'Something was missing', anon.;
http://www.afajournal.org/2005/september/905lesbianletter.asp

3. Post-Gay: Thank you for offending me

Michael Goeke

A recent article in the *San Francisco Chronicle* touted the merger of 1,400 'open and affirming' churches (meaning churches that affirm homosexual identity and behavior) with the National Gay and Lesbian Task Force. The article stated that leaders in the gay rights movement consider their biggest challenge to be that of convincing Christians that homosexual behavior is not a sin. I saw a part of this movement when I spoke recently at a gathering of pastors and church leaders from a denomination that is heavily divided over the issue of homosexuality. One man spoke of his desire that everyone be welcome at his church, and that they be 'inclusive' and, especially, that no one leave their church 'offended' by what they hear. Of course, this was not the first time I had heard these types of thoughts. Many people I talk to, including pastors and parents and friends, are concerned that they not 'offend' gay people.

Let me just say a hearty 'THANK YOU' to my wife, and my parents and family, and my friends, who cared enough about me to offend me! I get a sick feeling in the pit of my stomach when I consider the ramifications in my life had the people in my world bought into the lie that to love me was to affirm my homosexuality. When I left my wife to pursue homosexuality, she boldly told me that she knew God could work in me and in our marriage and that she would not pursue divorce. She protected her interests but always professed her love for me and her desire to work through this together. My parents (and other family members) told me that what I was doing was wrong. They found Exodus, got materials, and tried to get me to talk to a counselor. They also called frequently to check on me, sent me money when I needed it, came to see me on my birthday, and flew me home for holidays. My friends drove hours to talk to me about what I was doing, and told me what they believed. They flew from other towns to take me to dinner and tried to convince me to get help and to turn from what I was doing. They also sent me cards and letters full of love and affirmation of our friendship.

And each of them offended me. Each of them made me angry. I viewed them as bigoted, and unenlightened, and ignorant, and prejudiced, and hateful. If they truly loved me, I told them, they would accept my homosexuality and affirm me in the lifestyle I was living. I ignored their calls and I viewed them with skepticism. I did my best to sever my relationships with those who were offending me. But they would not let me go. They did not coddle me, but they refused to give up on me.

When I finally took *You Don't Have to be Gay* from my Dad, just to shut him up, I was ready to draw a line in the sand and cut all ties with my wife, my family and my friends. But the time planned by God for the piercing of my heart had come. As I have said many times, that book showed me more than the sentimental, saccharine love of Jesus that gay theology had sold me. It showed me the powerful love of the risen Savior, and I was compelled back to Him by that love. The offending parties in my life were waiting, as loving and gracious as they had ever been ... not holding my sin against me, but standing there, ready to walk the journey out of homosexuality alongside of me.

Today my marriage is restored and has grown beyond my imagination. I have three beautiful children and am living out the call on my life to vocational ministry. Healing has happened in my family relationships, and I am closer to that cadre of friends than ever before. As I listen to people debate the 'gay' issue and talk of affirmation and inclusivity of homosexuality, I wonder where I would be today had Stephanie accepted my claim that I had always been gay and would always be gay and pursued divorce like I wanted her to do. I wonder where I would be if my parents had joined PFLAG (Parents, Families and Friends of Lesbians and Gays) and supported me in my quest to live homosexually. I wonder where I would be if my friends had encouraged me to divorce Stephanie and had rallied around me in my homosexuality. I wonder where I would be if my pastors and spiritual shepherds had encouraged me to accept the very thing I needed to lay before the cross of Christ. I shudder at the thought. I know it must have killed them to think of losing me, but they loved me enough to take that risk. THANK YOU, dear friends, for your offense to me. At the time, the Truth you shared was the aroma of death to me (II Cor. 2:15) but today it is the sweet fragrance of LIFE.

Mike Goeke is the Director of Cross Poser Ministries in Midland, Texas, where he and his wife, Stephanie, minister to married couples impacted by homosexuality, and work to equip the church to minister love and redemption to anyone struggling with unwanted homosexuality. He can be reached via email at mgoekecpm@gmail.com. He and Stephanie have three children.

See also

'Pressing Questions about Homosexuality: Summer 04' by Fr Mario Bergner; http://74.1.174.242/redeemedlives/GetArticle.asp

'Homosexuality: The Person and the Act' by Rabbi Benzion Milecki; 'Let's Take a Deeper Look'; http://www.southhead.org/blog/2004/12/homosexuality-person-and-act.html

4.   Homophobia: An Unfinished Story

Professor J. Budziszewski

"Are you Professor Theophilus?"

I turned. "That's me. Come in."

"My name's Lawrence. I'm gay. I came to complain about your talk about constitutional liberties yesterday. It was bigoted and homophobic. I'm filing a formal protest to the people who run the Student Union speakers series."

At least he's direct, I thought. I waved him to a seat.

"Help me out, Mr. Lawrence. How could —"

"Just Lawrence."

"Thank you. Now how could my talk have been 'bigoted and homophobic' when it didn't mention homosexuality?"

"I didn't actually hear the talk itself. I came in during Q&A."

"I see. And what did I say during Q&A?"

"You said gays have sex with animals."

I'm used to this sort of thing, so I merely observed, "I'm afraid you weren't listening carefully."

"I remember distinctly," he declared. "A girl asked your opinion of laws against discrimination on the basis of sexual orientation, and you said gays have sex with animals."

"No, What I said was 'sexual orientation' can mean many things. Some people are 'sexually oriented' toward the opposite sex; others toward the same sex; others toward children; others toward animals; others toward cadavers. I said that I wondered where this trend will end."

"Then you admit that gays don't have sex with animals?"

"You brought that up," I reminded him. "I have no information on the point. I'm only suggesting that not all 'orientations' are morally equivalent."

He said nothing, but showed no inclination to leave. "Do *you* think all 'orientations' are morally equivalent?" I queried.

"I won't even dignify that question with an answer," he said. "But I know what you think of my orientation. I'm sick of you phony Christians with your filthy hypocrisy about the love of God."

"So you've heard that I'm a Christian."

"Who hasn't? The holy, the sanctimonious, the Most Excellent Professor Theophilus of Post-Everything State University — what else would he be? The whole school reeks of you, of you and the other so-called Christian so-called professors. That's why I walked in on your Q&A. I wanted to see you spit venom."

"My goodness. Have I said anything venomous?"

"It's what you're thinking that's venomous."

"I see," I smiled. "Why don't you stop being bashful, and tell me what's bothering you?"

"You must think you're funny."

"I'm serious. Tell your complaints one by one, and I'll answer them."

"You couldn't answer them. I have too many."

"Try me. I'll give short answers."

He cocked his head and peered at me. "You mean it, don't you?"

"I wouldn't say it if I didn't."

"One at a time?"

"One at a time."

"All right, here's the first. Christians are hypocrites. You're always running down gays, but what about the other things your Bible condemns, like divorce and remarriage? It's other people's sins that bother you, not your own."

I laughed. "If you'd spent any time around me, you'd know that I'm just as hard on the sins of heterosexuals as on those of homosexuals. Easy divorce is a prime example of how one bad thing leads to another — in our case the loss of the ability to make any distinctions about sexual acts at all."

Ignoring the reply, he went on to his next complaint. "You're intolerant. You reject people like me just because we're different than you."

"Me reject you?" I said. "Aren't you the one who rejects what is different than yourself? Don't you reject the challenge of the other sex?"

"I don't need the other sex. I have a committed relationship with my partner."

"Research shows that homosexuals with partners don't stop cruising, they just cruise less. When they don't think straights are listening, gay writers say the same."

"So what if it's true? There's nothing wrong with gay love anyway."

I spoke quietly. "Tell me what's loving about sex acts that cause bleeding, choking, disease and pain," I suggested. "You might start by explaining the meaning of the medical term 'Gay Bowel Syndrome,' or how people get herpes lesions on their tonsils."

"You're — how can you even say that?" he demanded. "How dare you tell me who to love?"

"I don't think I am telling you who to love."

"Oh, no? Then what are you telling me?"

"That there is nothing loving about mutual self-destruction."

"You must think my relationship with my partner is just dirt!"

"No, I respect friendship wherever I find it — your friendship with your partner included. It's just that sex doesn't make every kind of friendship better."

"Why not? Are you anti-sex or something?"

"Not at all," I said, "but would you say that sex improves the friendship of a father with his daughter?"

Seeing from his face that he didn't, I continued. "You get my point. Nor does sex improve the friendship of two men."

"That's where you're wrong. Gay sex is just as natural for some people as straight sex is for other people."

"What's 'natural'," I said, "is what unlocks our inbuilt potential instead of thwarting it. One of the purposes of marital sex is to get you outside your Self and its concerns, to achieve intimacy with someone who is Really Other."

Was he listening to any of this? "I'm sorry, Lawrence — I really am — but having sex with another man can't do that. It's too much like loving your reflection. That's what I meant before about refusing the challenge of the other sex."

I was about to go on, but abruptly he changed the subject: "It's attitudes like yours that killed Matthew Shepard."

"Surely you don't imagine that the thugs who killed Matthew Shepard were Christians, do you?" I smiled at the absurdity of the thought, but seeing that he misunderstood my smile I made my face serious and tried again.

"Lawrence, I deplore the violence that killed Matthew Shepard, and I'm glad those men were caught. But shouldn't we also grieve the urge which caused Matthew Shepard to be sexually attracted to violent strangers?"

He said only, "You hate me."

I paused to study him. Did he really believe that, or was it a smokescreen?

"I don't hate you," I said. "I love you." I paused. "I'd like to be with you forever, in heaven."

Lawrence's face displayed shock, as though he had been hit in the stomach. Then he looked confused. The expression of confusion was instantaneously replaced by an expression of anger.

For one split-second, it had looked as if the shutters were open. *"God in heaven,"* I thought, *"I need help."* How could they be pried back up?

"My love isn't really the issue for you, is it?" I asked.

"What do you mean?"

"It's God's. God's love is the issue for you." For a few seconds there was no reaction.

Then it came. "You're bleeping right God's love is the issue for me," he said. *"Your* God's love. The lying God who says He loves man, but who hates me for loving men."

"Do you think God hates you?"

"Doesn't He?"

"What makes you say that?"

"Doesn't your Bible say that? It calls people like me an abomination."

"It calls what you *do* abomination. There's a difference."

"There's no difference. I do what I am."

I considered his point. "Could it be," I said, "that you want God to love you *less?"*

"Less!" he spat.

"Yes. Don't you know what love is?"

"Acceptance."

"Acceptance of what kills you? Consider another view: Love is a commitment of the will to the true good of the other person."

"What?"

"I said love is a commitment of the will to the true good of the other person."

"I don't get what you're saying."

"Sure you do. The lover wants what's good for the beloved."

He hesitated. "I suppose."

"Good. Now think. If that's what love is, then a *perfect* Lover would want the *perfect* good of the Beloved. Do you see what that means? He would loath and detest whatever destroyed the beloved's good — no matter how much the beloved desired it."

I couldn't read the look on his face, so I plowed on. "That's what sin does — it destroys us. Yours destroys you, mine destroys me. And so the Lover doesn't 'accept' it; He hates it with an inexorable hatred. To cut the cancer out of us, He will do whatever it takes — like a surgeon. No, more than like a surgeon. If you let Him, He will even take the cancer upon Himself and die in your place."

Still inscrutable, he kept his eyes in front of him, just avoiding my own.

I asked "What happens, then, if you refuse to let go of what destroys you? What happens if you say this to the divine and perfect Lover who wants your complete and perfect good — if you say, 'I bind myself to my destruction! Accept me, and my destruction with me! I refuse to enter heaven except in the company of Death!'"

Neither of us spoke.

Lawrence rose from his chair and walked out the door.

The Seeker

This dialogue, like all Office Hours dialogues, is fiction, but it is based on actual events: the "second thoughts" of Theophilus' visitor closely resemble the real-life testimony of an ex-gay who is a friend of the author.

"It wasn't easy finding your office," said my visitor as he took a seat. "This building is like a rabbit warren."

"Yes," I said, "for the first couple of years I worked here, I had to leave a trail of crumbs each day to find my way back out. We haven't met, have we?"

"No, I'm over in Antediluvian Studies — I'm a grad student. My name's Adam, Adam Apollolas."

"M.E. Theophilus." We shook hands.

"You are the same Theophilus who wrote the *'Homophobia' dialogue* for Nounless Webzine, aren't you? I was hoping to talk with you about it."

"Busted," I smiled. "What would you like to know about it?"

"Was it based on a real conversation?"

"Yes and no; it was a composite. A homosexual student really did visit to accuse me of saying that 'gays have sex with animals,' and the rest is from real life too, but not necessarily from the same conversation."

"But it can't possibly be true that all of the homosexuals who speak with you are as angry and closed-minded as he was."

"No, of course not."

"Then why did you portray him that way in the dialogue?"

"Would you have me pretend that *nobody* in the homosexual life is angry and closed-minded? A good many are like that — you should see my letters — and I try to show my readers the dynamics of more than one kind of conversation. You see, when people have honest questions you try to answer them, but when they only churn out smokescreens, then you blow the smoke away."

"So you'd be open to different kinds of conversation."

"Of course," I said. I smiled. "Are we, perhaps, having one right now?"

His eyebrows lifted. "Am I that obvious?"

"It was just a shot in the dark. So what did you really want to talk about?"

"I'm not very ideological, but I guess you could call me a Seeker. See, I've been in the gay life for five years, but lately I've been having second thoughts. I'm not asking you to convert me, understand? I thought I'd just hear what you have to say, then go away and think about it."

"What have you been having second thoughts about?"

He hesitated. "Are you going to use this conversation in one of your dialogues?"

"If I did, I'd make sure you couldn't be identified. You can speak freely."

"Well —" he hesitated. "One thing is intimacy. I've never had problems finding sex, but it's more or less anonymous. That didn't bother me at first, but now it's getting me down."

"Is the sex always anonymous?"

"No, the first time I had gay sex was in a steady relationship. I've been in two or three others, too — for a month, two months, a year. But they were never what you'd call faithful, know what I mean? It's as though there had to be other sexual outlets for the relationship to work at all. I'm starting to want — I don't know. Something else."

"I follow you."

He paused. "Another thing. I want to be a Dad. That doesn't fit the stereotype, does it? Are you surprised to hear me say it?"

"Not at all."

"In that case you're the only one. My friends don't get it. One said, 'Why don't you just get a turkey baster and make an arrangement with a lesbian?' But that's not what I want." Another pause. "I used to say to myself, 'Get used to it. You can't have everything you want.' But that doesn't work for me any more."

After a second he spoke again. "There's one more thing."

"What's that?"

"God."

"God? How so?"

"Oh, I go to church sometimes. Now *that* must surprise you."

"No. What kind of church?"

"Different kinds. I didn't go to any church at first. My family never went to

54

church. Most of my gay friends don't have any use for God. Then I started going to a gay church, and that was okay for awhile. But I think I might want the real stuff, do you know what I mean? Or else nothing."

"I think so. You don't have any doubts about what the real stuff is?"

"No. I'm not saying I believe in Jesus, but —" He thought for a moment. "The gay church said you can be a Christian and still live a gay life. I don't think I ever really believed that. I read a book that the minister in the gay church recommended —"

"Yes?"

"The title was something like *Sex and Dirt*. I'm leaving something out. Hold on, it'll come to me."

"Never mind, I know the book."

"Oh, good. Then you probably remember how the author argues that when the Bible lays down rules about sex, they're just purity codes — not moral laws — so you don't have to keep them."

"Sure."

"He had me going for a while — right up to where he said 'that's why even having sex with animals is okay,' or words to that effect. Just what the guy in your dialogue accused *you* of saying gay people think. I could see that the author's conclusion followed from his premises — but after that, I didn't have any use for his premises, if you see what I mean."

"I see exactly what you mean. So where does all this leave you?"

"Like I said, I want to hear you out, and then I'll go away and think about it."

"That's fine, Adam, but just what is it that you want to hear me out about?"

"I think what I'm missing is the Big Picture about sex. If there is a Big Picture about sex."

"There is indeed a Big Picture about sex."

"Draw it, then. Paint it. Lecture me, even. That is," he added, "if you don't mind."

I had to laugh. "You asked me before if I was going to use this conversation in one of my dialogues. If I do, nobody will believe it. They'll call it contrived."

"Why?"

"Because you've set the stage too well. Your 'second thoughts' anticipate everything I'd like to say. And now you ask for a lecture!"

"After seven years of college, I'm used to lectures. You do your professor thing, and I'll listen. If I want to argue — believe me, I know how — I'll come back another day."

I collected my thoughts. "All right, Adam. The main point of Christian sexual morality is that human nature is *designed.* We need to live a certain way because we're designed to live that way."

He said, "I can see design in an organ like the heart. Human nature — that's a little too big for me."

"Then let's start with the heart. Do you see how every part works together toward its purpose, its function?"

"Sure. You've got nerves and valves and pumping chambers, all for moving blood."

"Right. If you think about the sexual powers instead of the heart, it's just the same. The key to understanding a design is to recognize its purposes. For the heart, the purpose is pumping blood; for the sexual powers — you tell me."

"Pleasure?"

"Think about it. Would you say pleasure is the purpose of eating?"

"No, I'd say nourishment is the purpose of eating, and pleasure is just the result."

"If you thought pleasure were the purpose of eating, what would you do if I offered you pleasant-tasting poison?"

"Eat it."

"And what would happen?"

"I'd get sick."

"But if you understood that nourishment were the purpose of eating and pleasure merely the result, *then* what would you do if I offered you pleasant-tasting poison?"

"Refuse it and ask for food instead."

"It's the same with the sexual powers. Pleasure is a result of their use, but not the purpose of their use. The purposes can tell you which kinds of sexual activity are good and which aren't; by itself, pleasure can't."

"So what are the purposes of the sexual powers?"

"You've told me already; you just didn't realize you were doing so."

"I have? When?"

"When you were telling me your second thoughts about the homosexual life. There were three of them. What was the first one about?"

"Intimacy. Bonding."

"And the second?"

"Having children."

"Then you won't be surprised to hear that one inbuilt purpose of the sexual powers is to bond a man with a woman, and another is to have and raise children."

"If bonding is good, why not use the sexual powers to bond a man with a man?"

"Has that worked in your case, Adam?"

"Well, no. That's what I was complaining about."

"You see, that's no accident. Bonding man with man is contrary to the design."

"You say that, but how do you *know?*"

"There are two reasons. First, man and woman are complementary. They're not just *different,* they *match.* There is something in male emotional design to which only the female can give completion, and something in female emotional design to which only the male can give completion. When same mates with same, that can't happen. Instead of balancing each other, they unbalance each other."

"What's the other reason?"

"The other reason is that the linkage of same with same is sterile. You've complained about that, too."

"But sometimes a man can't produce children with a woman, either."

"The mating of same with same isn't *accidentally* sterile, Adam, as the union of a particular man with a particular woman might be; it's *inherently* sterile. A husband and wife who are unable to have a baby haven't set themselves against their own inbuilt purposes. A man and man who have sex together have."

He grinned. "There's always the turkey baster."

"But when your friend made that suggestion, you refused, didn't you? What was your reason?"

"I'm not sure. I just think a kid needs a Mom and a Dad."

"That's exactly right. Male and female complement and complete each other not just in having children but in rearing them. Women are better designed for nurture, men are better designed for protection. Besides, two Dads can't model male-female relationships. Neither can two Moms. Neither can one."

Adam was silent as he digested this. "You know," he said finally, "this isn't at all what I expected you to talk about."

"What did you expect me to talk about?"

"Disease." He paused. "Now that I think about it, you didn't say much about disease in that dialogue I read either."

"I should think you already know the deadliness of your way of life."

"I suppose so. But it does seem unfair. Why should gay sex be less healthy than any other kind?"

"Don't we come right back to the design? Start with the fact that not all orifices are created equal."

"Hmmm."

"Hmmm?"

"I think I'll go do what I said I'd do: Go away and think about it all. In the meantime, Professor, I think you have a problem."

"Do I?"

"That is, if you do intend to use this chat of ours in one of your dialogues."

"And what might this problem be?"

"We've talked too long. Your dialogues are all 1500 words. This one is way over."

I smiled. "I'll talk to my editor about it."

Dr J. Budziszewski is a Professor of Government and Philosophy at the University of Texas, Austin, and a specialist on natural law. He is especially interested in moral self-deception – in what happens to us when we tell ourselves that we don't know what we really do. His eleven books cover a wide range, including one *Christianity Today* award winner (*Written on the Heart: The Case for Natural Law*), three for young people (*How to Stay Christian in College*, *Ask Me Anything*, and a forthcoming *Ask Me Anything 2*), and one with a double negative (*What We Can't Not Know: A Guide*). In the person of his alter-ego, Professor Theophilus, he also writes the monthly online column "Office Hours" at TrueU.org, from which these articles are taken. We have it on reliable authority that Dr Budziszewski is a former atheist, former socialist, former Anglican, and former lots of other things. In 2003, he was received into the Roman Catholic Church. Married for thirty-six years, he and his wife have several grown children.

Photo by Kevin Vandivier, Lakeway, Texas

See also

'Why meeting nice "gay" and lesbian persons should not lead to approval of homosexual practice', 2007 email exchange between Brien and Dr Rob Gagnon; http://www.robgagnon.net/AnswersToEMails.htm

God's Grace and the Homosexual Next Door by Alan Chambers and the Exodus International Leadership Team (Harvest House, 2006).

'Can't Anyone Tell Me Why?' by Dr J. Budziszewski; http://catholiceducation.org/articles/homosexuality/h00082.html

The Books, the Porn, the Truth
The Truth About the Homosexual Rights Movement

Dr Ronald G. Lee

Introduction by Chris Sugden

The following article will be shocking to some, and it will anger others; it is an account of one man's experience, his own story, his personal testimony. We include it, however, because personal experience is given a privileged status in the debates about homosexuality. Great emphasis is laid on the importance of listening carefully to people's individual stories, and attending to them with empathy.

It is our view that Dr Lee's narrative deserves a hearing equal to that given to the impassioned gay advocate. Surely equal opportunities work both ways? If this was the truth for Dr Lee, then we owe it to him to attend to his experience, and allow it to form part of the evidence which we need to take into account when discussing these issues. Though it may be hard to believe, we love those struggling with same sex attraction too much to do otherwise.

There was a "gay" bookstore called Lobo's in Austin, Texas, when I was living there as a grad student. The layout was interesting. Looking inside from the street all you saw were books. It looked like any other bookstore. There was a section devoted to classic "gay" fiction by writers such as Oscar Wilde, Gertrude Stein, and W.H. Auden. There were biographies of prominent "gay" icons, some of whom, like Walt Whitman, would probably have accepted the homosexual label, but many of whom, like Whitman's idol, President Lincoln, had been commandeered for the cause on the basis of evidence no stronger than a bad marriage or an intense same-sex friendship. There were impassioned modern "gay" memoirs, and historical accounts of the origins and development of the "gay rights" movement. It all looked so innocuous and disarmingly bourgeois. But if you went inside to browse, before long you noticed another section, behind the books, a section not visible from the street.

The pornography section.

Hundreds and hundreds of pornographic videos, all involving men, but otherwise catering to every conceivable sexual taste or fantasy. And you would notice something else too. There were no customers in the front. All the customers were in the back, rooting through the videos. As far as I know, I am the only person who ever actually purchased a book at Lobo's. The books were, in every sense of the word, a front for the porn.

So why waste thousands of dollars on books that no one was going to buy? It was clear from the large "on sale" section that only a pitifully small number of books were ever purchased at their original price. The owners of Lobo's were apparently wasting a lot of money on gay novels and works of gay history, when all the real money was in pornography. But the money spent on books wasn't wasted. It was used to purchase a commodity that is more precious than gold to the gay rights establishment. Respectability. Respectability and the appearance of normalcy. Without that investment, we would not now be engaged in a serious debate about the legalization of same-sex "marriage." By the time I lived in Austin, I had been thinking of myself as a gay man for almost 20 years. Based on the experience acquired during those years, I recognized in Lobo's a metaphor for the strategy used to sell gay rights to the American people, and for the sordid reality that strategy concealed.

This is how I "deconstruct" Lobo's. There are two kinds of people who are going to be looking in through the window: those who are tempted to engage in homosexual acts, and those who aren't. To those who aren't, the shelves of books transmit the message that gay people are no different from anyone else, that homosexuality is not wrong, just different. Since most of them will never know more about homosexuality than what they learned looking in the window, that impression is of the greatest political and cultural importance, because on that basis they will react without alarm, or even with active support, to the progress of gay rights. There are millions of well-meaning Americans who support gay rights because they believe that what they see looking in at Lobo's is what is really there. It does not occur to them that they are seeing a carefully stage-managed effort to manipulate them, to distract them from a truth they would never condone.

For those who are tempted to engage in homosexual acts, the view from the street is also consoling. It makes life as a homosexual look safe and unthreatening. Normal, in other words. Sooner or later, many of these people will stop looking in through the window and go inside. Unlike the first sort of window-shopper, they won't be distracted by the books for long. They will soon discover the existence of the porn section. And no matter how distasteful they might find the idea at first (if indeed they do find it distasteful), they will also notice that the porn section is where all the customers are. And they will feel sort of silly standing alone among the books. Eventually, they will find their way back to the porn, with the rest of the customers. And like them, they will start rooting through the videos. And, gentle reader, that is where most of them will spend the rest of their lives, until God or AIDS, drugs or alcohol, suicide or a lonely old age, intervenes.

Ralph McInerny once offered a brilliant definition of the gay rights movement: self-deception as a group effort. Nevertheless, deception of the general public is also vital to the success of the cause. And nowhere are the forms of deception more egregious, or more startlingly successful, than in the campaign to persuade Christians that, to paraphrase the title of a recent book, *Jesus Was Queer*, and churches should open their doors to same-sex lovers. The gay Christian movement relies on a stratagem that is as daring as it is dishonest. I know, because I was taken in by it for a long time. Like the owners of Lobo's, success depends on camouflaging the truth, which is hidden in plain view the whole time. It is no wonder *The Wizard of Oz* is so resonant among homosexuals. "Pay no attention to that man behind the curtain" could be the motto and the mantra of the whole movement.

No single book was as influential in my own coming out as the now ex-Father John McNeill's 1976 "classic" *The Church and the Homosexual*. That book is to Dignity what *The Communist Manifesto* was to Soviet Russia. Most of the book is devoted to offering alternative interpretations of the biblical passages condemning homosexuality, and to putting the anti-homosexual writings of the Church Fathers and scholastics into historical context in a way that renders them irrelevant and even offensive to modern readers. The first impression of a naïve and sexually conflicted young reader such as myself was that McNeill had offered a plausible alternative to traditional teaching. It made me feel justified in deciding to come out of the closet. Were his arguments persuasive? Frankly, I didn't care, and I don't believe most of McNeill's readers do either. They were couched in the language of scholarship, and they sounded plausible. That was all that mattered.

McNeill, like most of the members of his camp, treated the debate over homosexuality as first and foremost a debate about the proper interpretation of texts, texts such as the Sodom story in the Bible and the relevant articles of the *Summa*. The implication was that once those were reinterpreted, or rendered irrelevant, the gay rights apologists had prevailed, and the door was open for practicing homosexuals to hold their heads up high in church. And there is a certain sense in which that has proved to be true. To the extent that the debate has focused on interpreting texts, the gay apologists have won for themselves a remarkable degree of legitimacy. But that is because, as anyone familiar with the history of Protestantism should be aware, the interpretation of texts is an interminable process. The efforts of people such as McNeill don't need to be persuasive. They only need to be useful.

This is how it works. McNeill reinterprets the story of Sodom, claiming that it does not condemn homosexuality, but gang rape. Orthodox theologians respond, in a commendable but naïve attempt to rebut him, naïve because these theologians presume that McNeill believes his own arguments, and is writing as a scholar, not as a propagandist. McNeill ignores the arguments of his critics, dismissing their objections as based on homophobia, and repeats his original position. The orthodox respond again as if they were really dealing with a theologian. And back and forth for a few more rounds. Until finally McNeill or someone like him stands up and announces, "You know, this is getting us nowhere. We have our exegesis and our theology. You have yours. Why can't we just agree to disagree?" That sounds so reasonable, so ecumenical. And if the orthodox buy into it, they have lost, because the gay rights apologists have earned a place at the table from which they will never be dislodged. Getting at the truth about Sodom and Gomorrah, or correctly parsing the sexual ethics of St. Thomas, was never really the issue. Winning admittance to Holy Communion was the issue.

Even as a naïve young man, one aspect of *The Church and the Homosexual* struck me as odd. Given that McNeill was suggesting a radical revision of the traditional Catholic sexual ethic, there was almost nothing in it about sexual ethics. The Catholic sexual ethic is quite specific about the ends of human sexuality, and about the forms of behavior that are consistent with those ends. McNeill's criticism of the traditional ethic occupied most of his book, but he left the reader with only the vaguest idea about what he proposed to put in its place. For that matter, there was almost nothing in it about the real lives of real homosexuals. Homosexuality was treated throughout the book as a kind of intellectual abstraction. But I was desperate to get some idea of what was waiting for me on the other side of the closet door. And with no one but Fr. McNeill for a guide, I was reduced to reading between the lines. There was a single passage that I interpreted as a clue. It was almost an aside, really. At one point, he commented that monogamous same-sex unions were consistent with the Church's teaching, or at least consistent with the spirit of the renewed and renovated post-Vatican II Church. With nothing else to go on, I interpreted this in a prescriptive sense. I interpreted McNeill to be arguing that homogenital acts were only moral when performed in the context of a monogamous relationship. And furthermore, I leapt to what seemed like the reasonable conclusion that the author was aware of such relationships, and that I had a reasonable expectation of finding such a relationship myself. Otherwise, for whose benefit was he writing? I was not so naïve (although I was pretty naïve) as not to be aware of the existence of promiscuous homosexual men. But McNeill's aside, which, I repeat, contained virtually his only stab at offering a gay sexual ethic, led me to believe that in addition to the promiscuous, there existed a contingent of gay men who were committed to living in monogamy. Otherwise, Fr. McNeill was implicitly defending promiscuity. And the very idea of a priest defending promiscuity was inconceivable to me. (Yes, that naïve.)

Several years ago, McNeill published an autobiography. In it, he makes no bones about his experiences as a sexually active Catholic priest – a promiscuous, sexually active, homosexual Catholic priest. He writes in an almost nostalgic fashion about his time spent hunting for sex in bars. Although he eventually did find a stable partner (while he was still a priest), he never apologizes for his years of promiscuity, or even so much as alludes to the disparity between his own life and the passage in *The Church and the Homosexual* that meant so much to me. It is possible that he doesn't even remember suggesting that homosexuals were supposed to remain celibate until finding monogamous relationships. It is obvious that he never meant that passage to be taken seriously, except by those who would never do more than look in the window – in others words, gullible, well-meaning, non-homosexual Catholics, preferably those in positions of authority. Or, equally naïve and gullible young men such as me who were looking for a reason to act on their sexual desires, preferably one that did not do too much violence to their consciences, at least not at first. The latter, the writer presumed, would eventually find their way back to the porn section, where their complicity in the scam would render them indistinguishable from the rest of the regular customers. Clearly, there was a reason that in the earlier book he wrote so little about the real lives of real homosexuals, such as himself.

I don't see how the contradiction between *The Church and the Homosexual* and the autobiography could be accidental. Why would McNeill pretend to believe that homosexuals should restrict themselves to sex within the context of monogamous relationships when his life demonstrates that he did not? I can think of only one reason. Because he knew that if he told the truth, his cause would be dead in the water. Although to this day McNeill, like all gay Christian propagandists, avoids the subject of sexual ethics as if it were some sort of plague, his life makes his real beliefs clear. He believes in unrestricted sexual freedom. He believes that men and women should have the right to couple, with whomever they want, whenever they want, however they want, and as often as they want. He would probably add some sort of meaningless bromide about no one getting hurt and both parties being treated with respect, but anyone familiar with the snake pit of modern sexual culture (both heterosexual and homosexual) will know how seriously to take that. And he knew perfectly well that if he were honest about his real aims, there would be no Dignity, there would be no gay Christian movement, at least not one with a snowball's chance in Hell of succeeding. That would be like getting rid of the books and letting the casual window-shoppers see the porn. And we can't have that now, can we? In other words, the ex-Fr. McNeill is a bad priest and a con man. And given the often lethal consequences of engaging in homosexual sex, a con man with blood on his hands.

Let me be clear. I believe that McNeill's real beliefs, as deduced from his actual behavior, and distinguished from the arguments he puts forward for the benefit of the naïve and gullible, represent the real aims and objectives of the homosexual rights movement. They are the porn that the books are meant to conceal. In other words, if you support what is now described in euphemistic terms as "the blessing of same-sex unions," in practice you are supporting the abolition of the entire Christian sexual ethic, and its substitution with an unrestricted, laissez faire, free sexual market. The reason that the homosexual rights movement has managed to pick up such a large contingent of heterosexual fellow-travelers is simple: Because once that taboo is abrogated, no taboos are left. I once heard a heterosexual Episcopalian put it this way: "If I don't want the church poking its nose into my bedroom, how can I condone it when it limits the sexual freedom of homosexuals?" That might sound outrageous, but if you still believe that the debate is over the religious status of monogamous same-sex relationships, please be prepared to point out one church somewhere in the U.S. that has opened its doors to active homosexuals without also opening them to every other form of sexual coupling imaginable. I am too old to be taken in by "Father" McNeill and his abstractions anymore. Show me.

A few years ago, I subscribed to the Dignity Yahoo group on the Internet. There were at that time several hundred subscribers. At one point, a confused and troubled young man posted a question to the group: Did any of the subscribers attach any value to monogamy? I immediately wrote back that I did. A couple of days later the young man wrote back to me. He had received dozens of responses, some of them quite hostile and demeaning, and all but one – mine – telling him to go out and get laid because that was what being gay was all about. (This was a gay "Catholic" group.) He did not know what to make of it because none of the propaganda to which he was exposed before coming out prepared him for what was really on the other side of the closet door. I had no idea what to tell him, because at the time I was still caught up in the lie myself. Now, the solution seems obvious. What I should have written back to him was, "You have been lied to. Ask God for forgiveness and get back to Kansas as fast as you can. Auntie Em is waiting."

In light of all the legitimate concern about Internet pornography, it might seem ironic to assert that the Internet helped rescue me from homosexuality. For twenty years, I thought there was something wrong with me. Dozens of well-meaning people assured me that there was a whole, different world of homosexual men out there, a world that for some reason I could never find, a world of God-fearing, straight-acting, monogamy-believing, and fidelity-practicing homosexuals. They assured me that they themselves knew personally (for a fact and for real) that such men existed. They themselves knew such men (or at least had heard tell of them from those who did). And I believed it, although as the years passed it got harder and harder. Then I got a personal computer and a subscription to AOL. "O.K.," I reasoned, "morally conservative homosexuals are obviously shy and skittish and fearful of sudden movements. They don't like bars and bathhouses. Neither do I. They don't attend Dignity meetings or Metropolitan Community Church services because the gay 'churches' are really bathhouses masquerading as houses of worship. But there is no reason a morally conservative homosexual cannot subscribe to AOL and submit a profile. If I can do it, anyone can do it." So I did it. I wrote a profile describing myself as a conservative Catholic (*comme ci, comme ça*) who loved classical music and theater and good books and scintillating conversation about all of the above. I said I wanted very much to meet other like-minded homosexuals for the purposes of friendship and romance. I tried to be as clear as I knew how. I was not interested in one night stands. And within minutes of placing the profile, I got my first response. It consisted of three words: "How many inches?" My experience of looking for love on AOL went downhill rapidly from there.

When I first came out in the 1980s, it was common for gay rights apologists to blame the promiscuity among gay men on "internalized homophobia." Gay men, like African Americans, internalized and acted out the lies about themselves learned from mainstream American culture. Furthermore, homosexuals were forced to look for love in dimly lit bars, bathhouses, and public parks for fear of harassment at the hands of a homophobic mainstream. The solution to this problem, we were told, was permitting homosexuals to come out into the open, without fear of retribution. A variant of this argument is still put forward by activists such as Andrew Sullivan, in order to legitimate same-sex marriage. And it seemed reasonable enough twenty years ago. But thirty-five years have passed since the infamous Stonewall riots of 1969 in New York, the

Lexington and Concord of the gay liberation movement. During that time, homosexuals have carved out for themselves public spaces in every major American city, and many of the minor ones as well. They have had the chance to create whatever they wanted in those spaces, and what have they created? New spaces for locating sexual partners.

There is another reason, apart from the propaganda value, that bookstores like Lobo's peddle porn as well as poetry. Because without the porn, they would soon go out of business. And, in fact, most gay bookstores have gone out of business, despite the porn. Following an initial burst of enthusiasm in the 1970s and 80s, gay publishing went into steep decline, and shows no signs of coming out of it. Once the novelty wore off, gay men soon bored of reading about men having sex with one another, preferring to devote their time and disposable income to pursuing the real thing. Gay and lesbian community centers struggle to keep their doors open. Gay churches survive as places where worshippers can go to sleep it off and cleanse their soiled consciences after a Saturday night spent cruising for sex at the bars. And there is no danger of ever hearing a word from the pulpit suggesting that bar-hopping is inconsistent with believing in the Bible. When I lived in the United Kingdom, I was struck by the extent to which gay culture in London replicated gay culture in the U.S. The same was true in Paris, Amsterdam, and Berlin. Homosexuality is one of America's most successful cultural exports. And the focus on gay social spaces in Europe is identical to their focus in America: sex. Cyberspace is now the latest conquest of that amazing modern Magellan: the male homosexual in pursuit of new sexual conquests.

But at this point, how is it possible to blame the promiscuity among homosexual men on homophobia, internalized or otherwise? On the basis of evidence no stronger than wishful thinking, Andrew Sullivan wants us to believe that legalizing same-sex "marriage" will domesticate gay men, that all that energy now devoted to building bars and bathhouses will be dedicated to erecting picket fences and two-car garages. What Sullivan refuses to face is that male homosexuals are not promiscuous because of "internalized homophobia," or laws banning same-sex "marriage." Homosexuals are promiscuous because when given the choice, homosexuals overwhelmingly choose to be promiscuous. And wrecking the fundamental social building block of our civilization, the family, is not going to change that.

I once read a disarmingly honest essay in which Sullivan as much as admitted his real reason for promoting the cause of same-sex "marriage." He faced up to the sometimes sordid nature of his sexual life, which is more than most gay activists are prepared to do, and he regretted it. He wished he had led a different sort of life, and he apparently believes that if marriage were a legal option, he might have been able to do so. I have a lot more respect for Andrew Sullivan than I do for most gay activists. I believe that he would seriously like to reconcile his sexual desires with the demands of his conscience. But with all due respect, are the rest of us prepared to sacrifice the institution of the family in the unsubstantiated hope that doing so will make it easier for Sullivan to keep his trousers zipped?

But isn't it theoretically possible that homosexuals could restrict themselves to something resembling the traditional Catholic sexual ethic, except for the part about procreation – in other words, monogamous lifelong relationships? Of course it is theoretically possible. It was also theoretically possible in 1968 that the use of contraceptives could be restricted to married couples, that the revolting downward slide into moral anarchy we have lived through could have been avoided. It is theoretically possible, but it is practically impossible. It is impossible because the whole notion of stable sexual orientation on which the gay rights movement is founded has no basis in fact.

René Girard, the French literary critic and sociologist of religion, argues that all human civilization is founded on desire. All civilizations have surrounded the objects of desire (including sexual desire) with an elaborate and unbreachable wall of taboos and restrictions. Until now. What we are seeing in the modern West is not the long overdue legitimization of hitherto despised but honorable forms of human love. What we are witnessing is the reduction of civilization to its lowest common denominator: unbridled and unrestricted desire. To assert that we have opened a Pandora's Box would be a stunning understatement. Fasten your seatbelts, ladies and gentlemen, it looks to be a bumpy millennium.

When I was growing up, we were all presumed to be heterosexual. Then homosexuality was introduced as an alternative. That did not at first seem like a major revision because, apart from procreation, homosexuality, at least in theory, left the rest of the traditional sexual ethic in tact. Two people of the same gender could (in theory) fall in love and live a life of monogamous commitment. Then bisexuality was introduced, and the real implications of the sexual revolution became clear. Monogamy was out the window. Moral norms were out the window. Do-it-yourself sexuality became the norm. Anyone who wants to know what that looks like can do no better than go online. The Internet offers front row seats to the circus of a disintegrating civilization.

Over the years, I have attended various gay and gay-friendly church services. All of them shared one characteristic in common: a tacit agreement never to say a word from the pulpit – or from any other location for that matter – suggesting that there ought to be any restrictions on human sexual behavior. If anyone reading this is familiar with Dignity or Integrity or the Metropolitan Community churches or, for that matter, mainline Protestantism and most of post-Vatican II Catholicism, let me ask you one question: When was the last time you heard a sermon on sexual ethics? Have you ever heard a sermon on sexual ethics? I take it for granted that the answer is negative. Do our priests and pastors honestly believe that Christians in America are not in need of sermons on sexual ethics?

Here is the terrifying fact: If we as a nation and as a Church allow ourselves to be taken in by the scam of monogamous same-sex couples, we will be welcoming to our Communion rails (presuming that we still have Communion rails) not just the statistically insignificant number of same-sex couples who have lived together for more than a few years (most of whom purchased stability by jettisoning monogamy); we will also be legitimizing every kind of sexual taste, from old-fashioned masturbation and adultery to the most outlandish forms of sexual fetishism. We will, in other words, be giving our blessing to the suicide of Western civilization.

But what about all those images of loving same-sex couples dying to get hitched with which the media are awash these days? That used to confuse me too. It seems that *The New York Times* has no trouble finding successful same-sex partners to photograph and interview. But despite my best efforts, I was never able to meet the sorts of couples who show up regularly on Oprah. The media are biased and have no interest in telling the truth about homosexuality.

I met Wyatt (not his real name) online. For five years he was in a disastrous same-sex relationship. His partner was unfaithful, and an alcoholic with drug problems. The relationship was something that would give Strindberg nightmares. When Vermont legalized same-sex "marriage," Wyatt saw it as one last chance to make their relationship work. He and his partner would fly to Vermont to get "married." This came to the attention of the local newspaper in his area, which did a story with photos of the wedding reception. In it, Wyatt and his partner were depicted as a loving couple who finally had a chance to celebrate their commitment publicly. Nothing was said about the drugs or the alcoholism or the infidelity. But the marriage was a failure and ended in flames a few months later. And the newspaper did not do a follow-up. In other words, the leading daily of one of America's largest cities printed a misleading story about a bad relationship, a story that probably persuaded more than one young man that someday he could be just as happy as Wyatt and his "partner." And that is the sad part.

But one very seldom reads about people like my friend Harry. Harry (not his real name) was a balding, middle-aged man with a potbelly. He was married, and had a couple of grown daughters. And he was unhappy. Harry persuaded himself that he was unhappy because he was gay. He divorced his wife, who is now married to someone else, his daughters are not speaking to him, and he is discovering that pudgy, bald, middle-aged men are not all that popular in gay bars. Somehow, Oprah forgot to mention that. Now Harry is taking anti-depressants in order to keep from killing himself.

Then there was another acquaintance, who also happened to have the same name as the previous guy. Harry (not his real name) was about 30 (but could easily pass for 20), and from a Mormon background, with all the naïveté that suggests. Unlike the first Harry, he had no difficulty getting dates. Or relationships for that matter. The problem was that the relationships never lasted more than a couple of weeks. Harry was also rapidly developing a serious drinking problem. (So much for the Mormon words of wisdom.) If you happened to be at the bar around two in the morning, you could probably have Harry for the night if you were interested. He was so drunk he wouldn't remember you the next day, and all he really wanted at that point was for someone to hold him.

Gay culture is a paradox. Most homosexuals tend to be liberal Democrats, or in the U.K., supporters of the Labour Party. They gravitate toward those Parties on the grounds that their policies are more compassionate and sensitive to the needs of the downtrodden and oppressed. But there is nothing compassionate about a gay bar. It represents a laissez faire free sexual market of the most Darwinian sort. There is no place in it for those who are not prepared to compete, and the rules of the game are ruthless and unforgiving. I remember once being in a gay pub in central London. Most of the men there were buff and toned and in their 20s or early 30s. An older gentleman walked in, who looked to be in his 70s. It was as if the Angel of Death himself had made an entrance. In that crowded bar, a space opened up around him that no one wanted to enter. His shadow transmitted contagion. It was obvious that his presence made the other customers nervous. He stood quietly at the bar and ordered a drink. He spoke to no one and no one spoke to him. When he eventually finished his drink and left, the sigh of relief from all those buff, toned pub crawlers was almost audible. Now all of them could go back to pretending that gay men were all young and beautiful forever.

Gentle reader, do you know what a "bug chaser" is? A bug chaser is a young gay man who wants to contract HIV so that he will never grow old. And that is the world that Harry left his wife, and the other Harry his Church, to find happiness in.

I have known a lot of people like the two Harrys. But I have met precious few who bore more than a superficial resemblance to the idealized images we see in Oscar-winning movies such as *Philadelphia*, or in the magazine section of *The New York Times*. What I find suspicious is that the media ignore the existence of people like the two Harrys. The unhappiness so common among homosexuals is swept under the carpet, while fanciful and unrealistic "role models" are offered up for public consumption. There is at the very least grounds for a serious debate about the proposition that "gay is good," but no such debate is taking place, because most of the mainstream media have already made up their (and our) minds.

But it is hard to hide the porn forever. When I was living in London, I had a wonderful friend named Maggie. Maggie (not her real name) was a liberal. Her big heart bled for the oppressed. Like most liberals, she was proud of her open-mindedness and wore it like a badge of honor. Maggie lived in a house as big as her heart and all of her children were grown up and had moved out. She had a couple of rooms to rent. It just so happened that both the young men who became her tenants were gay. Maggie's first reaction was enthusiastic. She had never known many gay people, and thought the experience of renting to two homosexuals would confirm her in her open-mindedness. She believed it would be a learning experience. It was, but not the sort she had in mind. One day Maggie told me her troubles and confessed her doubts. She talked about what it was like to stumble each morning down to the breakfast table, finding two strangers seated there, the two strangers her tenants brought home the night before. · It was seldom the same two strangers two mornings running. One of her tenants was in a long-distance relationship but, in the absence of his partner, felt at liberty to seek consolation elsewhere. She talked about what it was like to have to deal on a daily basis with the emotional turmoil of her tenants' tumultuous lives. She told me what it was like to open the door one afternoon and find a policeman standing there, a policeman who was looking for one of her tenants, who was accused of trying to sell drugs to school children. That same tenant was also involved in prostitution. Maggie didn't know what to make of it all. She desperately wanted to remain open-minded, to keep believing that gay men were no worse than anyone else, just different. But she couldn't reconcile her experience with that "tolerant" assumption. The truth was that when the two finally moved out, an event to which she was looking forward with some enthusiasm, and it was time to place a new ad for rooms to let, she wanted to include the following proviso: Fags need not apply. I didn't know what to tell Maggie because I was just as confused as she was. I wanted to hold on to my illusions too, in spite of all the evidence.

I am convinced that many, if not most, people who are familiar with the lives of homosexuals know the truth, but refuse to face it. My best friend got involved in the gay rights movement as a graduate student. He and a lesbian colleague sometimes counseled young men who were struggling with their sexuality. Once, the two of them met a young man who was seriously overweight and suffered from terrible acne. The young man waxed eloquent about the happiness he expected to find when he came out of the closet. He was going to find a partner, and the two of them would live happily ever after. The whole time my friend was thinking that if someone looking like this fat, pustulent young man ever walked into a bar, he would be folded, spindled, and mutilated before even taking a seat. Afterwards, the lesbian turned to him and said, "You know, sometimes it is better to stay in the closet." My friend told me that for him this represented a decisive moment. This lesbian claimed to love and admire gay men. She never stopped praising their kindness and compassion and creativity. But with that one comment she in effect told my friend that she really knew what gay life was all about. It was about meat, and unless you were a good cut, don't bother coming to the supermarket.

On another occasion, I was complaining to a lesbian about my disillusionment. She made a remarkable admission to me. She had a teenage son, who so far had not displayed signs of sexual interest in either gender. She knew as a lesbian she should not care which road he took. But she confessed to me that she did care. Based on the lives of the gay men she knew, she found herself secretly praying that her son would turn out to be straight. As a mother, she did not want to see her son living that life.

A popular definition of insanity is to keep doing the same thing, while expecting a different result. That was me, the whole time I was laboring to become a happy homosexual. I was a lunatic. Several times I turned for advice to gay men who seemed better adjusted to their lot in life than I was. First, I wanted confirmation that my perceptions were accurate, that life as a male homosexual really was as awful as it seemed to be. And then I wanted to know what I was supposed to do about it. When was it going to get better? What could I do to make it better? I got two sorts of reactions to these questions, both of which left me feeling hurt and confused. The first sort of reaction was denial, often bitter denial, of what I was suggesting. I was told that there was something wrong with me, that most gay men were having a wonderful time, that I was generalizing on the basis of my own experience (whose experience was I supposed to generalize from?), and that I should shut up and stop bothering others with my "internalized homophobia."

I began seeing a counselor when I was a graduate student. Matt (not his real name) was a happily married man with college-age children. All he knew about homosexuality he learned from the other members of his profession, who assured him that homosexuality was not a mental illness and that there were no good reasons that homosexuals could not lead happy, productive lives. When I first unloaded my tale of woe, Matt told me I had never really come out of the closet. (I still have no idea what he meant, but suspect it is like the "once saved, always saved" Baptist who responds to the lapsed by telling him that he was never really saved in the first place.) I needed to go back, he told me, try again, and continue to look for the positive experiences he was sure were available for me, on the basis of no other evidence than the rulings of the American Psychiatric Association. He had almost no personal experience of homosexuals, but his peers assured him that the book section at Lobo's offered a true picture of homosexual life. I knew Matt was clueless, but I still wanted to believe he was right.

Matt and I developed a therapeutic relationship. During the year we spent together, he learned far more from me than I did from him. I tried to take his advice. I was sharing a house that year with another grad student who was in the process of coming out and experiencing his own disillusionment. Because I had been his only gay friend, and had encouraged him to come out, his bitterness came to be directed at me, and our relationship suffered for it. Meanwhile, I developed a close friendship with a member of the faculty who was openly gay. When I first informed Matt, he was ecstatic. He thought I was finally come out properly. The faculty member was just the sort of friend I needed. But the faculty member, as it turned out, despite his immaculate professional facade, was a deeply disturbed man who put all of his friends through emotional hell, which I of course shared with a shocked and silenced Matt. (I tried to date but, as usual, experienced the same pattern that characterized all my homosexual relationships. The friendship lasted as long as the sexual heat. Once that cooled, my partner's interest in me as a person dissipated with it.) It was not a good year. At the end of it, I remember Matt staring at me, with glazed eyes and a shell-shocked look on his face, and admitting, "You know, being gay is a lot harder than I realized."

Not everyone I spoke to over the years rejected what I had to say out of hand. I once corresponded with an English ex-Dominican. I was ecstatic to learn that he was gay, and was eventually kicked out of his order for refusing to remain in the closet. He included an e-mail address in one of his books, and I wrote him, wanting to know if his experience of life as a homosexual was significantly different from mine. I presumed it must be, since he had written a couple of books, passionately defending the right of homosexuals to a place in the Church. His response to me was one of the last nails in the coffin of my life as a gay man. To my astonishment, he admitted that his experiences were not unlike mine. All he could suggest was that I keep trying, and eventually everything would work out. In other words, this brilliant man, whose books had meant so much to me, had nothing to suggest except that I keep doing the same thing, while expecting a different result. There was only one reasonable conclusion. I would be nuts if I took his advice. It took me twenty years, but I finally reached the conclusion that I did not want to be insane.

So where am I now? I am attending a militantly orthodox parish in Houston that is one of God's most spectacular gifts to me. My best friend Mark (not his real name) is, like me, a refugee from the homosexual insane asylum. He is also a devout believer, though a Presbyterian (no one is perfect). From Mark I have learned that two men can love each other profoundly while remaining clothed the entire time.

We are told that the Church opposes same-sex love. Not true. The Church opposes homogenital sex, which in my experience is not about love, but about obsession, addiction, and compensation for a compromised masculinity.

I am not proud of the life I have lived. In fact, I am profoundly ashamed of it. But if reading this prevents one naïve, gullible man from making the same mistakes, then perhaps with the assistance of Our Lady of Guadalupe; of St. Joseph, her chaste spouse; of my patron saint, Edmund Campion; of St. Josemaría Escrivá; of the blessed Carmelite martyrs of Compiègne; and, last but not least, of my special supernatural guide and mentor, the Venerable John Henry Newman, I can at least hope for a reprieve from some of the many centuries in Purgatory I have coming to me.

So, what do we as a Church and a culture need to do? Tear down the respectable façade and expose the pornography beneath. Start pressuring homosexuals to tell the truth about their lives. Stop debating the correct interpretation of Genesis 19. Leave the men of Sodom and Gomorrah buried in the brimstone where they belong. Sodom is hidden in plain view from us, here and now, today. Once, when preparing a lecture on Cardinal Newman, I summarized his classic Essay on the Development

73

of Christian Doctrine in this fashion: Truth ripens, error rots. The homosexual rights movement is rotten to the core. It has no future. There is no life in it. Sooner or later, those who are caught up in it are going to wake up from the dream of unbridled desire or else die. It is just a matter of time. The question is: how long? How many children are going to be sacrificed to this Moloch?

Until several months ago, there was a Lobo's in Houston too. Not accidentally, I'm sure, its layout was identical to the one in Austin. It was just a few blocks from the gas station where I take my car for service. Recently, I was taking a walk through the neighborhood while my tires were being rotated. And I noticed something. There was a padlock on the door at Lobo's. A sign on the door read, "The previous tenant was evicted for nonpayment of rent." The books and the porn, the façade and what it conceals, are gone now. Praise God.

Dr Ronald G. Lee is a librarian in Houston, Texas. He holds a Ph.D. in modern European history from the University of Notre Dame in Indiana.

(Detail from Rembrandt's *Return of the Prodigal Son* © Hermitage Museum)

See also

'Let's Talk About Sex' by Esther Addley;
 http://www.guardian.co.uk/gayrights/story/0,,2015220,00.html
'A Sad Scene' by Miles Douglas;
 http://catholiceducation.org/articles/homosexuality/h00108.htm,
'Guess What's Coming to the American Academy of Religion This Year, Courtesy of the Gay Men's Group?' by Professor Robert A. J. Gagnon;
 http://www.robgagnon.net/AARGayMen'sGroup.htm
After the Ball: How America Will Conquer Its Fear and Hatred of Gays in the 90s by Marshall Kirk and Hunter Madsen (Doubleday, 1989), pp. 275-373.

6.   Same Sex Attraction (SSA): Is it innate, and immutable?

Dr Neil Whitehead

1.   Summary

From the available literature, Same Sex Attraction (SSA) is shown to be less innate than most behaviour-related conditions. Identified genes have not yet been shown to be clearly involved, despite searching. Studies of twins show that ultimately a number of genes may be involved, but with effects that, both individually and collectively, are weak and indirect, like most links for other behaviours. Twin studies also show that the effects of genes on SSA will not be deterministic, and that this finding takes into account all future discoveries of linked factors. SSA is shown to have its origin in a number of sources, any one of which will have only a temporary effect on the great majority of people exposed to it. However, in individual cases these factors may become very important. At various times, individuals have asserted that the following factors have effects ranging from 'some impact' to 'vital impact': sexual abuse, childhood gender non-conformity, reaction to physical features of the body, chance sexual encounters, gay porn, rejection by peers, rebellion against cultural standards for their sex, the general cultural milieu, and family dynamics. Sociological surveys show that between heterosexuality and homosexuality, spontaneous change takes place in both directions, to a considerable and underappreciated degree. SSA is neither innate nor immutable. In contrast, opposite sex attraction (OSA) in today's cultural milieu is much less mutable. This is because substantial sexual experience, whether exclusive SSA or exclusive OSA, renders spontaneous change much less common.

2.   General Background

Although popular media accounts tend to suggest that genetic or pre-natal factors alone dictate the abilities and behaviours we will have from birth onwards, mainstream scientific opinion disagrees, and has disagreed for about thirty years. Where an individual human reacts with the environment, it is a truism that both genes and environment are involved, and arguments about whether a behaviour is "nature" or "nurture" are illegitimate – both are always involved. It must therefore be assumed from the outset that any human trait which involves behaviour is most unlikely to be innate only. This is so well established that if an attempt is made to link SSA with biological features only, it would be necessary to produce, at the least, a large volume of solid evidence that SSA is the exception it is made out to be. This evidence does not exist. In fact, we will show that there is solid evidence that the overall biological links with SSA are weaker than for most traits, and that this situation is not going to change with future research.

In a recent book-length review of the overall genetics field, Professor Sir Michael Rutter (Rutter, 2006), dismissed an exclusively genetic origin for behaviours, saying, "None of the findings are in the least bit compatible with a genetically deterministic view" and, similarly, "It should be noted that the evidence is equally incompatible with any suggestions that environmental influences account for all individual variation. Any dispassionate but critical, review of the research leads to the clear conclusion that there are substantial genetic and environmental effects on almost all types of behavior".

He also said, "The great bulk of psychological traits ... is multifactorial in origin." That is, genetic *and* environmental influences, and many factors within each sector. We show below that SSA fits this general pattern.

3.   *Same Sex Attraction*

A search for perhaps 40 years has failed to find one single factor, whether genetic or environmental, which *always* causes SSA in a majority of those exposed to it. The nearest is childhood gender non-conformity, or Gender Identity Disorder. Of those who have this trait so severely that they are referred to clinics, 50-75% develop SSA in longitudinal studies. But only a small minority of those who appear merely "sissy" as youngsters go on to develop SSA, and this pattern is universal. Assuming that SSA does have observable causes, these are likely to be highly individualistic, and/or multifactorial.

The impression from the media is that there are many studies which show that SSA is innate. However, modern original papers are always careful to say that only a link has been demonstrated. For example, when a difference in brain structure or function is demonstrated between heterosexual and homosexual, e.g. (Safron et al. 2007), the authors say explicitly that it cannot be determined whether the observed difference is due to sexual behaviour or is innate. No difference of this type has ever been demonstrated to be independent of learning and environment. What is more, although the brain is known to be structurally plastic, even in adulthood, and to respond to learning by changing its microstructure, it cannot be known or demonstrated that differences are innate, or that they persist unmodified until adulthood, except for gross morphological features.

When the strength of the alleged links can be mathematically calculated, these links are found, without exception, to be important for only a minority of those possessing them.

The results of attempts to link regions on the DNA or genes with SSA have not produced any results that can be replicated at the conventional probability of $p=0.05$ (Mustanski et al. 2005 and references therein). This means that no genes are known to be clearly linked to SSA, in spite of about seventeen years of research. In contrast, nearly twenty years of research have found far more significant links between specific genes and various conditions, e.g. schizophrenia, autism, dyslexia. The functions of the genes are always (almost surprisingly) indirect, compared with the conditions investigated. The strength of the links is such that in several cases appropriate drugs to ameliorate the condition are being sought. That cannot apply to SSA because no such links are known. It is highly likely that some such genes will ultimately be found, but each will be responsible for only a very small part of SSA, and their effects, although affecting all the population, gay or straight, will be very indirect and inconsequential for most of the population.

So many biological links with SSA are publicized, it might seem that their sum must be overwhelming, or that in future a factor will be discovered which will be. We now show that neither possibility is true, because of the already known results of twin studies.

4.   Twin Studies

There are several varieties of twin studies, but for illustration's sake we will consider only the simplest. Identical twins have the same genes, and essentially the same pre-natal environment and upbringing. This raises the crucial question: if one twin has SSA does the other have it as well? This is called the pairwise concordance. It is a kind of summation of the effects of both factors, genes and environment. For SSA the study that is commonly acknowledged to be the best and largest available (Bailey et al. 2000) has pairwise concordance, using strict SSA criteria, of 11% for men and 14% for women. (It is generally acknowledged that earlier studies with higher concordances were grossly biased through "volunteer error".) If one twin has SSA the other usually doesn't. It should be noted that this result includes the summation of all factors currently known or *yet to be discovered*. There are three other smaller studies which are consistent with this result, none contradicting it, and it is not expected to change greatly with further research. This shows that it is the factors which make twins *different* that are critical, and the predominant causes of SSA.

Before passing on we consider briefly the idea sometimes put forward that genes for SSA are actually present, but are not exerting their influence for complex genetic reasons; the result is called "low penetrance". This relies on such genes actually existing, and none are known. It would also be unlikely for SSA because low penetrance is itself unusual, and penetrance as low as this, very unusual. At least two layers of speculation are needed to entertain this idea, making it a concept requiring much evidence before it can be accepted.

The 11-14% degree of concordance for SSA is unusually low, whereas concordance for other traits has a mean of approximately 50%. This means that genetic factors are minor for SSA, where "genetic" means all pre-natal influences including hormonal conditions. The pairwise concordance for left-handedness (Medland, et al. 2006) is 13.8%, which is similar, but the link between left-handedness and genes on chromosome 2 is very well established (Francks et al. 2003). By contrast, there is no link for SSA. On the other hand the pairwise concordance for heterosexuality is 94%, arising from some combination of common genes and common environmental factors. This shows that SSA and OSA are quite different: SSA arises from non-shared unusual factors, OSA arises from common shared factors. The standard interpretation of the low concordance for SSA is that SSA shows *unusually* little evidence of innateness.

The interpretation of this low SSA concordance is that the twins have either had experiences which have been different, or have reacted in different ways to the same experiences, which could, however, include reaction to innate bodily features.

The list of factors volunteered by various people with SSA as having had some influence on their psycho-sexual development is very varied and individualistic, indeed "post-modern". Clearly, some can happen to one identical twin and not another. These include sexual abuse, childhood gender non-conformity, reaction to physical features of the body, chance sexual encounters, bad experiences with the opposite sex, encounters with gay porn, rejection by peers, rebellion against cultural standards for their sex, the general cultural milieu, and family dynamics. For example, the same parenting style may be mistakenly perceived, by each young twin, as having different meanings. Perceived or real favoritism is commonly experienced as a factor by some children, but for most it does not result in SSA. In lists supplied to researchers, subjects each endorsed several factors, on average, as having had at least some importance in the origin of their SSA (Otis and Skinner, 2004). Thus even for an individual the origin may be multifactorial.

More complex twin methodology in Bailey et al, above, also supported the idea that difference-creating factors were predominantly responsible. In general, research has found (Oliver and Plomin, 2007) that genes tend to make twins more alike, and factors in the environment tend to make them more different.

5.   *Stability of SSA*

How stable is SSA? The evidence is clear that the percentages in the population of people with SSA, meaning people who have each of the same-sex factors – i.e. identity, attraction and activity – generally come down by at least a half when those in their thirties are compared with those in their late fifties (Kinsey, 1948, table 149, Laumann et al.1994). Since this was seen both in the Kinsey surveys and the Laumann survey, fifty years apart, it cannot be an effect of societal values, which change.

The following evidence shows that SSA, far from being innate and immutable, is much less stable than OSA. First of all there is adolescent changeability, with a few fleeting same-sex encounters, and second, change by those who have considerable sexual experience. All surveys show that, in adolescence particularly, there is much movement on the sexual continuum scale. Many young people may have a few same-sex experiences, but do not continue (e.g. Laumann et al. 1994). It is doubtful anyone would claim that these young people had SSA in any deep sense. However, the change is more profound for a small proportion of the population. Five surveys (Whitehead and Whitehead, 1999 and references therein) show that half of those now with SSA were at one time convinced they were OSA. A similar number of those once convinced they had stable SSA are now equally convinced they have stable OSA. This translates to a result that 50% of the SSA population once thought themselves OSA, but only about 1-2% of the OSA population once thought of themselves as SSA. (According to Kinsey a significant number of these changes were in adulthood). This indicates that OSA is, by a large factor, more stable than SSA, for whatever reason. There is thus a few percent of the population who have experienced a significant change, through the vicissitudes of life, rather than through therapy of some kind. Within these changes, the most common described within the literature are within the various degrees of bisexuality. The extreme ends of the sexual orientation continuum scale are more stable.

There are some general conclusions to be drawn from the relationships between genes and behaviour. For instance, one can expect a significant environmental component. Then, change is possible in principle. This means that the allegation of innateness should never be used to close off the Christian virtue of Hope – in this case the hope of change – in relation to any kind of behaviour for those who may want it.

6. Conclusion

SSA is neither innate nor immutable, and the degree of hidden change in the population from SSA to OSA is generally considerably underestimated. In today's increasingly censorious cultural climate, most people will never even be aware of the existence of this phenomenon, nor the potential for significant change that it demonstrates. In relation to individuals with SSA, it could reasonably be expected that the greater the degree of active and continued participation in this particular orientation, the greater the difficulty of change.

Dr Neil Evan Whitehead, of Whitehead Associates, Lower Hutt, New Zealand, did an interdisciplinary Ph.D, and says things have got worse ever since. After working for the New Zealand Government and the United Nations as a scientist for more than three decades, he is now an independent consultant, and just back from being a visiting professor at Hiroshima University. He continues to publish on many subjects. He lives in Lower Hutt, New Zealand with his wife Briar, and cycles, reads extensively, writes haiku, and makes what some call music on his bagpipes.

Reference List

Bailey, J.M., Dunne, M.P. and Martin, N.G. (2000) Genetic and Environmental influences on sexual orientation and its correlates in an Australian twin sample. *Journal of Personality and Social Psychology* **78** 524-536.

Francks, C. , DeLisi, L.E., Shaw, S.H., Fisher, S.E., Richardson, A.J., Stein, J.F., Monaco, A.P. (2003) Parent-of-origin effects on handedness and schizophrenia susceptibility on chromosome 2p12–q11. *Human Molecular Genetics* **12** 3225-3230

Kinsey, A.C., Pomeroy, W.B. and Martin, C.E. (1948) *Sexual Behavior in the Human Male*. Philadelphia: W.B.Saunders.

Laumann, E.O., Gagnon, J.H., Michael, R.T. and Michaels, S. (1994) *The Social Organization of Sexuality*, Chicago: University of Chicago Press.

Medland, S.E., Duffy, .D.L., Wright., M.J., Geffen, .G.M. .and Martin,.N.G. (2006) Handedness in Twins: Joint Analysis of Data From 35 Samples. *Twin Research and Human Genetics,* **9**, 46-53.

Mustanski, B.S., DuPree, M.G., Nievergelt, C.M., Bocklandt, S., Schork, N.J. and Hamer, D.H. (2005) A genomewide scan of male sexual orientation. *Human Genetics* **116** 272-278.

Oliver, B.R. and.Plomin.R. (2007) Twins' early development study (TEDS): a multivariate, longitudinal genetic investigation of language, cognition and behavior problems from childhood through adolescence. *Twin Research and Human Genetics* **10**, 95-105.

Otis, M.D. and Skinner, W.F. (2004) An exploratory study of differences in views of factors affecting sexual orientation for a sample of lesbians and gay men. *Psychological Reports* **94** 1173-1179.

Rutter, M. (2006) *Genes and Behavior,* Malden, Maryland: Blackwell.

Safron, A., Barch, B., Bailey, J.M., Gitelman, D.R., Parrish, T.B. and Reber, P.J. (2007) Neural correlates of sexual arousal in homosexual and heterosexual men. *Behavioral Neuroscience* **121**, 237-48.

Whitehead, N.E. and Whitehead, B.K. (1999) *My Genes Made Me Do It!,* Layfayette, Louisiana: Huntington House.

See also

'"Homosexuality Is Not Hardwired," concludes Dr Francis S. Collins, Head of The Human Genome Project' by A. Dean Byrd, PhD, MBA, MPH;
http://www.narth.com/docs/nothardwired.html

Under 'Update: An Alternative View' with Glynn Harrison, Consultant Psychiatrist and Norah Cooke Hurle Professor of Mental Health at Bristol University;
http://timescolumns.typepad.com/gledhill/2007/03/sors_back_in_th.html#more

'Childhood family correlates of heterosexual and homosexual marriages: a national cohort study of two million Danes', M. Frisch, A Hviid, October 2006; Department of Epidemiology Research, Danish Epidemiology Science Center, Statens Serum Institut, 5 Artillerivej, DK-2300, Copenhagen S, Denmark;
http://www.ncbi.nlm.nih.gov/sites/entrez?db=pubmed&uid=17039403&cmd=showdetailview&indexed=google

Dr Neil Whitehead and Briar Whitehead, 'Chapter Twelve: Can You Change Your Sexual Orientation?' Excerpt from *My Genes Made Me Do it - a scientific look at sexual orientation;* http://www.mygenes.co.nz/Ch12.pdf

7. How Might Homosexuality Develop? Putting the Pieces Together[1]

Dr Jeffrey Satinover, M.D.

It may be difficult to grasp how genes, environment, and other influences interrelate to one another, how a certain factor may "influence" an outcome but not cause it, and how faith enters in. The scenario below is condensed and hypothetical, but is drawn from the lives of actual people, illustrating how many different factors influence behavior.

Note that the following is just one of the many developmental pathways that can lead to homosexuality, but a common one. In reality, every person's "road" to sexual expression is individual, however many common lengths it may share with those of others.

(1) Our scenario starts with birth. The boy (for example) who one day may go on to struggle with homosexuality is born with certain features that are somewhat more common among homosexuals than in the population at large. Some of these traits might be inherited (genetic), while others might have been caused by the "intrauterine environment" (hormones). What this means is that a youngster without these traits will be somewhat less likely to become homosexual later than someone with them.

What are these traits? If we could identify them precisely, many of them would turn out to be gifts rather than "problems," for example a "sensitive" disposition, a strong creative drive, a keen aesthetic sense. Some of these, such as greater sensitivity, could be related to – or even the same as – physiological traits that also cause trouble, such as a greater-than-average anxiety response to any given stimulus.

No one knows with certainty just what these heritable characteristics are; at present we only have hints. Were we free to study homosexuality properly (uninfluenced by political agendas) we would certainly soon clarify these factors – just as we are doing in less contentious areas. In any case, there is absolutely no evidence whatsoever that the

---

[1] Excerpted from 'The Complex Interaction of Genes and Environment: A Model for Homosexuality'

behavior "homosexuality" is itself directly inherited.

(2) From a very early age potentially heritable characteristics mark the boy as "different." He finds himself somewhat shy and uncomfortable with the typical "rough and tumble" of his peers. Perhaps he is more interested in art or in reading – simply because he's smart. But when he later thinks about his early life, he will find it difficult to separate out what in these early behavioral differences came from an inherited temperament and what from the next factor, namely:

(3) That for whatever reason, he recalls a painful "mismatch" between what he needed and longed for and what his father offered him. Perhaps most people would agree that his father was distinctly distant and ineffective; maybe it was just that his own needs were unique enough that his father, a decent man, could never quite find the right way to relate to him. Or perhaps his father really disliked and rejected his son's sensitivity. In any event, the absence of a happy, warm, and intimate closeness with his father led to the boy's pulling away in disappointment, "defensively detaching" in order to protect himself.

But sadly, this pulling away from his father, and from the "masculine" role model he needed, also left him even less able to relate to his male peers. We may contrast this to the boy whose loving father dies, for instance, but who is less vulnerable to later homosexuality. This is because the commonplace dynamic in the pre-homosexual boy is not merely the absence of a father – literally or psychologically – but the psychological defense of the boy against his repeatedly disappointing father. In fact, a youngster who does not form this defense (perhaps because of early-enough therapy, or because there is another important male figure in his life, or due to temperament) is much less likely to become homosexual.

Complementary dynamics involving the boy's mother are also likely to have played an important role. Because people tend to marry partners with "interlocking neuroses," the boy probably found himself in a problematic relationship with both parents.

For all these reasons, when as an adult he looked back on his childhood, the now-homosexual man recalls, "From the beginning I was always different. I never got along well with the boys my age and felt more comfortable around girls." This accurate memory makes his later homosexuality feel convincingly to him as though it was "preprogrammed" from the start.

(4) Although he has "defensively detached" from his father, the young boy still carries silently within him a terrible longing for the warmth,

love, and encircling arms of the father he never did nor could have. Early on, he develops intense, nonsexual attachments to older boys he admires – but at a distance, repeating with them the same experience of longing and unavailability. When puberty sets in, sexual urges – which can attach themselves to any object, especially in males – rise to the surface and combine with his already intense need for masculine intimacy and warmth. He begins to develop homosexual crushes. Later he recalls, "My first sexual longings were directed not at girls but at boys. I was never interested in girls."

Psychotherapeutic intervention at this point and earlier can be successful in preventing the development of later homosexuality. Such intervention is aimed in part at helping the boy change his developing effeminate patterns (which derive from a "refusal" to identify with the rejected father), but more critically, it is aimed at teaching his father – if only he will learn – how to become appropriately involved with and related to his son.

(5) As he matures (especially in our culture where early, extramarital sexual experiences are sanctioned and even encouraged), the youngster, now a teen, begins to experiment with homosexual activity. Or alternatively his needs for same-sex closeness may already have been taken advantage of by an older boy or man, who preyed upon him sexually when he was still a child. (Recall the studies that demonstrate the high incidence of sexual abuse in the childhood histories of homosexual men.) Or oppositely, he may avoid such activities out of fear and shame in spite of his attraction to them. In any event, his now-sexualized longings cannot merely be denied, however much he may struggle against them. It would be cruel for us at this point to imply that these longings are a simple matter of "choice."

Indeed, he remembers having spent agonizing months and years trying to deny their existence altogether or pushing them away, to no avail. One can easily imagine how justifiably angry he will later be when someone casually and thoughtlessly accuses him of "choosing" to be homosexual. When he seeks help, he hears one of two messages, and both terrify him; either, "Homosexuals are bad people and you are a bad person for choosing to be homosexual. There is no place for you here and God is going to see to it that you suffer for being so bad;" or "Homosexuality is inborn and unchangeable. You were born that way. Forget about your fairytale picture of getting married and having children and living in a little house with a white picket fence. God made you who you are and he/she destined you for the gay life. Learn to enjoy it."

(6) At some point, he gives in to his deep longings for love and

begins to have voluntary homosexual experiences. He finds – possibly to his horror – that these old, deep, painful longings are at least temporarily, and for the first time ever, assuaged.

Although he may also therefore feel intense conflict, he cannot help admit that the relief is immense. This temporary feeling of comfort is so profound – going well beyond the simple sexual pleasure that anyone feels in a less fraught situation – that the experience is powerfully reinforced. However much he may struggle, he finds himself powerfully driven to repeat the experience. And the more he does, the more it is reinforced and the more likely it is he will repeat it yet again, though often with a sense of diminishing returns.

(7) He also discovers that, as for anyone, sexual orgasm is a powerful reliever of distress of all sorts. By engaging in homosexual activities he has already crossed one of the most critical and strongly enforced boundaries of sexual taboo. It is now easy for him to cross other taboo boundaries as well, especially the significantly less severe taboo pertaining to promiscuity. Soon homosexual activity becomes the central organizing factor in his life as he slowly acquires the habit of turning to it regularly – not just because of his original need for fatherly warmth of love, but to relieve anxiety of any sort.

(8) In time, his life becomes even more distressing than for most. Some of this is in fact, as activists claim, because all-too-often he experiences from others a cold lack of sympathy or even open hostility. The only people who seem really to accept him are other gays, and so he forms an even stronger bond with them as a "community." But it is not true, as activists claim, that these are the only or even the major stresses. Much distress is caused simply by his way of life – for example, the medical consequences, AIDS being just one of many (if also the worst). He also lives with the guilt and shame that he inevitably feels over his compulsive, promiscuous behavior; and too over the knowledge that he cannot relate effectively to the opposite sex and is less likely to have a family (a psychological loss for which political campaigns for homosexual marriage, adoption, and inheritance rights can never adequately compensate).

However much activists try to normalize for him these patterns of behavior and the losses they cause, and however expedient it may be for political purposes to hide them from the public-at-large, unless he shuts down huge areas of his emotional life he simply cannot honestly look at himself in this situation and feel content.

And no one – not even a genuine, dyed-in-the-wool, sexually insecure "homophobe" – is nearly so hard on him as he is on himself.

Furthermore, the self-condemning messages that he struggles with on a daily basis are in fact only reinforced by the bitter self-derogating wit of the very gay culture he has embraced. The activists around him keep saying that it is all caused by the "internalized homophobia" of the surrounding culture, but he knows that it is not.

The stresses of "being gay" lead to more, not less, homosexual behavior. This principle, perhaps surprising to the layman (at least to the layman who has not himself gotten caught up in some pattern, of whatever type) is typical of the compulsive or addictive cycle of self-destructive behavior; wracking guilt, shame, and self-condemnation only causes it to increase. It is not surprising that people therefore turn to denial to rid themselves of these feelings, and he does too. He tells himself, "It is not a problem, therefore there is no reason for me to feel so bad about it."

(9) After wrestling with such guilt and shame for so many years, the boy, now an adult, comes to believe, quite understandably – and because of his denial, needs to believe – "I can't change anyway because the condition is unchangeable." If even for a moment he considers otherwise, immediately arises the painful query, "Then why haven't I...?" and with it returns all the shame and guilt.

Thus, by the time the boy becomes a man, he has pieced together this point of view: "I was always different, always an outsider. I developed crushes on boys from as long as I can remember and the first time I fell in love it was with a boy, not a girl. I had no real interest in members of the opposite sex. Oh, I tried all right – desperately. But my sexual experiences with girls were nothing special. But the first time I had homosexual sex it just 'felt right.' So it makes perfect sense to me that homosexuality is genetic. I've tried to change – God knows how long I struggled – and I just can't. That's because it's not changeable. Finally, I stopped struggling and just accepted myself the way I am."

(10) Social attitudes toward homosexuality will play a role in making it more or less likely that the man will adopt an "inborn and unchangeable" perspective, and at what point in his development. It is obvious that a widely shared and propagated worldview that normalizes homosexuality will increase the likelihood of his adopting such beliefs, and at an earlier age. But it is perhaps less obvious – it follows from what we have discussed above – that ridicule, rejection, and harshly punitive condemnation of him as a person will be just as likely (if not more likely) to drive him into the same position.

(11) If he maintains his desire for a traditional family life, the man may continue to struggle against his "second nature." Depending on whom

he meets, he may remain trapped between straight condemnation and gay activism, both in secular institutions and in religious ones. The most important message he needs to hear is that "healing is possible."

(12) If he enters the path to healing, he will find that the road is long and difficult – but extraordinarily fulfilling. The course to full restoration of heterosexuality typically lasts longer than the average American marriage – which should be understood as an index of how broken all relationships are today.

From the secular therapies he will come to understand what the true nature of his longings are, that they are not really about sex, and that he is not defined by his sexual appetites. In such a setting, he will very possibly learn how to turn aright to other men to gain from them a genuine, nonsexualized masculine comradeship and intimacy; and how to relate aright to woman, as friend, lover, life's companion, and, God willing, mother of his children.

Of course the old wounds will not simply disappear, and later in times of great distress the old paths of escape will beckon. But the claim that this means he is therefore "really" a homosexual and unchanged is a lie. For as he lives a new life of ever-growing honesty, and cultivates genuine intimacy with the woman of his heart, the new patterns will grow ever stronger and the old ones engraved in the synapses of his brain ever weaker.

In time, knowing that they really have little to do with sex, he will even come to respect and put to good use what faint stirrings remain of the old urges. They will be for him a kind of storm-warning, a signal that something is out of order in his house, that some old pattern of longing and rejection and defense is being activated. And he will find that no sooner does he set his house in order that indeed the old urges once again abate. In his relations to others – as friend, husband, professional – he will now have a special gift. What was once a curse will have become a blessing, to himself and to others.

Dr Jeffrey Satinover is an author, psychiatrist and physicist, currently doing research into complex systems theory at the University of Nice, France. During his research and practice in psychology, he developed an interest in the treatment of homosexuality which, contrary to pop theory, he found to be reversible in motivated men and women. He has written extensively on the subject, approaching it variously from clinical, legal and political perspectives. He has taught physics at Yale University and civil liberties and constitutional law at Princeton. He will be taking position at the ETH Zurich (Swiss Federal Institute of Technology) in physics and economics beginning fall 2008. He lives in Connecticut, USA with Julie, his wife of twenty-five years, and his three teenage daughters. When not dealing with the rigors of the latter, he enjoys alpinism, J.S. Bach and jazz keyboard.

8.   Post-Gay: The Primacy Of Affect: A Psychotherapeutic Approach

Dr Joseph Nicolosi

Healing moments occur when the client feels seemingly "unbearable" affect, while at the same moment, experiencing the support of the therapist.

Recent advances in psychotherapy have focused on the central importance of affect in the therapeutic process.

Evidence is mounting for our understanding the therapeutic alliance as an "affective correcting experience" (Schore, 1991). Affects – the neurotransmitters of human relations – connect the person with his emotional environment. Affect-Focused Therapy (AFT) is about the way we attach, detach, and re-attach. Treatment focuses on the removal of blocks that disconnect the client from his core feelings.

The particular meeting place of reparative therapy and Affect-Focused Therapy lies in our view that homosexuality is fundamentally an attachment problem. For many of our clients, same-sex behavior appears to be an attempt to repair an insecure attachment to the father. Emotional disregulation, most often in the form of shame blocking masculine assertion, drives many of our same-sex attracted (SSA) clients toward unwanted homosexual enactment. Homosexual activity, fantasy and ideation serve as temporary compensation for failure of the attachment bond.

But we do not reduce SSA solely to father-son attachment failure; in fact, we believe that some homosexual development may well have begun with problems in mother-son attunement. Indeed, the effectiveness of reparative therapy is increased by use of techniques that also explore early mother-son attachment problems. Because the mother-child bond shapes and refines our earliest sense of self, therapy must also revisit that attachment.

Interpersonal rapport is, in the final analysis, what characterizes our deepest humanity and determines our internal equilibrium. Thus our treatment process has moved away from more traditional attempts at resolving intra-psychic conflict, and more in the direction of affect regulation, with the therapist as affect-regulation facilitator.

The quintessential model of affective contact is the Double Loop, a powerful therapeutic achievement between client and therapist.

1.　A Radical Therapeutic Resonance

The flow of affect is determined by attachment. Traditional psychodynamic concepts such as "internalized objects" are metaphors for this biologically based phenomenon of neurological transmission. What we call "internalization of the object," for example, is actually a body-held memory – a conditioned affective response.

AFT requires the therapist to exert a level of emotional engagement and empathy that is far beyond, even contradictory to, the traditional psychotherapeutic approach. AFT concentrates upon the fine details of the effective intersubjective therapeutic exchange. The therapist must be fully emotionally "present" in order to elicit, and deeply share, the client's visceral experience.

Affective expansion has been shown to occur when there is a radical level of client-therapist resonance. Utilizing AFT techniques, the reparative therapist attempts to evoke the client's expression of core affects and to expand his somatic awareness. As trust and confidence build within their exchange, the client begins to feel confident enough to experience an authentic exchange with other men. Later, he can begin to more authentically engage women.

2.　Attunement Changes Brain Structure

Each person's neurological structure is designed to be synchronized with other neurological structures. As Stern reminds us, "Our brains were designed to lock in with other brains" (2002). But human attachments can break down (as illustrated by the Double Bind) and then reconnect (through the Double Loop). Interruptions of affect – through anxiety, shame, and other inhibitors – disconnect the person from his emotional environment, causing a shutdown.

Personal identity development is the cumulative result of years of attunement with others. Our level of attunement with others, determines our inner relationship with ourselves. Traumatic malattunement – the inevitable consequence of Double Bind communication – creates shame, and shame creates intrapsychic detachment. In contrast, attunement with the therapist in the Working Alliance (a consequence of the Double Loop experience) resolves this barrier of shame and fosters self-reattachment.

Thus, an affective "turning on," or openness, is the goal of reparative therapy. In AFT, the therapist maintains empathic attunement in the Working Alliance to facilitate unification of the left brain and right brain hemispheres. In so doing, the he metaphorically "embeds" himself between the client's right brain and his left brain.

It is through this connectedness with the therapist that the client allows himself to feel the bodily sensations that are associated with his painful early experiences. Healing moments occur when the client can feel what seems to be unbearable core feeling, while at the same moment, experiencing the care and support of the therapist. Thus, in a process of interactive repair, their attuned relationship actually changes the neurological structure of the brain.

For the client who grew up in the narcissistic family, the early trauma of the parental Double Bind has created an attunement split. Through reattunement, the Double Loop unifies the client with himself, then unifies the self with others. Attunement with another leads back to greater attunement with self.

3.   From Anxiety to Spontaneity

Affect-Focused Therapy rapidly accelerates the client's encounter with his fear-filled affective life. The therapist encourages him to feel and express his anxiety-provoking bodily feelings and sensations, while at the same time, supporting him in maintaining their interpersonal contact. Toleration of this previously unbearable affect is possible because of their mutual emotional rapport.

Through that Double Loop experience, the client learns that painful emotions are not intolerable in themselves – but rather, it was the early sense of parental abandonment associated with those emotions that actually rendered them intolerable.

The goal of therapy, therefore, is the integration of conflicting affects. When the client experiences the reintegration of these once negative-seeming affects, he experiences a surprising eruption of spontaneity, authenticity, vitality, and a feeling of self-integrity – all of which is prompted by the restructuring of the True Self. This restructuring is expressed as a greater outflow of energy in relating to others, and less preoccupation with oneself.

With the emergence of the True Self, we gradually see the establishment of new friendships and the strengthening of old and long-neglected family ties.

4.   A Subtle Synchronicity

When Affect-Focused Therapy functions at its best, we see a corrective experience of sublime attunement with subtle, highly nuanced human communication. Therapist and client share an implicit knowledge – that non-verbal, pre-explicit experience that can occur between two people in the recognition that "*I* know that *you* know that *I* know."

In many hours of analyzing audio- and videotape recordings of actual psychotherapy sessions at my clinic, I have seen how this subtle synchronicity emerges, with each person in the therapeutic dyad eventually having the sense of what the other is trying to express. Stern offers the example of two people kissing: the speed, direction, angle of approach – all perfectly coordinated for a "soft landing" (without crashing teeth) – is a miracle of psychic intimacy with "maximal complexity" of thinking, intending and then doing. Stern says it simply:

> Our minds are not created alone; they are co-created. Our nervous system is ready to be taught by other peoples' nervous systems, which transforms us.

Psychotherapy is the second opportunity to integrate one's emotional life. In attempting to explain how this therapeutic second opportunity works through the model of sublime attunement, Stern speaks of the importance of setting the correct tempo for "moving along" – the unspoken regulation of the rhythm and intensity of the back-and-forth between two people. He also notes the importance of "field regulation," which is the assessment of the other's receptivity with questions such as "Do you really like me?" and "What's actually happening between us right now?" He is particularly interested in what he calls "'now' moments," when the entire frame of the picture alters to zoom in on two people as they are pulled into the present moment, while experiencing an intense "existential presentness."

These "now moments" contain a heightened anxiety and the sense that somehow, "this moment is important," either for good or ill in the relationship. Personal exposure and vulnerability are a basic part of these moments; we see an excitement, a recognition of each other on a deeper level, and perhaps a slight, embarrassed smile that recognizes this sometimes-awkward vulnerability and personal exposure. Such moments, which Martin Buber calls "moments of meeting," cannot be forced; but as therapists, we can certainly, as Stern says, "be ready to coax such opportunities into existence."

Stern's description of the textured aspects of these central moments constitutes our Double Loop.

5. Two Binary Affects: Assertion vs. Shame

AFT helps us distinguish the basic "on" (attaching) affects versus the "off" (detaching) affects. Common detaching affects include anxiety, fear, and shame. Attaching affects are trust, empathy, and love. This fundamental "open/closed" distinction, described by Fosha as the "green signal" versus the "red signal," is equivalent to the sympathetic versus the parasympathetic neurological response.

Making the same distinction but in different words, Schore identifies affective openness and attunement, in contrast to a "freeze" response. This freeze response is much like reparative therapy's "shame" response – the consequence of the boy's feeling humiliated for his masculine gestures.

Clients have expressed this experience of the affective shift as the difference between:

Exploding	–	imploding
heart open	–	heart closed
Inflated	–	deflated
expansive	–	constrictive

These vitality affects versus inhibitory affects are illustrated by the Pike Phenomenon (Wolverton, 2005). In an experiment, a pike fish is placed in a tank with live minnows. The pike immediately begins eating all the minnows it sees. Then an invisible glass cylinder is placed over the pike, separating it from the minnows. Attempts to eat the minnows result in the pike hitting its nose on the glass cylinder, causing it pain. The cylinder is then removed, but the pike, anticipating pain, makes no more attempt to eat the minnows. The vitality response has been lost and the inhibitory response is substituted.

The Pike Phenomenon illustrates a conditioned response that inhibits healthy assertion. For our clients, there is an anticipation of shame for their gendered assertion.

Anticipatory shame represents a somatic "flashback" which switches the body into a defensive, shut-down mode.

6.   *Emotional Shutdown on a Biological Level*

It is sometimes helpful to explain to the client that his shutdown is a physiological, bodily reaction. This explanation helps him observe his own bodily shifts as they occur in the moment. Developing a self-observant stance can increase the client's ego strength as he observes his body (not "himself," but "his body") shift to the shut-down mode. The facilitation of the client's observation of his own bodily response is similar to Eye-Movement Desensitization Therapy's repeated instruction to the client to "go back to" and then "let go of" the traumatic image.

Another term for the Shame Moment is the "freeze response," in which the person loses his somatic vitality and the body becomes rigid and stiff. This is similar to the Freudian concept of dissociation, the earliest phenomenon of study in the history of psychoanalysis, which is triggered when the person anticipates a recurrence in the present of some past trauma. In dissociation there is a "segmentation of minds," each possessing its own "cluster of thoughts, feelings and memories" (Jung) which are held in the body. When someone is "in one mind" (a cluster of embodied memories), it is hard for him to recall the other "mind," and if the other mind is recalled – i.e., felt in the body – then it has already left the first mind.

For example, when a person walks into a restaurant feeling hungry and smelling good food, he is in one "mind"; two hours later, when he has eaten his dinner and walks out, he is in a very different "mind," and it is virtually impossible for him to recapture the totality of that earlier mindset of hunger and anticipation.

A client reported going on a weekend trip where he was camping and shooting with his friends. This experience put him into the Assertion state, where couldn't recall the other "mind" of homosexual temptation. A week later, when he was back into the shame zone, the opposite had occurred: he couldn't recall the mindset of Assertion.

7.   *Shame Posture vs. the Assertive State*

Reparative therapy carefully examines the self-states, especially regarding the scenario preceding homosexual enactment. The simultaneous experience of feeling shame in the body, and at the same time experiencing the acceptance and understanding of the attuned therapist, works to diminish the physiological "charge" of shame.

When clients are in the Assertive Stance, they can vaguely recall, but cannot intensely feel, their homoerotic attractions. When they shift into the Shame Posture, they cannot recall what it was like not to have compelling homoerotic feelings.

Shame, as we have noted, has, like all the other self-states, an evolutionary survival function. It is a powerful controlling tool used by the "pack" for socialization that aids survival of the group – and thus the individual. (Shame, it should be noted, is not the same as guilt – guilt results from a negative judgment of one's own behavior, while shame is a basic physiological response.) A child will be shamed – which is to say, threatened by expulsion from the pack – for behaviors that risk the stability and survival of the group. (Some researchers posit that this autonomic response of shame may be the biological basis for conscience.)

The self-state of shame brings to mind the work of Freud's mentor, Pierre Janet, known as the father of dissociation. Janet laid the foundation for Freud's later work on hysteria – where past events, when held outside of consciousness, still retain an influence on present behavior. Dissociation represents the mind's attempt to block out traumatic childhood memories which still, on an unconscious level, feel overwhelmingly threatening.

8.   *Somatic Shift Leads to New Meaning*

Reparative therapy focuses on Body Work because we understand the unconscious mind to hold a buried "body memory" that operates without cognitive awareness. The body does not deceive us, but the mind can do so. Freud said the goal of psychoanalysis was that "Where 'id' was, there ego shall be"(1933). He meant that psychoanalysis replaces unconscious, irrational impulses with self-awareness and rationality. We may revise this dictum to propose that "Where the somatic shift is, there new meaning shall be," because the mind can give new understanding to body memories as they are reexperienced.

For example, the gay-identified man sees an attractive male and experiences a sexual arousal. His self-understanding is "I'm sexually attracted to him because I'm gay. Such attractions are normal and natural for me." For this man, an attractive male is associated with sexual gratification, and he comes to believe that such feelings authentically define him.

However, the non-gay homosexual has the same somatic reaction to the same attractive man, but his internal narrative is quite different. He says: "I'm attracted to that man because he possesses qualities of masculinity that I feel are lacking right now within myself. And what can I do to change that?"

This is the essential difference between the gay-identified man and the non-gay homosexual – the way they interpret their body responses.

What the gay-identified man takes at face value, the non-gay homosexually oriented man instead, chooses to question. The gay man believes this attraction is "out there," reflecting his true self-identity.

But the "non-gay" SSA man sees the same feeling as a catalyst for asking himself, "It's not about the other guy's attractiveness. What is going on *'in here'* right now to generate these feelings that contradict my true, designed nature?'"

Dr Joseph Nicolosi is a licensed psychologist and founder and Clinical Director of the Thomas Aquinas Psychological Clinic in Encino, California. He specializes in the treatment of men who wish to diminish their same-sex attractions and develop their heterosexual potential, and has been practising as a psychologist since 1980.

Dr Nicolosi is a former president of NARTH – The National Association of Research and Therapy of Homosexuality – which is the only U.S. professional group organized to protect the right of homosexual clients to receive change-oriented therapy.

He is the author of *Reparative Therapy of Male Homosexuality* (Jason Aronson, Inc., 1991), *Healing Homosexuality: Case Stories of Reparative Therapy* (Jason Aronson, Inc., 1993), and co-author with his wife, Linda Ames Nicolosi, of the book *A Parent's Guide to Preventing Homosexuality* (Intervarsity Press, 2002).

He is also co-author of a research study, 'Retrospective Self-Reports of Changes in Homosexual Orientation: A Consumer Survey of Conversion Therapy Clients', which was published in *Psychological Reports*, June 2000, vol. 86, pp. 1071-1088, and of several other peer-reviewed papers.

References

Fosha, Diana (2000). The Transforming Power of Affect: A Model for Accelerated Change. N.Y.: Basic Books.

Freud, S. (1933). New introductory lectures on psychoanalysis. S.E., volume 22, p. 80.

Schore, A. (1991) "Early Superego development: The emergence of shame and narcissistic affect regulation in the practicing period," Psychoanalysis and Contemporary Thought, 14, pp. 187-205.

Stern, D. (2002). "Why Do People Change in Psychotherapy?" Presentation. University of California at Los Angeles, March 9, 2002; Continuing Education Seminars, 1023 Westholme Ave., Los Angeles, CA 90024:
Wolverton Mountain Enterprises, 2005:
http://www.wolverton-mountain.com/articles/pike.htm

See also

'"Do You Do Reparative Therapy?": The Making of a NARTH Psychologist' by Dr Philip M Sutton; http://www.narth.com/docs/coll-sutton.html

9. Post-Gay: Understanding SSA As A 'Signal'

Dr Joseph Nicolosi

July 5, 2007 – Several media stories recently have promoted the message that no one ever transitions out of same-sex attractions (SSA). As proof, reporters cite the words of prominent ex-gay ministry leaders. These leaders – who consider themselves profoundly changed – nevertheless admit to the media that they sometimes struggle, even today, with unwanted temptation.

People who oppose our message – particularly, many reporters – seized upon the ministry leaders' message, which was subtle, ambiguous and requiring nuanced consideration, and reduced it to a more attractive (to them) idea that was "short and dumb" but missed the truth of the matter.

As the truism goes, "For every complex question there is one simple answer – and it is usually wrong." "See?" the media stories seemed to say. "No one ever changes."

Here, instead, is the nuanced message.

The early Christian ex-gay movement portrayed the overcoming of homosexuality in absolute terms – offering a nice, clean picture of complete transition: With sufficient prayer, faith, and support, a person was said to have overcome SSA once and for all. Once a person repented, if his faith was sufficient, he would enjoy full restoration to heterosexuality.

The result of that overly optimistic view was an angry backlash by another, newly emerging celebrity – the man who once thought he was ex-gay, but now says he is happily gay once again – and wishes he had *never tried* to change. These "EX-EX-gays" have gone to the media with a story that is very appealing to many ears – the message of absolute sexual liberation.

It was out of concern about this angry backlash that ex-gay ministries have now become very cautious in delivering their message of hope. But they seem to be telling the struggler that he must be prepared to face unending trials. This is not an appealing message to the confused young man who is trying to decide whether to go ahead and tackle the change process, or "just give it up and be gay."

This bleak message also appears to support the pro-gay claim that homosexuality is fixed and intrinsic for some people. It gives "comfort to the enemy" and to his insistence that although behavioral change may be possible, beneath it all, "Gay is who you really are – it's your true nature."

Perhaps we should look at the big picture behind these opposing claims.

I. *A Psychological Solution To An Either-Or Predicament*

A solution to this "complex question demanding a simple answer" can be found in the psychological understanding of homosexuality. Following in a long-established – and never disproven – psychodynamic tradition, reparative therapists see SSA as a symbolic defense against the trauma of attachment loss.

Having failed to fully identify with his own gender, the man with SSA romanticizes what he lacks – falling in love with something "out there" that a normal developmental process would have caused to be internalized, not eroticized. (As one gay-activist psychologist, Daryl Bem, aptly explained, the man with SSA "eroticizes what was exotic" in childhood. Bem, though, thinks it is perfectly normal for one's own gender to feel mysterious and "exotic.")

Men in reparative therapy disagree; they want to "de-mystify" males and maleness – making them no longer "exotic" – and to have relationships with men characterized by mutuality and authenticity. They believe their biological design makes it clear that humanity was created to partner with the opposite sex.

Nevertheless, these men still have strong unmet needs for male affection, understanding, and affirmation. Utilizing their new adaptive skills to recognize same-sex attractions as "signals," they know that when homosexual impulses recur, this is an internal indicator that "something in my life is out of balance."

The client now knows his unwanted attraction is not about "that other guy," but about himself. He understands that it is not about sex, but about his present feelings about himself as he relates to others. The recurrence of temptation is a warning that he has compromised his healthy self-needs – most often, through a lack of authentic relational engagement. By authentic engagement, we mean consistently relating to other men in the assertive stance; freeing themselves of shame; maintaining deeply affirming relationships with close male friends; and not allowing themselves to be disempowered or "drained" in relationships with women.

One man, at the very end of his therapy, said, "Thank you, homosexuality. You have forced me to look at deeper issues I tried to avoid." Similarly, psychotherapist Richard Cohen, when asked by a TV interviewer if he had any further same-sex temptations, answered, "Yes, I do – when I am not taking care of myself."

Here is what a former client says he learned in therapy:

Therapy has helped me to connect more with men as brothers to be trusted. For most of my adult life, I only felt fearful of and alienated around men – especially men of my own age group. I never felt I belonged to their circle and always feared their rejection.

The general pattern these last few years has tended to be the opposite: I feel connected to most men and at ease in their company, and if and when I feel self-conscious and fearful, I challenge myself to surrender my fears, so that I can reconnect with both my inner man and the men around me.

I've becoming more emotionally assertive in situations where formerly I'd be controlled by shame, and in due course, I have developed an unprecedented level of authenticity with others, especially men. I am much better able to read the emotions I am feeling in my body, and I have more access to my overall emotional experiences.

If one thing angers me in life it is this: when gay apologists claim that to reject a 'gay identity' is to be in denial of my true self. My personal experience tells me the opposite! My therapy has helped bring about in me more self-acceptance, peace and feeling accepted by men, more than was ever conceivably the case in the years since puberty started. When I feel masculine within, I have no emotional need to draw on the men 'out there' who are external to me. This is because I feel at one with them. If, however, I don't deal with my shame, then my masculinity becomes 'covered over' and my heart then gravitates to symbols of masculinity found outside myself. I then feel disconnected both from myself, others – particularly men, and from God.

I have abandoned most of the suspicion and discomfort of women I carried around for all my adult life. I see more of the beauty of the opposite sex now than I ever did previously.

Were these changes an 'accident,' unconnected to my therapy? I think not. Was my therapy 'dangerous,' as some critics with an ideological axe to grind try to claim? Well, if growing in self-acceptance, and feeling now that I belong around men is 'dangerous,' then I want more of it!!!!!!

The extent to which my therapy has reaped, and is still reaping results depends largely on how much I challenge myself to continue to implement what I have learned.

2.   *Coming Back Home*

The Judeo-Christian concept of humanity and traditional psychodynamic psychology share the same understanding that human nature is supposed to *"function according to its design."* Both envision mankind as part of a universal heterosexual natural order, where some people struggle with SSA, but it is not intrinsic to their designed nature.

This "signal" view of SSA acknowledges the ongoing nature of the change process, and contradicts the "intrinsically gay" claim. Thus, we see the occasional reemergence of the homosexual impulse not as proof of the truth of gay anthropology, but a call to come back home again to one's authentic self. Looking at the issue from this "signal" perspective, we see that a gay worldview – both as a personal and political force – is not vindicated, but disempowered.

Dr Joseph Nicolosi is a licensed psychologist and founder and Clinical Director of the Thomas Aquinas Psychological Clinic in Encino, California. He specializes in the treatment of men who wish to diminish their same-sex attractions and develop their heterosexual potential, and has been practising as a psychologist since 1980.

Dr Nicolosi is a former president of NARTH – The National Association of Research and Therapy of Homosexuality – which is the only U.S. professional group organized to protect the right of homosexual clients to receive change-oriented therapy.

He is the author of *Reparative Therapy of Male Homosexuality* (Jason Aronson, Inc., 1991), *Healing Homosexuality: Case Stories of Reparative Therapy* (Jason Aronson, Inc., 1993), and co-author with his wife, Linda Ames Nicolosi, of the book *A Parent's Guide to Preventing Homosexuality* (Intervarsity Press, 2002).

He is also co-author of a research study, 'Retrospective Self-Reports of Changes in Homosexual Orientation: A Consumer Survey of Conversion Therapy Clients', which was published in *Psychological Reports*, June 2000, vol. 86, pp. 1071-1088, and of several other peer-reviewed papers.

See also

'How a "gay rights" leader became straight' by Michael Glatze;
    http://www.wnd.com/news/article.asp?ARTICLE_ID=56487
'Interview with Michael Glatze: A former gay activist explains how he left homosexuality';
    http://www.narth.com/docs/glatze.pdf

10. What If I Don't Change?

Dr Joseph Nicolosi

Over the years, many men have come to my office for help in changing their sexual orientation. Homosexuality doesn't work in their lives. It just never feels right or true. To these men, it is clear that gay relationships don't reflect who they are as gendered beings, and that they have been designed – physically and emotionally – for opposite-sex coupling.

But reorientation therapy is a long and difficult process, with no guarantee of success. What if the man doesn't change? Will he have gained anything of value?

People are often surprised to hear that in reparative therapy, typically there is very little discussion about sex. In fact, it is a mistake for any psychotherapy to focus exclusively on one particular symptom. Clients come in with a difficulty that they want removed from their life – an eating disorder, gambling obsession, or unwanted same-sex attraction – but good therapy addresses the whole person.

I typically tell my clients in the very first session, "Rule Number One is, never accept anything I say unless it resonates as true for you." The experience of the client, whatever that may be, must always trump any preconceived theory. Reparative theory holds that the origin of SSA is in unmet emotional and identification needs with the same sex, and the client is free to accept or reject that premise. If that doesn't feel true to him, he will usually decide to leave therapy after one or two sessions.

But if he continues, the therapeutic setting will provide a "holding environment," an opportunity in which he can explore, reexperience and assimilate past, painful trauma. Here, he begins to liberate himself from old patterns of self-sabotage. He grows beyond the emotional isolation and chronic loneliness that have so long limited him, and develops a renewed emotional investment in authentic relatedness.

Through a relationship with an attuned therapist, the client discovers how it feels to emotionally disclose to another man – revealing those long-buried, shame-evoking feelings. He experiences from him a deep acceptance of wherever he is in his life, at that point in time, whether he changes or not. Such an experience is always deeply therapeutic.

Besides an enhanced ability to develop genuine male friendships, the client will discover healthier relationships with females – where he learns to prohibit the boundary violations with women that have caused him to surrender his separate, masculine selfhood.

He will also learn how to examine himself with appropriate criticism – no longer "beating himself up" with self-blame – and in the process, he will better distinguish between constructive critiques and shame-based distortions. As one client put it,

> In the past, I made the worst self-appraisals and simply assumed the worst about myself. But now, there is a clarity of wants and needs – strength in my voice – and a deeper way of communicating.

With time, he develops the conviction that he must accept the people in his life as they are, without the need to defensively distort reality in order to remember them as having been better than they were. Further, any hurt and anger at parents and peers turns into a certain benevolent acceptance: "They were what they were." "In their own way, I know my parents loved me." "Those other guys had their own insecurities." Here, the man comes to understand the attachments he has formed with a new attitude of humility and compassion – even toward those who have hurt him.

One man told me:

> Last night I had a salient conversation with myself about giving to others. I can empathize with other people more – because now, I can feel my own feelings more.
>
> I think I've finally quit hiding from myself – and I want my personal journey to end with deeper relationships with people.

Rather than focusing on sexual-orientation change, the primary work of therapy is, in fact, to teach the client to relate from a place of authenticity, openness and honesty. This way-of-being in the world is what we call the Assertive Stance, where the person matches up his inner feelings with his outer dealings – to paraphrase Fosha, who defines the healthy individual as the person who is actively "feeling and dealing."[1]

We, too, believe that "feeling and dealing" is the essential ingredient to the healing of SSA: teaching the person to live and love from his authentic self. When he truly does so, we believe, his unwanted SSA will

---

[1] Diana Fosha, Ph.D, *The Transforming Power of Affect: A Model for Accelerated Change* (New York: Basic Books 2000).

powerfully diminish and ultimately disappear.

Besides this growth in human connectedness, the client learns to reject the Shame Posture that has so long paralyzed him. As one man explained:

> In the center of my chest I feel the heavy truth that I've spent 40 years of my life not taking action; afraid of men – afraid of women – afraid of living. I've let my shame-wound separate me from people.

The client should conclude therapy with a better understanding of why he has those attractions that feel so alien to his ego, and what he can do, if he wishes, to continue to diminish them.

But what about the client who fails to change; will he be left in a sort of "intimacy limbo" – not heterosexual, yet unable to be intimate with men? The truth is, our client was never intimate with men. That is why he came to therapy. He also came to us because he believes that true sexual intimacy with a person of the same gender is, in fact, not possible: same-sex eroticism simply fails to match his biological and emotional design, and does not reflect who he is on the deepest level.

Some clients, of course, change their worldview over time. "Jason" recently left reparative therapy to live in a gay relationship. He had come to believe that homosexuality was, contrary to his earlier beliefs, truly compatible with his religion. His worldview had changed so much that he and I were no longer in fundamental agreement about the meaning of homosexuality, and we agreed to end our working relationship. He told me, "I didn't change sexual orientation, but I can truly say that I've learned to be my own person."

Other men enter reparative therapy as gay-identified from the start. With those clients, we agree on a precondition to our working together – that is, we will not address the issue of sexual-identity change, but we will work on all of their other problems in living. And so we work on issues like capacity for intimacy, problems with self-esteem, internalized shame, childhood trauma, and the search for identity.

The good therapist always conveys his complete acceptance of the client, even if that client eventually decides to gay-identify. Like Jason, some of our clients decide to change course and embrace homosexuality as "who they are." Some never lose their conviction that they were designed to be heterosexual, and they persist toward that goal. Others remain ambivalent about change, while going in and out of gay life over a period of months. We accept their choices even if we don't agree with them, because we accept the person.

Dr Joseph Nicolosi is a licensed psychologist and founder and Clinical Director of the Thomas Aquinas Psychological Clinic in Encino, California. He specializes in the treatment of men who wish to diminish their same-sex attractions and develop their heterosexual potential, and has been practising as a psychologist since 1980.

Dr Nicolosi is a former president of NARTH – The National Association of Research and Therapy of Homosexuality – which is the only U.S. professional group organized to protect the right of homosexual clients to receive change-oriented therapy.

He is the author of *Reparative Therapy of Male Homosexuality* (Jason Aronson, Inc., 1991), *Healing Homosexuality: Case Stories of Reparative Therapy* (Jason Aronson, Inc., 1993), and co-author with his wife, Linda Ames Nicolosi, of the book *A Parent's Guide to Preventing Homosexuality* (Intervarsity Press, 2002).

He is also co-author of a research study, 'Retrospective Self-Reports of Changes in Homosexual Orientation: A Consumer Survey of Conversion Therapy Clients', which was published in *Psychological Reports*, June 2000, vol. 86, pp. 1071-1088, and of several other peer-reviewed papers.

See also

'Ex-Gays? A Longitudinal Study of Religiously Mediated Change in Sexual Orientation (by) Stanton L. Jones (Wheaton College) and Mark A. Yarhouse (Regent University), Author Q&A', IVP Academic; http://www.ivpress.com/media/exgays-qa.pdf

'New Book Details Benefits and Limits of Gay Change', by Dr Warren Throckmorton; http://www.drthrockmorton.com/article.asp?id=205

'Is Anyone Ever Totally Healed?' by Alan Medinger; http://www.regenerationministries.org/newsletters/200603.pdf

II. A Faithful Church: The Bible and Same-Sex Sex

Professor Robert A. J. Gagnon

1. *Preface*

A paper entitled "Making the Case: The Blessing of Same Sex Unions in the Anglican Church of Canada" (May 2007) has been circulated to all the delegates at the 2007 General Synod of the Anglican Church of Canada (29 pages – or 31 if one counts the two-page list appendix at the end). The writer of the paper is a certain John Thorp, who is a professor of philosophy at the University of Western Ontario.[1]

Although Thorp apologizes in his preface for the limited scope of his essay, this does not stop him from making many bold claims. He ends with the following: "Gay liberation is *clearly* the work of the Spirit. How can it reasonably be judged otherwise?" (p. 29; his emphasis). He believes that the case he has made for blessing homosexual unions at three levels – Scripture, Tradition, and Reason – "*easily* overcomes the surface prohibitions" against homosexual practice in Scripture (p. 19; my emphasis).

The reality of the matter is quite different. I see very little evidence that he is even aware of the major counterarguments to his position, much less that he responds effectively to these arguments. This circumstance apparently forms the basis for his overconfidence. True, he has some understanding of the philosophical discussions in ancient Greece; see, for example, his essay "The Social Construction of Homosexuality" in *Phoenix* 46.1 (1992): 54-61[2]. But his lack of expertise in biblical studies, theology, and science shows throughout the essay. Even where one would expect him to be strongest, namely in his own area of philosophical argumentation, the presentation is surprisingly weak.

Even so, I never assume that what appears as a markedly weak case to the trained eye will also appear so to the untrained eye. The rebuttal below presents in relatively short order some of the major

---

[1] A copy of the paper can be found on the web at the Anglican Church of Canada website at http://www.anglican.ca/faith/ethics/documents/Making-the-Case-Thorp.pdf.
[2] online at http://www.fordham.edu/halsall/med/thorp.html.

counterarguments, following in order the basic outline of his essay. We can only be cursory here given the short turnover time that delegates will have to read and digest this material. Fuller documentation of my arguments can be obtained by reading material from the abridged bibliography. Hopefully Prof. Thorp will begin reading some of these resources.

2. Introduction: A Faithful, Not "Frozen," Church in Matters of Significance

In his introduction (pp. 1-3), Thorp repeatedly warns against a "frozen" church. Sadly, he shows precious little concern for a *faithful* church. His straw man consists of groups in the church that allegedly hold to "eternal and unchanging religious law, enshrined in the Bible and governing human life in *every last one of its details*" (p. 1; emphasis added). Thorp contends that "if at first" embracing homosexual unions "appears to be a radical break in the faith and order of the Church, it is in fact not so." In response I lift up the following points for reflection:

(i)   *The two-sexes prerequisite is no little "detail" in Scripture but a core value in sexual ethics.*

The universal witness of Scripture to a male-female prerequisite for valid sexual unions – the flip side of which is the witness of Scripture against every form of homosexual practice – is no little "detail." It is a core value among Scripture's sexual ethics. It is a value held:

- *pervasively*, that is, within each Testament and across Testaments;

- *absolutely*, that is, without exception;

- *strongly*, that is, as or more offensive than adultery and the worst forms of consensual adult incest;

- *counterculturally*, that is, in opposition to broader cultural trends.

As such, retaining the Bible's position on this matter renders the church faithful, not frozen. Violating this foundational stance is not "dynamic," as Thorp claims, but profoundly disobedient.

(ii)   *Thorp's attack on a position of "no change" beats a dead horse.*

Perhaps surprisingly for Thorp virtually *no one* is arguing for the eternal and unchanging character of every one of Scripture's commands. Indeed, such a position would be patently unbiblical inasmuch as Jesus himself overruled the Law of Moses when he revoked exemptions to the monogamy principle that had been given for men but never women (Mark 10:2-12 par. Matt 19:3-9).

Jesus acknowledged that these exemptions in the Law were nothing more than concessions made to human (chiefly male) hardness of heart. Now Jesus was declaring that such concessions would no longer be allowed. So clearly Jesus accepted the view that the Old Testament or covenant could be improved upon; that is, aligned more closely to the perfect will of God. Thorp is beating a dead horse of his own making when he argues against the unchangeable character of "every last detail" of the Bible.

(iii)   Jesus himself is Thorp's main obstacle for discounting a two-sexes prerequisite.

What was the basis for Jesus' unilateral amendment of the Law of Moses that eliminated the right of men to more than one wife? Here the matter becomes embarrassing for Thorp's position, for Jesus cited as his justification God's creation of "male and female" in Gen 1:27 and the marriage standard of a "man" and his "woman" being joined together in Gen 2:24 – two texts that Thorp seeks to circumvent by endorsing homosexual unions.

Jesus' declared these two texts as constituting the foundation for his limitation of the number of parties in a sexual bond to two. In other words, the 'twoness' or duality of a sexual bond is predicated on the 'twoness' or duality of the sexes. Eliminating the significance of the latter for defining appropriate sexual bonds leaves the church without basis for a monogamy principle. God's creation of two primary sexes is the foundation for prohibiting additional persons beyond two in a sexual bond, whether concurrently (polygyny) or serially (repeat divorce/remarriage). The union of the two sexes into one makes a third party both unnecessary and undesirable.

That was Jesus' opinion, which should have considerably more significance than Thorp's opinion or that of any bishop who also seeks to contravene Jesus' view. Since Jesus lifted up Gen 1:27 and 2:24 as normative, with proscriptive implications, for all matters of human sexual ethics, it is not surprising that when Paul indicts homosexual practice absolutely in Rom 1:24-27 and 1 Cor 6:9 he has these same two texts from Genesis in the background. He simply shows himself to be a good disciple of Jesus.

(iv)   *The male-female prerequisite is the foundation or prior analogue*
           for defining other critical sexual norms.

A powerful indicator of the significance of a male-female prerequisite is its
relationship to other key sexual standards.

For Jesus the two-sexes prerequisite grounded in God's creation will
in Scripture must have been more important than his rulings against
polygyny and divorce/remarriage inasmuch as the foundation is greater
than the positions predicated on the foundation.

The Bible's stance against adult, consensual incest cannot be more
important than its stance against homosexual practice since:

- Though both are rejected in Scripture on grounds of too much formal
  or structural sameness (incest on a familial level, homosexual practice
  on the level of sex or gender), this degree of structural sameness is felt
  more keenly in the case of homosexual practice. For sex or gender is a
  more integral component of sexual relations, and more foundationally
  defines it, than is and does the degree of blood relatedness.

- While the Old Testament accommodated at different points of Israel's
  history to some forms of incest, Scripture never makes an
  accommodation for homosexual practice of any sort.

- An implicit proscription of homosexual behavior can be grounded in
  the creation narratives in Gen 1-2 (as Paul certainly did, see below) but
  as regards incest at most only an implicit prohibition of
  intergenerational incest might be found.

- Adultery becomes an applicable offense only when the sexual bond that
  the offender is cheating on is a valid sexual bond. One can't cheat
  against a union that is structurally invalid, and thus immoral, from the
  beginning – or at least the notion of cheating must be considerably
  diluted (much as the idea of 'cheating' on a mistress must, by
  definition, be diminished in significance). Consequently, incest and
  homosexual practice violate God's sexual standards at a more
  foundational level than adultery.

(v)   *Same-sex intercourse radically offends against God's intentional*
          creation of humans as "male and female" (Gen 1:27) and the
          definition of marriage as a union between a man and a woman
          (Gen 2:24).

Genesis 1:27 links God's image imprinted on humans with the
complementary sexual differentiation of humans into male and female.

Although animals are similarly differentiated, only in humans is that differentiation connected with being created in God's image. This suggests that what humans do sexually can affect either negatively or positively the stamp of God's image on them. It also suggests that, while male and female each have individual integrity as God's image, the union of male and female brings together complementary expressions of the divine image into a full-orbed sexuality. Entering into a homosexual union disregards the sacred foundation on which Gen 1 predicates sexual activity and dishonors one's God-given sex by merging with a person of the same sex as though that person were the complement to one's sex.

Genesis 2:21-24 give a beautiful illustration in story form of the inherent complementarity of a man-woman sexual bond and so the implicit, inherent discomplementarity of a same-sex sexual bond. Woman is drawn from the "side" of the human (a better translation than "rib"). She is the missing part, sexually speaking, to a man – the missing sexual complement if one is seeking a sexual relationship with another. Man and woman may be (re-)joined into one flesh because the two emerged out of one flesh. This is a lovely picture of the basic point that men and women are each other's sexual "other halves" – not two males or two females.

(vi)   Every text in Scripture that treats the issue of homosexual practice treats it as a high offense abhorrent to God.

A triad of stories about extreme depravity – attempted sexual assault of male visitors by the men of Sodom (Gen 19.4-11), the attempted sexual assault of the Levite passing through Gibeah (Judg 19.22-25), and (as I and others have argued elsewhere) Ham's offense against his father Noah (Gen 9.20-27) – feature man-male intercourse as an integral element of the depravity. Arguing that these stories indict only homosexual practice characterized by coercion (rape) is like arguing that a story about an adult raping a parent (which, incidentally, is probably what the story of Ham and Noah is about) only indicts coercive forms of incest. If one examines these stories in their historical and literary contexts – the ancient Near Eastern evidence, other texts written by the same author, other texts in ancient Israel presupposing a male-female prerequisite or indicting homoerotic activity, and the history of interpretation – one sees that the same-sex dimension of the acts is a significant *compounding* offense, not an incidental act.

The Levitical prohibitions of homosexual practice (18:22; 20:13) treat it as a first-tier sexual offense (20:10-16), specifically tag it with the label *to'evah* ("abomination, abhorrent act") that is normally reserved for high moral offenses, and in all other respects treat the act as a matter of moral impurity. Unlike merely ritually impure acts, homosexual practice is not contagious through physical contact and is not rectified by ritual bathing; nor does the prohibition encompass unintentional or inadvertent acts.

Jesus, as we have seen, predicated his view of marital monogamy and indissolubility on a male-female prerequisite for valid sexual bonds given in Gen 1-2. His view on homosexual practice is clear not only from this but also from: his view of the Old Testament as holy Scripture and his retention of the Law of Moses even on relatively minor matters such as tithing; his intensification of the Law's sexual ethic in matters involving adultery of the heart and divorce and in his saying about cutting over body parts (Matt 5:27-32); the fact that the man who baptized him, John the Baptist, was beheaded for defending Levitical sex laws; early Judaism's univocal opposition to homosexual practice; the early church's united opposition to homosexual practice; the distinction that he drew between the non-defiling effect of food and the body-defiling character of gratifying sexual desires for behavior that God forbids (Mark 7:21-23); and other arguments.

Paul in Rom 1:24-27 treated homosexual practice as comparable to idolatry insofar as both radically suppress the truth (one about the Creator, the other about the way the Creator made us) transparent in the material structures of creation/nature. He refers to homosexual practice, both female and male, as an act of sexual "uncleanness" or "impurity" (*akatharsia*), an "indecency" or "shameful act" (*aschēmosune*), a "dishonoring (*atimazesthai*) of their bodies among themselves," the product of "dishonorable passions" (*pathē atimias*), and an act "contrary to nature" (*hē para phusin*) that, in part, was its own "payback" (*antimisthia*). Twice later in the same letter he alludes back to homosexual practice as a paradigmatic example of sexual impurity and immorality that believers must put aside or else still face God's coming judgment (6:19-23; 13:13-14). The continuation of the vice list from 1:19-27 to 1:28-31 does not mean that Paul regarded idolatry and homosexual practice as "just two of many vices," nor does the continuation of the argument in ch. 2 suggest that Paul is opposed to the Christian community judging idolatry and homosexual practice as high moral offenses.

Paul in 1 Cor 6:9 lists "soft men" (*malakoi*, i.e. men who feminize themselves to attract male sex partners) and "men who lie with a male" (*arsenokoitai*; cf. also 1 Tim 1.10) among a series of sexual offenders that include adulterers and, implied in the context, men who engage in incest and men who have sex with prostitutes (*pornoi*, cf. 5.9-11; 6.15-16). Such persons, whether they claim to be believers or not, "shall not inherit the kingdom of God" if they do not repent (6.9-10; cf. 2 Cor 12:21).

The reasons given above make clear that the Bible's male-female prerequisite for sexual unions is no little "detail". Deviating from this foundation for sexual ethics is indeed a "radical break in [i.e. from] the faith and order of the Church."

3. Moral Evolution

Thorp appeals to Richard Hooker's three-stranded cord (later identified as a three-legged stool) consisting of Scripture, Reason, and Tradition (Thorp subsumes experience under reason). However, he does not use this hermeneutical model in the manner that Hooker would have. Particularly problematic is the short shrift that Thorp gives Scripture, which for Hooker occupied "that first place" to which "both credit and obedience is due." In a 29-page paper Thorp gives Scripture a grand total of two-and-one-third pages, discussing it only after he treats both "Moral Evolution" and "Reason". Even his handling of "moral evolution," "reason," and "tradition" contain fatal errors and misinterpretations. We will begin with his section on "Moral Evolution" (pp. 4-9).

Thorp makes the single point here that "*morals change*" (p. 9) and cites the church's stance on usury and slavery to make his point. That changing circumstances may result in changing moral standards from those enunciated in Scripture *within limits* is, as I have already observed, patently obvious. Making this point, however, does not in any way establish Thorp's case for changing in the specific area of homosexual practice. Indeed, proper analogical reasoning shows the matter to be otherwise. Here there are three main problems with Thorp's argument.

First, the concept of "moral evolution" implies steady improvement in the morality of society in all, or virtually all, areas over the centuries. Any minimal understanding of history will show this assumption to be false. There is at least as much moral *devolution* over time, as witnessed not least in the sexual looseness and infidelity that characterizes modern Western society.

Second, valid moral change is not always in the direction of greater permissiveness. One need only look at the six antitheses that kick off the Sermon on the Mount, two of which have to do with sex, where Jesus summarizes his message as: You used to be able to get away with the following things; I tell you that such is no longer the case because I'm closing these loopholes (Matt 5:17-48).

Third, the two analogues that Thorp cites for jettisoning the Bible's stance on homosexual practice are poor analogues. In fact, Thorp has chosen to eschew near analogues (incest, polyamory) in favor of adopting more remote analogues (usury, slavery). He has done so for the obvious reason that the closer analogues won't get him to his desired ideological outcome.

Usury

The Bible's stance on usury does not remotely approach the consistency, severity, absoluteness, and strongly countercultural character of the Bible's stance on homosexual practice. Thorp's analogy is akin to comparing usury law and incest law. In other words it makes little sense.

Slavery

The analogy with slavery also has insurmountable problems. Note the following differences between the Bible's stance on slavery and the Bible's stance on homosexual practice:

- *No mandate.* There is no scriptural mandate to enslave others, nor does one incur a penalty for releasing slaves. No noble values ever 'rode' on the preservation of the institution of slavery. Selling oneself into slavery was seen as a last-ditch measure to avoid starvation – at best a necessary evil in a state with limited welfare resources (Lev 25:39). There *is*, however, a scriptural mandate to limit sexual unions to heterosexual ones, with a severe penalty (in this life or the next) imposed on violators.

- *Not pre-Fall.* Unlike the opposite-sex prerequisite, Scripture does not ground slavery in pre-Fall structures. Even if one were to contend that this is a de-historicizing argument, based on myth, the creation story still tells us that the biblical writers viewed heterosexual unions, unlike slavery, as normative and transcultural.

- *The Bible's critical edge toward slavery.* One can discern within the Bible a significant critical edge toward slavery. Front and center in Israelite memory was its remembrance of God's liberation from slavery in Egypt (e.g., Exod 22:21; 23:9; Lev 25:42, 55; Deut 15:15). Christian memory adds the paradigmatic event of Christ's redemption of believers from slavery to sin and people (1 Cor 6:20; 7:23; and often). Israelite law put various restrictions on enslaving fellow Israelites – mandatory release dates, the right of near-kin redemption, not returning runaway slaves, and insisting that Israelites not be treated as slaves.

- The "undisputed Paul" in 1 Cor 7:21 and Phlm 16 regarded liberation from slavery as at least a penultimate good. The ultimate good, of course, was freedom of moral purpose, something that not even slavery could deprive someone of. First Corinthians 7:21 is best translated as: "Were you, a slave, called? Don't let it trouble you. But if also (or: even if, if indeed) you are able to become free, all the more (or: rather) use (it, i.e. your freedom)," that is, to redouble your efforts to serve God. As regards Philemon, Thorp inaccurately characterizes Paul's message as: "And, of course, the whole of the letter to Philemon is about the return to him of his runaway slave Onesimus, whom Paul had encountered in prison" (p. 8). No, the whole of the letter is about Paul getting Philemon to look at Onesimus in an entirely new light, including as a person who should be treated "no longer as a slave but more than a slave, as a beloved brother ... both in the flesh and in the Lord" (i.e., in the sphere of both society and church; v. 16).

- The canon of Scripture shows considerable discomfort with the institution of slavery. Yet there is not the slightest indication anywhere in the canon that same-sex intercourse is anything other than a detested practice to be utterly eschewed by the people of God in all circumstances. The discomfort that Scripture shows is not with any opposition to same-sex intercourse but rather with any accommodation to it.

- *The Bible's countercultural witness.* Although the contemporary church has gone beyond the Bible in its total opposition to slavery, the biblical stance was generally more critical of slavery than were the surrounding cultures out of which the Scriptures emerged. The countercultural edge was in the direction of criticizing and weakening the institution of slavery. The precise opposite happens to be the case with the Bible's stance on same-sex intercourse. The authors of Scripture expressed far greater disapproval of such behavior and maintained a far more rigorous male-female sexual prerequisite than did the cultures of their day. The countercultural edge was decidedly in the direction of intensifying opposition to homosexual practice. For Paul liberation in the Christian life here meant freedom from the tyranny of intense urges that dishonor the human creation as male and female, not necessarily by losing the intense urges but rather by gaining a new power, that of the Spirit, to enable obedience amidst hardship (compare Rom 1:24-27; 6:19-22; 7:5-6; 8:12-17).

- Simply put, *Scripture nowhere expresses a vested interest in preserving slavery but rather in many ways strong reservations, whereas Scripture does express a clear countercultural and creational vested interest in preserving an exclusive male-female dynamic to human sexual relationships*. Scripture itself does not provide the kind of clear and unequivocal witness *for* slavery that it exhibits *against* same-sex intercourse.

- An emancipation movement would not have appalled Jesus and Paul but acts of same-sex intercourse would have done just that. There is much to suggest that Jesus and Paul would have condoned an emancipation movement, though they might have questioned: (1) how it could be accomplished without massive violence (they did not live in democratic states and lacked political power); (2) how some particularly destitute persons would survive (they did not live in welfare states so some people might face starvation); and (3) how the disciples of Jesus would survive if it made emancipation a cornerstone (they would confirm for authorities suspicions that Christian faith was a seditious threat to the Roman Empire). Thorp's stance on same-sex intercourse represents a fundamental challenge to the authority of Scripture and Jesus that far supersedes any challenge posed by emancipation movements. It is a challenge to Scripture's core values.

- What the authors of Scripture, and Jesus, meant by "slavery" was also something significantly different from what we Americans normally mean by slavery. Slavery in the ancient world was not predominantly race-based, often did not mean lifelong servitude, often served as a form of criminal justice (in the absence of long-term prison facilities), often allowed private enterprise, sometimes led to social advancement, and operated in a social and political economy that made complete abolition of the institution problematic (totalitarian states that disallowed such political reform; no welfare net). These differences are well documented and help to mitigate the problem of different stances toward the institution of slavery held by ancient and modern believers.

Better analogues: incest and polyamory. Instead of fixating on the relatively remote analogies of usury and slavery, why doesn't Thorp focus attention on the much closer analogies of incest and polyamory? After all, these are also sexual offenses. Incest is closest to homosexual practice as a severe sexual offense in Scripture. Both incest and homosexual practice are rejected, ultimately, because they constitute an attempt at merging with someone who is too much of a structural same. As noted above, polyamory (multiple-partner sexuality) is rejected by Jesus on the ground that it violates the twoness of the sexes established by God at creation. So clearly there is a logical link that can be made between homosexual practice and incest, on one hand, and homosexual practice and polyamory, on the other.

Homosexual practice, incest, and polyamorous unions all can be conducted by adults as consensual, loving relationships. Homosexual practice and incest can also be monogamous, while even a polyamorous bond can express fidelity in a lifelong commitment. None of these relationships is *intrinsically* harmful, if by harm we mean *scientifically measurable* harm. Absolute prohibitions for all three depend significantly on a principle of embodied structural congruity that transcends the will and orientation of the participants.

The best analogies are obviously those that share the greatest number of points of correspondence with the thing to which they are being compared. Thorp has ignored the best analogies. It is clear that Thorp doesn't want to focus attention on the analogues of incest and polyamory because doing so would lead the church to the conclusion that it should continue to oppose homosexual practice. For we continue to oppose absolutely in the church incest and polyamory – even those instances of an adult, consensual, and committed sort. Since Thorp doesn't want to reach the conclusion that a prohibition of homosexual practice be maintained, he chooses the more remote analogues of usury and slavery. That is an intellectually dishonest form of analogical reasoning.

In promoting homosexual practice Thorp is actually pushing for a reinstitution of slavery, the kind of slavery that Paul warns against in Rom 6:1-8:17: a slavery to the sinful impulses of the flesh to do what God expressly forbids.

4.   Reason

Thorp's argument from reason is thin on reasons even though this represents his only hope of overturning Scripture and Tradition (pp. 10-16). His argument has two parts.

The first part claims that the church originally did not regard homosexual practice as a severe offense but "just one vice among others" with "the grounds for its disapproval" being "quite various" (p. 11). This claim is false. From its roots in ancient Israel, through the New Testament, and to the Church Fathers and beyond, homosexual practice has consistently been regarded as (1) a high moral offense that is (2) contrary to God's design in nature/creation. Thorp's contention that homosexual practice first becomes a high offense in the work of Peter Damian (ca. 1050) is historically absurd. Certainly there is no justification in the New Testament for hating persons who engage in homosexual practice. There is justification, however, for being repulsed by homosexual practice in a manner akin to the revulsion felt for incest between a man and his mother

(1 Cor 5). At the same time offenders are not to be consigned to hell and done with, but rather sought out for the purposes of being recovered for the kingdom of God.

Typical of Thorp's misreading of texts is his handling of *Didache* 2:2-3. Thorp assumes that because pederasty is mentioned in the *Didache* among an array of offenses it is being viewed as "just one vice among others." *Didache* 2:2-3 simply constructs a vice list based on the second half of the Decalogue without attempting to provide a ranking. To give an analogous example, Paul is clearly morally outraged by the case of the incestuous man in 1 Cor 5, a person whom Paul refers to as a *pornos*, i.e. a sexually immoral man. He clearly does not regard incest as "just one vice among others," say, as merely the equivalent of the sin of fornication (i.e., non-incestuous, heterosexual intercourse outside of marriage). Yet he simply includes the *pornoi* as one among many offenders in the vice lists in 1 Cor 5:9-10 and 6:9-10 from whom the church should temporarily disassociate (pending repentance) and who (if repentance is not forthcoming) run the risk of exclusion from God's kingdom.

The second part of Thorp's argument from reason is that "the secular understanding of homosexuality has changed in recent decades" in that we now know, allegedly, that homosexuality, "like left-handedness, ... is a normal abnormality" and that it is a proclivity that is "either inborn, or at any rate acquired so early in life that the agent has no say in its acquisition" (p. 15). Persons who engage in homosexual practice are "sexual minorities," on the analogy of "racial and religious minorities" (ibid.). They can live well-adjusted lives.

A later section of his paper entitled "Other Considerations" (pp. 23-26) also belongs here. Thorp argues that homosexual practice cannot be "contrary to nature" inasmuch as it is exhibited in many animal populations (to stress the point Thorp even appends a 2-page list of mammals exhibiting homosexual behavior, drawn from Bruce Bagemihl's book, *Biological Exuberance*, pp. 30-31). Against a procreation argument, Thorp argues that the church has accepted non-procreative sexuality among heterosexuals.

None of these are strong arguments for overturning the powerful witness of Scripture against homosexual practice. Consider the following:

Innateness as anticipated in the ancient world and as irrelevant for assessing an act as moral. The argument about innateness of homosexual desire is a complete wash, for two reasons. First, already in the ancient world congenital causation factors for at least some forms of same-sex attraction were posited. As classicist Thomas K. Hubbard notes in his *Homosexuality in Greece and Rome: A Sourcebook of Basic Documents*

(University of California Press, 2003): "Homosexuality in this era [viz., of the early imperial age of Rome] may have ceased to be merely another practice of personal pleasure and began to be viewed as an essential and central category of personal identity, exclusive of and antithetical to heterosexual orientation" (p. 386).

Second, as even Thorp has to admit (p. 26), the "born that way" argument does not do justice to the Christian view of original sin, nor the fact that humans experience a wide array of innate impulses that are sinful. Quite simply, "no clear conclusions about the morality of a behavior can be made from the mere fact of biological causation, because all behavior is biologically caused" (J. Michael Bailey and Brian S. Mustanski, "A therapist's guide to the genetics of human sexual orientation." *Sexual and Relationship Therapy* 18.4 [2003]: 429-36, here p. 432). Pedophilia, for example, is every bit as "innate," that is, not a product of willful choice, as homosexuality. The same can be said for "polysexual" impulses, the common (especially male) dissatisfaction for lifelong monogamy. While at present it is more difficult to tie "orientation" to incest, incest would (or should) not be acceptable even if there were such a thing as an orientation to incest on the part of some. None of God's commands are predicated on people lacking or losing any innate desire to violate the command in question.

The absurdity of analogies with left-handedness and ethnicity. Left-handedness is a bad analogue for homosexuality because left-handedness is not an impulse to do something God expressly forbids. It is not a desire to merge sexually with another structurally discordant to oneself.

Comparisons between benign non-sexual conditions and disputed forms of sexual relationship are fraught with difficulties. Sexual intercourse has its own distinctive rules. For example, it would be absurd to argue, as Thorp and other proponents of homosexual unions do, that the love commandment validates all sexual unions where love is present. The problem with such a use of the love commandment would be readily apparent if one realized that, while Jesus commanded us to love everyone, he at the same time restricted the number of persons with whom one could have sex to one other person lifetime (based, as we have seen, on a two-sexes prerequisite). Obviously, then, Jesus had a distinctive sex ethic. He absolutely prescribed love of everyone with whom one comes into contact, including an enemy, while absolutely proscribing sex with more than one other person and limiting that one other person to a person of the other sex.

Sexual intimacy is not just more love. It has its own distinctive character from generic, non-sexual love. Accordingly, parents who "love" their children by having sex with them go to prison. A few years ago at the American Academy of Religion national meeting the Gay Men's Issues in Religion Group had a theme session that advocated for "polyfidelity" (faithful, multiple-partner sexual unions). One of the presenters compared an erection to a particularly warm handshake. Another likened the Trinity to a sexual 'threesome.' These presenters did not realize that sexual unions have their own unique prerequisites that are not required by, and sometimes are at diametrical odds with, the command to love everyone.

A polysexual orientation is a much closer, and thus better, analogue than the non-sexual and non-moral condition of left-handedness. Again, Thorp doesn't want the closer analogues because they lead to a conclusion that Thorp finds undesirable.

The attempt to develop the category of "sexual minorities," on analogy to ethnic minorities, leads to ludicrous results. An ethnicity is a condition that is 100% heritable, absolutely immutable, primarily non-behavioral, and therefore inherently benign. Homosexual orientation is a sexual impulse and, like many sexual impulses, it is:

> Not 100% heritable. Homosexual development cannot be predicted with the degree of certainty that one can predict that two people, say, of French ancestry will always produce a child of French ancestry.

> Open to some change in the course of life, at least as regards the intensity of the impulse. Needless to say, persons of French ancestry do not become more or less French in the course of life.

> Primarily a behavioral desire to do something. Being French or any other ancestry or ethnicity is more a condition of being than of behavior.

Thus homosexuality, unlike ethnicity but like polysexuality (i.e. polyamory), pedosexuality (pedophilia), and desires to have sex with close blood relations, is not an inherently benign condition. Of course, a person is not held culpable merely for experiencing an impulse to do what God forbids. But such an impulse is a sinful impulse because it seeks to violate God's commands. If it were not a sinful impulse there would be no need to refrain from expressing it. When an individual acquiesces to the impulse in thought and/or deed, then the individual becomes culpable for sin.

Why homosexuality in the animal kingdom does not make homosexual practice natural in the deepest sense.

Thorp's argument about homosexuality in the animal kingdom is irrelevant even for making his nature argument. I never used my dear departed dog "Cocoa" and her instinctive sexual habits as a basis for determining what is "natural" behavior. You can find animals of various species where some part of the population at least practices incest, pedophilia, extreme polyamory, and cross-species sex, along with same-sex sexual activity. Does this make all such activity "natural"? In one sense, perhaps, but not in all senses.

Nature cannot be limited to impulses but rather must be broadened to include the formal, embodied structures of human existence. The sheer structural incongruence of an incestuous bond, a sexual bond involving more than two persons concurrently, and an adult-child sexual bond are enough for people to categorize such bonds as unnatural. The unnatural character of homosexual practice does not stem in the first instance from what animals do or don't do. It stems from the totality of embodied maleness, if male, or femaleness, if female, each of which represent only one half of the sexual spectrum. In other words, it stems from the structurally incongruous character (anatomically, physiologically, and psychologically) of same-sex sexual unions. Homosexuality is unnatural in the sense that it is narcissistic arousal for the distinctive features of one's own sex; or the self-deluded desire to complement one's own sex (which is intact) through merger with someone of the same sex, as if one were only half one's own sex.

Why an otherwise well-adjusted life does not validate homosexual practice.

The fact that some homosexual persons live otherwise well-adjusted lives does not establish the validity of homosexual practice.

First, the definition of immorality is not limited to what produces *intrinsic, scientifically measurable* harm. If it were otherwise, society would have to endorse some type of virtually every sexual bond. Even adult-child contact does not produce inherent measurable harm, as two APA studies have noted, to say nothing of adult incest or faithful polyamory. Homosexual persons do not become complete moral werewolves simply because they engage in homosexual practice. People compartmentalize their impulses and behaviors, being good in some areas and bad in others. The good doesn't convert the bad into good.

Second, Thorp's claim overlooks the fact that homosexual persons experience disproportionately high rates of measurable harm *in ways that typify their specific sex.* Same-sex erotic bonds lack a person of the other sex to moderate the extremes of a given sex or to fill in the gaps of that given sex. Not surprisingly, homosexual men experience on average markedly higher numbers of sex partners in the course of life and a markedly higher rates of sexually transmitted disease. Homosexual women experience on average unions of shorter duration and higher rates of mental health issues, probably due to the greater personal expectations that women put on sexual relationships (thus putting added pressure on the relationship) and a higher investment of self-worth in the success of the relationship (which, when the relationship fails, leads to greater depression). Because men and women were designed by God to complement each other in a sexual bond, not men and men or women and women, the former type of union is natural, the latter type unnatural.

This leads to the third point: Such problems are symptomatic of a deeper root problem; namely, conceiving a person of the same sex as the appropriate sexual complement to one's own sex.

A proper use of a procreation argument.

Thorp dismisses a procreation argument on the grounds that heterosexual relationships are blessed even when lacking a procreative capacity. Procreation was clearly not Paul's main concern either (cf. 1 Cor 7) but that didn't stop him from issuing a severe indictment of homosexual practice in his letters. The procreation argument is a heuristic device – one more clue for why God did not design two persons of the same sex for sexual pairing. There is a big difference between having equipment failure (infertility among heterosexual couples) and not having the equipment at all (the inherent incapacity for procreation in homosexual bonds).

Thorp's argument from reason is thus badly constructed. He seems not even to be aware of the main counterarguments to his position, much less answer them effectively.

Thorp's misogyny argument

A final point needs to be said about Thorp's predictable use of a misogyny argument in this section of his paper. He suggests that "the *deep* reason for the loathing of homosexuals that our culture has known" stems "ultimately from the disprizing of women that was a common feature of the cultures of the Mediterranean basin" (pp. 14-15). But this argument will not work, for at least three reasons.

First, even Greco-Roman critiques of homosexual practice were more broadly motivated than simply a desire to keep women down. Greco-Roman moralists also appealed to the structural complementarity of the sexes, as regards both anatomical and procreative design. "Basic to the heterosexual position [against homosexual practice in the first few centuries

C.E.] is the characteristic Stoic appeal to the providence of Nature, which has matched and fitted the sexes to each other" (Hubbard, *Sourcebook*, 444). The misogyny argument ignores concerns for formal or structural congruence that they applied (and we still apply) to various forbidden sexual practices.

Second, in the Greco-Roman milieu opposition to male homosexual practice intensified as appreciation for women grew. Advocates for the superiority of male-female love generally espoused a *higher* view of women as suitable companions and friends deserving of equal pleasure in the sexual bond.

Third, the illogical but inevitable corollary of the misogyny argument is that ancient Israel, early Judaism, and early Christianity were the most misogynistic cultures in the ancient world. For it is in these cultures that one finds the strongest opposition to homosexual practice. As it is, the idea that these cultures were more deeply misogynistic than "pagan" cultures is absurd. Therefore, it is also absurd to argue that the *primary* stimulus for opposing homosexual practice in the pages of the Bible was a fundamental fear or hatred of women.

5.   Scripture

As we have already noted, Thorp's discussion of Scripture (pp. 17-19) is poor indeed. At no point does he provide a careful examination of any texts of Scripture. Instead he focuses on two main philosophical arguments that are more asserted than substantiated.

A. Why a prohibition of "committed" homosexual unions is both reasonable and scriptural.

Thorp first contends that "it seems extremely unlikely" that the Bible could be expressing opposition to "lifelong, committed, nurturing" homosexual relationships since "the language is too harshly dismissive to allow us to think it is motivated by any knowledge" of such (p. 18).

Before offering my main critique an aside is in order. First, one should bear in mind that the characterization "lifelong" is problematic given that only a tiny fraction of all homosexual relationships turn out to be lifelong – certainly less than 5% and probably less than 1% in cases where there is not premature death through AIDS. A more realistic expectation for about 10-25% of committed homosexual unions is "long-term," meaning something like a union of 5-20 years duration.

I offer two main points in response to Thorp's argument.

First, this is nothing at all unusual or unreasonable about an absolute prohibition of homosexual unions, even of a committed sort. In fact, Thorp would presumably apply the same logic to dismissing absolutely all adult consensual incestuous bonds, say, between a man and his (widowed or divorced?) mother or between a woman and her brother. Surely he would not argue here that our retention of an absolute prohibition of such unions is "too harshly dismissive" when it does not make exceptions for adult incestuous bonds that are "lifelong, committed, nurturing" (and, I might add, that are infertile or that use birth control)? Presumably, he would recognize that formal or structural prerequisites exist for sexual bonds irrespective of whether the sexual union exhibits love and commitment. As I have argued, the structural discomplementarity of homosexual bonds is even more severe than that of incestuous bonds.

We have also noted that faithful polyamorous arrangements – whether a traditional polygamous bond or non-traditional "threesomes" and the like – are not as severe a violation of God's sexual norms as are homosexual unions. Jesus predicated his view of monogamy on a two-sexes prerequisite and the foundation must be more important than the structure built on the foundation. And yet in the Western Church we don't make any allowances for polygamy, even in circumstances where consenting adults are involved and love and commitment are evident. Thorp refers to the tolerance of polygamy "in many Anglican jurisdictions in Africa ... in cases where men who [already] have several wives convert to Christianity" (p. 18). Yet presumably even Thorp would not make exceptions (not even in Africa) for Christians who want to enter into a *new* polygamous arrangement. But isn't this view "too harshly dismissive"?

Thorp's problem here is that he simply assumes in the case of homosexual practice (though apparently only here) that love and commitment ultimately trump all formal requirements for a sexual union, so long as intrinsic measurable harm cannot be demonstrated. But such a position leads to absurd results that not even he would accept (hopefully).

Parenthetically, Thorp makes an argument based on the church's partial accommodation to divorce and remarriage in modern times, an accommodation that he attributes to changing circumstances (p. 18). However, the argument won't get him to where he wants to go as regards validating homosexual unions, for at least two reasons. First, as we have already noted, Jesus and the entire apostolic witness (to say nothing of the Old Testament witness) understood the two-sexes prerequisite for marriage to be more, not less, important than the lifelong character of such bonds. The dissolution of a natural bond cannot be compared to an active entrance into a strongly unnatural bond. This is particularly true in cases where one has largely been the victim of the dissolution rather than the perpetrator but it is even true in the case of the perpetrator. It is not possible to reason correctly from accommodation for a lesser offense to an accommodation for a greater offense. For the same reason I've not heard anyone arguing that greater laxity on divorce/remarriage permits greater laxity on "committed" incest. Second, the church doesn't ordain anybody who has been divorced and remarried five times, let alone someone who declares that s/he will continue to get divorced and remarried monthly with the fewest negative side-effects. Yet that is precisely what Thorp and other advocates of homosexual unions want the church to do with someone who is actively and unrepentantly engaged in serial homosexual practice.

My second point to Thorp's assumption that the Bible's indictment of homosexual unions could not have embraced committed homosexual bonds is this: Demonstrating that homosexual practice is rejected absolutely (i.e., without exception) by the authors of Scripture is easy to demonstrate. I will lay out only a brief outline here with respect to Paul's view because (1) Thorp himself has made no attempt to document his conclusions by careful exegesis of Scripture in its historical context and (2) demonstrating this fully would add at least another ten pages of text to this paper when I have already demonstrated this fully in many other writings that Thorp and others simply need to take the time to read. Here are six main arguments:

(i)   Appeal to the creation texts.

Paul clearly had in view the creation texts in Gen 1:27 and 2:24 behind his two main indictments of homosexual practice, Rom 1:24-27 (note eight points of correspondence, in a parallel tripartite structure, between Gen 1:26-27 and Rom 1:23-27) and 1 Cor 6:9 (see the citation of Gen 2:24 in 1 Cor 6:16). These echoes establish that Paul's main problem with homosexual practice was that it was a violation of God's will for male-female pairing established in creation, not that it was typically exploitative.

(ii)   The nature argument.

Paul's nature argument in Romans 1.24-27 does not lend itself to distinctions between exploitative and non-exploitative manifestations of homosexual behavior but rather to an absolute rejection of all homosexual bonds. By *para phusin* ("beyond nature" in the sense of "contrary to, against nature") Paul meant that the evidence from the material structures of creation – here the complementary embodied character of maleness and femaleness – gives clear evidence of God's will for human sexual pairing (cf. the quote from Hubbard above against the misogyny argument).

(iii)   *The absolute wording of Rom 1:24-27.*

In Rom 1:24-27 Paul emphasizes the *mutuality* of the homoerotic desires ("inflamed with their yearning for one another" and "their bodies being dishonored among themselves"). This proves that Paul is not restricting his remarks to coercive, exploitative acts.   Moreover, the wording of "exchanging" and "leaving behind" the other sex for the same sex is absolute. The text does not say that men and women exchanged or left behind committed relationships with either sex for exploitative relationships with either sex. It states clearly that the problem was solely the exchange or leaving behind of other-sex sexual unions to pursue same-sex sexual unions.

(iv)   *The indictment of lesbian intercourse in Rom 1:26*

does not support the view that Scripture's indictment is limited to exploitative homosexual acts, since lesbianism in antiquity was not characterized by pederasty, prostitution, or abuse of slaves. Indeed, Greco-Roman moralists in antiquity who wanted to argue against man-male intercourse in its entirety sometimes cited intercourse between women as the ultimate trump card inasmuch as lesbian intercourse was disapproved of even by men who advocated for man-male intercourse. Thorp contends in a footnote that "it has been persuasively argued" that Rom 1:26 refers to heterosexual anal intercourse" rather than lesbian behavior. This is false, given the following facts: (a) the parallel phrasing of Rom 1:26 and 1:27, where "even their females exchanged the natural use" parallels "likewise also the males, having left the natural use *of the female*"; (b) Paul's attribution of blame exclusively to "females" with no mention of males in 1:26; (c) instances in ancient sources where one finds a pairing male homoeroticism and female homoeroticism; (d) references to lesbianism as unnatural in ancient "pagan" literature but no such references to heterosexual anal intercourse as unnatural; (e) the uniformly negative view of female homosexual practice among men in the Greco-Roman world; and (f) the dominant history of interpretation of Rom 1:26 as lesbianism by the Church Fathers.   On the last point Augustine (ca. 410) is a notable exception, but (as B. Brooten notes) this may have been due to his debates with the Pelagians, who in Augustine's view had an overly positive view of sex in marriage apart from its procreative function. All the other Church Fathers from Augustine's time or earlier who commented on what Paul meant by unnatural female intercourse in Rom 1:26 understood it as lesbian intercourse: Clement of Alexandria (ca. 200), Tertullian (ca. 200), "Ambrosiaster" (ca. 370), and John Chrysostom (ca. 390; cf. Bernadette Brooten, *Love Between Woman* [University of Chicago Press, 1996]).

(v) *The inclusive character of the terms malakoi and arsenokoitai in the historical and literary context for 1 Cor 6.9.*

As regards the meaning of *malakoi* (lit., "soft men," in the sense of men who feminize themselves to attract male sex partners) note:

> Its place in amidst other participants in illicit sexual intercourse and its pairing with the immediately following word *arsenokoitai*.

> Philo of Alexandria's use of cognate words to refer to men who actively feminize themselves for the purpose of attracting other men.

> Greco-Roman uses of *malakoi* and the parallel Latin word *molles* (soft men) to denote effeminate *adult* males who are biologically and/or psychologically disposed to desire penetration by men.

As regards the meaning of *arsenokoitai* (literally, "men lying [*koitō*] with a male [*arsōn*]") note (among other reasons):

> That the word is a specifically Jewish/Christian word formulated from the prohibitions of man-male intercourse in Lev 18:22 and 20:13, which Jews of the period interpreted absolutely to include consensual adult male contact.

> Actual usage of *arsenokoitai* and cognates in Christian texts written after 1 Corinthians, which was not limited to pederasts or men who had sex with call boys.

> The implications of the broad context in 1 Cor 5-7, such as the parallel case of incest in ch. 5, the presumption of consent in the vice list in 6:9-10, the citation of Gen 2:24 in 6:16, and the presumption of a male-female prerequisite in the treatment of marriage in ch. 7 (cf. also 1 Cor 11:2-16).

> The fact that sex between two free adult males in the Roman Imperial Age was regarded as more offensive, not less so, than sex with an adolescent boy.

(vi) *The existence of committed homosexual love in the Greco-Roman world.*

A conception of caring homoerotic unions already existed in Paul's cultural environment. Yet even homosexual unions of this sort were rejected by some Greco-Roman moralists. For example, in a debate over heterosexual and homosexual bonds, Plutarch's friend Daphnaeus admits that homosexual relationships are not necessarily exploitative, for "union contrary to nature does not destroy or curtail a lover's tenderness." Yet, he declares, even when a "union with males" is conducted "willingly" it remains "shameful" since males "with softness (malakia) and effeminacy (thēlutēs) [are] surrendering themselves, as Plato says, 'to be mounted in the custom of four-footed animals' and to be sowed with seed contrary to nature" (Dialogue on Love 751).

Historically speaking, then, the evidence is overwhelming that Paul, like all other Jews and Christians of the period, opposed homosexual practice categorically and absolutely. Louis Compton was correct when he stated in his massive *Homosexuality and Civilization* (Harvard University Press, 2003):

> According to [one] interpretation, Paul's words were not directed at "bona fide" homosexuals in committed relationships. But such a reading, however well-intentioned, seems strained and unhistorical. Nowhere does Paul or any other Jewish writer of this period imply the least acceptance of same-sex relations under any circumstance. The idea that homosexuals might be redeemed by mutual devotion would have been wholly foreign to Paul or any other Jew or early Christian. (p. 114)

B. *Why the "Big Picture" of Scripture doesn't disavow a prohibition of homosexual practice.*

Thorp's second line of reasoning is that "even if Paul means to condemn such relationships," we should read the Bible "for the big picture," which "urges us in the direction of love and acceptance of gay and lesbian people" and "abstinence from judgment" (pp. 18-19).

The problem with this argument is that there is nothing in the "big picture" of the Bible on sexual ethics that moves "in the direction of" support for homosexual practice. The New Testament, to say nothing of the Old Testament, certainly doesn't define love as tolerating behaviors that Scripture strongly, pervasively, and counterculturally forbids. "Love does not rejoice over wrongdoing (or: unrighteousness, *adikia*) but rejoices in conjunction with the truth" (1 Cor 13:6). In a context having to do with sexual behavior Paul insisted that what counts is "keeping the commandments of God" (1 Cor 7:19). An outraged Paul asked in the case of the incestuous man, "Isn't it the case that you are to judge those inside (the church)?" (1 Cor 5:12). He intended this rule to apply equally to men who have sex with a male and to adulterers (6:9).

Jesus was no different. Jesus coupled his outreach to tax collectors and sexual sinners with a call for repentance as an essential precondition for inheriting the kingdom of God (Mark 1:15 par.; 6:12 par.; Matt 11:20-21 par.; 12:41 par.; Luke 13:3-5). In the paradigmatic story of the woman caught in adultery Jesus prevented the crowd from stoning the woman – dead people don't repent – but clearly commanded the woman to "no longer be sinning" (John 8:11). This command is combined elsewhere in John with the warning "lest something worse happen to you" (i.e., loss of eternal life; John 5:14). In Matthew's Sermon on the Mount the saying about cutting off offending body parts in order to avoid being sent to hell full-bodied is sandwiched in between two sets of teaching on the importance of sexual purity (Matt 5:27-32). Jesus viewed rebuke of the recalcitrant as an integral part of what it meant to love one's neighbor (compare Luke 17:3-4 par. Matt 18:15, 21-22 with Lev 19:17-18). He repeatedly warned about the perils of the coming judgment for those who only hear his words but do not do them (e.g., Matt 7:13-27). He defined discipleship to him as taking up one's cross, denying oneself, and losing one's life (Mark 8.34-37; Matt 10.38-39; Luke 14.27; 17.33; John 12.25) – in short, radical death to self, not accommodation to preexisting intense bodily urges to do what God forbids.

As we have seen, the command to "love your neighbor as yourself" that Jesus lifted from Lev 19:18 as the second greatest commandment does not lead us to accept a wider array of sexual behaviors. For Jesus interpreted "neighbor" as broadly as possible to mean "everyone with whom one might come into contact, including one's enemy." Yet he developed a sexual ethic that narrowed further the sexual ethics of the Old Testament by restricting the number of persons with whom one could have sex to one other person of the other sex lifetime – an interpretation, as we have seen, derived from the male/female, man/woman prerequisite enunciated in Gen 1:27 and 2:24. Now perhaps Thorp understands Jesus' interpretation of the love commandment better than Jesus himself did. But I seriously doubt it.

Another person who understood the love commandment was Augustine.

> Do not imagine that ... you then love your neighbor when you do not rebuke him. This is not love, but mere feebleness. Let love be fervent to correct, to amend ... Love not in the person his error, but the person; for the person God made, the error the person himself made. (*Ten Homilies on the First Epistle of John* 7.11; *NPNF*, slightly modified)

Tolerating or accepting sinful behavior would only convey to the perpetrators that the sin in question is "no big deal," leave the individual exposed to the wrath of God, and put such a one at risk of exclusion from an eternal relationship with God – not to mention the harmful effects of undermining the community's resolve to resist sexual impurity (1 Cor 5.6-7: a little leaven leavens the whole lump of dough) and provoking God's judgment on the community as a whole.

As an aside, we should note that Thorp's understanding of the Spirit/letter contrast does not mean in Scripture (i.e. Paul in 2 Cor 3:6; Rom 2:27, 29; 7:6) what Thorp alleges that it means. Whereas Thorp understands it to mean "surface rules" versus "the deep lessons of Scripture" (p. 28), Paul meant a mere script that does not empower one to do what is commanded versus the impartation of the gift of the Spirit that enables us to do what God commands (i.e., the law written on the heart). In short, the issue is not one of overturning God's foundational commands (Thorp) but rather one of being empowered at long last to keep these commands. Of course, I prefer Paul to Thorp.

Given the arguments that can be mounted against Thorp's use of Scripture and reason, there seems to be unwarranted arrogance in Thorp's statement: "A deep reading of the Scripture ... combined with what Reason tells us about homosexuality, *easily* overcomes the surface prohibitions" (p. 19; my emphasis). Thorp has offered neither "a deep reading of the Scripture" nor even a convincing presentation of the case from reason.

6. Tradition

As regards his treatment of "Tradition" (pp. 20-22), Thorp offers nothing positive to bolster his case. Indeed, he tacitly admits that there is nothing in the long history of the church that might lead to an openness toward homosexual practice –other than the fact that the church has changed on some other issues (usury, slavery), none of which, as we have seen, remotely approximates the extensive change that would be required to affirm homosexual practice. Rather than offer something positive from tradition, Thorp performs two 'rear guard' actions.

First, he argues that "what has been believed everywhere, at all times, by everyone" (*quod ubique, quod semper, quod ab omnibus creditum est*) is not necessarily "reliably catholic teaching." Thorp goes so far as to argue that the Church "*should* change" its teachings "in the light of evolving *circumstances*" (p. 22, his emphases). Such a statement, however, requires qualification. "Evolving circumstances" are only relevant if they fundamentally refute the primary premise on which the scriptural teaching is based. We have already shown that Thorp has not made this case with regard to the issue of homosexual practice. Indeed, the evidence indicates that the premise for Scripture's opposition – namely, that men and women are each other's sexual "other halves," not men and men or women and women – is not fundamentally affected by the existence of "lifelong" or "loving" homosexual unions. Scripture doesn't indict homosexual practice on the sole basis of a lack of longevity or loving affect.

Then, secondly, Thorp defines what Hooker meant by "tradition" as that which the Church believes to be true on the basis of Reason (note: Thorp says "Scripture and Reason" but his whole discussion indicates Reason as the driving force). In effect, although Thorp refers to Hooker's three-legged stool, Thorp's own understanding of Hooker leaves one with a two-legged stool since he interprets Tradition to be the virtual equivalent of Reason. Since we have already shown that Thorp is far from making his case from reason, let alone from Scripture, his discussion of Tradition gets him nowhere.

7.   Conclusion

Thorp concludes as follows:

> This essay set out to make an Anglican case, in an Anglican way, for the blessing of same sex unions in the Canadian Church. It has undertaken to show that the introduction of such a practice ... would sit comfortably on the three-legged stool of Scripture, Tradition and Reason. (p. 27)

As it is, though Thorp may have "set out to make an Anglican case, in an Anglican way," the case that he has attempted to make is no different from the case that other proponents of homosexual practice have attempted to make from their own denominational heritage – whether it be Catholic, Presbyterian, Lutheran, Methodist, or Baptist. Neither Hooker's delineation of Scripture, Tradition, and Reason, on the one hand, nor Thorp's contention that circumstances may change the "details" of the Bible's commands, on the other, represents a peculiarly Anglican approach to hermeneutics.

Rather than demonstrating that blessing homoerotic unions "sits comfortably on the three-legged stool of Scripture, Tradition, and Reason," Thorp has rather shown that his position has no leg to stand on (or, to fit the image, sit on). Scripture is decisively against any blessing of homosexual unions, inasmuch as blessing such a union would constitute implicit endorsement for the homosexual activity that constitutes the union. In the same way, blessing an adult, committed incestuous relationship or polyamorous relationship would imply an endorsement of the incest or polyamory that establishes the sexual bond. Neither Reason nor Tradition provides substantive grounds for deviating from Scripture's two-sexes prerequisite for valid sexual unions. Indeed, Reason and Tradition actually support Scripture's stance rather than stand in tension with it.

The truth is that Thorp adopts a distinctly anti-Anglican position both in the secondary or even tertiary status that he gives Scripture (contrast the primacy that Hooker gave Scripture in his three-legged stool) and in the way that he mishandles Reason and Tradition. His position is anti-Anglican because it is anti-Christian. Christians can hold deeply anti-Christian positions and this is apparently one such case.

Recapping our main points:

In the Introduction, we argued that Scripture's two-sexes prerequisite for marriage (and thus all sexual bonds) is no little "detail" but a core value in Scripture's sexual ethics. We showed this in several ways.

We pointed to Jesus' use of this core value in sexual ethics, which he believed to be firmly ensconced in the creation stories (Gen 1:27 and 2:24), as a foundation for extrapolating a more demanding approach to monogamy and marital indissolubility.

We noted that the male-female prerequisite is the foundation or prior analogue for defining other critical sexual norms, including prohibitions of incest, polyamory, and adultery.

Consistent with Jesus' and Paul's teaching, we showed that same-sex intercourse radically offends against God's intentional creation of humans as "male and female" (Gen 1:27) and the definition of marriage as a union between a man and a woman (Gen 2:24).

To this we added the fact that every text in Scripture that treats the issue of homosexual practice treats it as a high offense abhorrent to God. Along the same lines we noted that the assumption of a male-female prerequisite and the attendant opposition toward homosexual practice in ancient Israel, early Judaism, and early Christianity was pervasive, absolute, and countercultural.

In our treatment of Thorp's argument for "Moral Evolution," we noted that Thorp took no account of (1) the more common pattern of moral devolution and (2) the fact that for Jesus moral evolution meant a tightening, not loosening, of God's moral standards. We also showed that (3) Thorp's attempt at analogical reasoning, comparing the Church's current stance on homosexual practice to its earlier positions on usury and slavery, failed at two key levels:

It failed to note the major differences between these alleged analogies and the Church's appropriation of a core value in Scripture's sexual ethics. Here we focused on the slavery argument, demonstrating that Scripture exhibits a decisively critical edge toward slavery while maintaining a deep, vested interest in a male-female prerequisite.

Moreover, it failed in ignoring the much closer analogues that can be found in the Church's stance against incestuous and polyamorous relationships of an adult, committed, and caring sort. We noted that Thorp apparently fixated on more remote analogues in order to 'fix' the game of analogical reasoning; that is, he accommodated the results to his desired ideological objective. This, we suggested, was a dishonest use of analogical reasoning. Fair use of analogical reasoning demands that one follow the lead of the closest analogies, even when doing so leads one to results that one would prefer not to reach.

In our discussion of Reason, we noted (1) that (contrary to Thorp's profile of historical development) the Church has maintained a consistent stance against homosexual practice as a high moral offense that is contrary to the Creator's design embedded in nature. (2) As regards allegedly radical new knowledge about homosexuality, we made a number of points.

We underscored, first, that already in the Greco-Roman milieu of Paul's day orientation theories had been formulated for at least some forms of homosexual practice; and, second, that the innateness of a given impulse is no argument for the morality of that impulse since all impulses have a biological basis.

We showed the attempted analogies to left-handedness and ethnicity to be fatally flawed since neither of these analogies involves an impulse to do what God expressly forbids. We argued that Jesus himself did not believe that application of the love commandment was a *sufficient* standard for defining acceptable sexual relationships; that sexual relationships necessitated special formal or structural prerequisites which did not apply to love generically construed. If it were otherwise, then having sex with everyone (including close blood relations, multiple persons concurrently, and children) would be an appropriate fulfillment of the command to love one's neighbor as oneself.

We also demonstrated that evidence of homosexuality in the animal kingdom does not prove that homosexual practice is "natural" in the deepest sense. For animals regularly engage in lots of behavior that we would consider "unnatural" because "nature" entails not just innate urges but considerations of embodied complementarity. As unnatural characteristics of homosexuality, we referred both to the narcissism of being erotically aroused by the distinctive features of one's own sex and the self- and other-dishonoring delusion of imaging a person of the same sex as the sexual complement to one's own sex.

We argued that Thorp's point about well-adjusted homosexual persons is mitigated by two facts: first, that no form of consensual sexual behavior that we currently regard as immoral produces intrinsic, scientifically measurable harm; and, second, that homosexual males and homosexual females do experience disproportionately high rates of measurable harm in ways that typify the extremes and gaps of their given sex.

We indicated that a procreation argument had validity as a heuristic device; namely, as a clue about God's larger design for human sexual pairing.

We showed that Thorp's attempt to blame the Church's opposition to homosexual practice on a latent misogynistic impulse was misguided for three reasons: first, that it took no account of arguments based on formal or structural congruence employed in the ancient (and modern) world; second, that it failed to recognize that higher views of women in antiquity led to increasing opposition to homosexual practice; and, third, that it led to the manifestly absurd corollary that the most misogynistic cultures in antiquity were ancient Israel, early Judaism, and early Christianity.

As regards Scripture, we noted the serious deficiencies in the attention and priority that Thorp gave to the subject, which is understandable in light of Scripture's profound opposition to homosexual practice and preservation of a two-sexes prerequisite.

We first established that, contra Thorp, there was nothing "extremely unlikely" or "harshly dismissive" about the view that Scripture is absolutely opposed to homosexual practice, for this is comparable to Scripture's stance against committed incestuous unions and to the New Testament's consistent opposition to committed polyamorous bonds (note too the Old Testament's opposition to polyandry). Quite simply, there are formal or structural prerequisites for sexual bonds, involving the complementarity of embodied existence, that transcend the question of how two (or more) people feel about each other sexually.

We then showed that the modern ecclesiastical accommodation to divorce and remarriage is a less helpful analogue, both because Scripture doesn't treat divorce and remarriage as significant an infraction as homosexual practice and because divorce/remarriage doesn't approach the serial or highly repetitive character of homosexual practice.

We followed this with six main arguments (and many subarguments) for concluding that Paul's opposition to homosexual practice – consistent with the opposition everywhere in early Judaism and early Christianity (including Jesus) – was absolute and inclusive of caring homosexual bonds. Most of these arguments Thorp appears not even to be aware of and to none does he mount a credible counterargument.

We concluded by showing that Scripture's "big picture" in no way disavows a prohibition of homosexual practice; that love in Scripture is always "love in truth" (perhaps a better phrasing than "truth in love") and cannot be reduced to toleration or affirmation of behaviors which God declares to be abhorrent and which put persons in jeopardy; that Scripture demands that the Church should make judgments against sexual immorality while lovingly seeking to recover the lost for an eternal relationship with God; and that Jesus' call to discipleship involves a radical denial of self.

Finally, in our discussion of Tradition we indicated that Thorp could derive no positive argument from tradition to substantiate the radical change in Christian sexual ethics that Thorp and others are advocating. The best that Thorp could come up with is (1) contending that "what has been believed everywhere, at all times, by everyone" is not necessarily "reliably catholic teaching," restating his fatally flawed "moral evolution" examples of usury and slavery; and (2) reinterpreting Tradition to be the virtual equivalent of the Church's use of Reason, which is not helpful to Thorp's overall argument since he failed to make the case from both Reason and Scripture.

Thorp ends with two final thoughts. First, he presents as the only two alternatives for the Anglican Church of Canada: either continue "loathing" homosexual persons or "fully accept" homosexual persons by blessing homosexual unions. These are false alternatives. Replace "homosexual persons" with "polysexual persons" and you get the point. Persons who experience homosexual desires are like any persons who experience desires to do what God expressly forbids (which, ultimately, takes in everyone). They are welcome in the Church but not to engage unrepentantly in behavior that Scripture treats (and, I might add, Reason confirms) as abhorrent to God – irrespective of whatever intense impulses are experienced. The Church obviously should not loathe persons struggling with same-sex attractions either by consigning them callously to hell *or* by blessing behavior that will put their inheritance in God's kingdom at risk. The Church expresses its love *precisely in* a refusal to condone homosexual practice, coupled with efforts at meeting intimacy needs short of violating God's clear commands.

Thorp's second point is that homosexual persons are capable of exhibiting fruits of the Spirit. The point, however, is both trivial and problematic: trivial because most persons in the church are able to exhibit such fruit in some areas of their life even as they sin in other areas; problematic because the very act of engaging in same-sex intercourse (like incest and 'polyfidelity') is itself evidence that insufficient fruit has been borne.

The fruit-bearing analogy was used by the early Church to bring in Gentile believers who were uncircumcised and who did not observe the full array of dietary commands in the Law of Moses. However, both Jesus and Paul expressly *rejected* comparisons between such ritual observances and moral matters involving sexual practice (Mark 7:21-23; 1 Cor 6:12-20; 7:18-19). Scripture does not ground circumcision in creation structures but it does so ground a two-sexes prerequisite for sexual activity. Circumcision and dietary laws were Jewish ritual prescriptions enjoined only on proselytes and, like ritual generally, affected the body only superficially. But Judaism included a prohibition of homosexual practice among its "Noahide laws" enjoined on all Gentiles. And both Judaism and the early church understood that sexual immorality affected the body holistically. Gentile inclusion in the first-century Church was about welcoming persons, not about accepting the sexual practices (including homosexual practice) that typified much of Gentile life. Such practices, according to both the Apostolic Decree and Paul's letters, were distinctly unwelcome (Acts 15:20; 1 Thess 4:3-8).

I trust that Prof. Thorp is sincere in his beliefs. However, when he ends by saying that

> Gay liberation is *clearly* the work of the Spirit. How can it reasonably be otherwise?

one can only shake one's head in astonishment at the degree to which he is sadly mistaken, *and* in loving concern at the prospect that he might contribute to the self-deception of those struggling with same-sex attractions, *and* in holy fear at the danger of God's judgment faced by the Anglican Church of Canada. May it be otherwise.

Professor Robert A. J. Gagnon. Robert has served as a professor of New Testament at Pittsburgh Theological Seminary since 1994, specializing in biblical sexual ethics and Paul's letters. Prior to that he taught classes in Scripture, early Judaism, and Gnosticism for a year at Middlebury College in Middlebury, Vermont. A high school valedictorian, Robert has degrees from Dartmouth College (B.A., with highest honors in the department of history), Harvard Divinity School (M.T.S.), and Princeton Theological Seminary (Ph.D., *magna cum laude*). He is author of *The Bible and Homosexual Practice* (Abingdon Press, 2001; 500 pages), *Homosexuality and the Bible: Two Views* (Fortress Press, 2003; co-author with Dan O. Via), and many articles, both in scholarly journals and online at www.robgagnon.net. Robert's website, carrying an enormous amount of material on the issue of the Bible and homosexual practice, is regularly updated as he responds to strange developments and arguments in the Presbyterian Church (U.S.A.), the ELCA, the Anglican Communion, and the United Methodist Church. He regularly speaks at denominationally related events, although it has become increasingly difficult to find anyone who is willing to debate or dialogue with him. A middle child in a competitive and fun family (third of six children, the first five of whom were born one year after the other for five years), Robert grew up in Massachusetts and New Hampshire. His religious journey has taken him from a nominal faith in Roman Catholicism to a Baptist church, nondenominational charismatic churches, and finally to the Presbyterian Church (USA) where he is an ordained elder. He lives in Pittsburgh, Penn. (USA) with his wife Carol, whom he first met when they were both 13 years old (it took him four years to get Carol to notice him, following the uncreative but persistent slow-drip method of securing a date!). They have two young girls, Caris and Eliana, both of whom were born when mom and dad were well along in years and who thus are a source of unspeakable joy to their parents (at least at this stage in their young lives). Robert is a history buff, likes to play board games with his family and friends, and watch classic films.

Additional Resources by Professor Robert Gagnon

For some of the resources cited below and other materials go to www.robgagnon.net.

Bible and Homosexual Practice: Texts and Hermeneutics. (Nashville: Abingdon 2001).

"Are There Universally Valid Sex Precepts? A Critique of Walter Wink's Views on the Bible and Homosexuality," *Horizons in Biblical Theology* 24, pp. 72-125 (2002). Online: http://www.robgagnon.net/articles/homoWinkHBTResp.pdf.

Homosexuality and the Bible: Two Views, with Dan O. Via. (Minneapolis: Fortress 2003). Also: "Notes to Gagnon's Essay in the Gagnon-Via *Two Views* Book." 50 pgs. Online: http://www.robgagnon.net/2Views/HomoViaRespNotesRev.pdf.

"Does the Bible Regard Same-Sex Intercourse as Intrinsically Sinful?" pp. 106-155 in *Christian Sexuality: Normative and Pastoral Principles.* Ed. R. E. Saltzman. (Minneapolis: Kirk House 2003).

"A Comprehensive and Critical Review Essay of Homosexuality, Science, and the 'Plain Sense' of Scripture, Part 2." *HBT* 25: pp. 179-275. (2003)
    Online: http://www.robgagnon.net/articles/homoBalchHBTReview2.pdf.

"An Open Letter to the Presiding Bishop Frank Griswold." 3 pages (2003).
    Online: http://www.robgagnon.net/articles/homoGriswoldLetter.pdf.

"Response to Countryman's Review in *Anglican Theological Review*. On Careful Scholarship." 18 pages (2003).
    Online: http://www.robgagnon.net/Reviews/homoCountrymanResp.pdf.

"Old Testament and Homosexuality: A Critical Review of the Case Made by Phyllis Bird." *Zeitschrift für die Alttestamentliche Wissenschaft* 117: pp. 367-394 (2005).

"Scriptural Perspectives on Homosexuality and Sexual Identity." *Journal of Psychology and Christianity* 24: pp. 293-303. (2005)

"Sexuality." Pp. 739-48 in *Dictionary for Theological Interpretation of the Bible*. Eds. K. J. Vanhoozer, et al. London: SPCK; (Grand Rapids: Baker Academic 2005).

"Why the Disagreement over the Biblical Witness on Homosexual Practice? A Response to Myers and Scanzoni, *What God Has Joined Together?*" *Reformed Review* 59: 19-130. (2005) Online: http://www.westernsem.edu/files/westernsem/gagnon_autm05_0.pdf

"Homosexuality." Pp. 327-32 in *New Dictionary of Christian Apologetics*. Eds. C. Campbell-Jack, G. J. McGrath, and C. S. Evans. (Leicester, U.K.: Inter-Varsity Press, 2006)

"Does Jack Rogers's New Book 'Explode the Myths' about the Bible and Homosexuality and 'Heal the Church?' Part 3." 15 pgs. (2006)
    Online: http://www.robgagnon.net/articles/RogersBookReviewed3.pdf.

"Does Jack Rogers's New Book 'Explode the Myths' about the Bible and Homosexuality and 'Heal the Church?' Part 4." 16 pgs. (2006)
    Online: http://www.robgagnon.net/articles/RogersBookReviewed4.pdf.

"Is Rowan Williams wrong on the meaning of Romans?" *Church of England Newspaper* (The Record), 4 May 2007, pp. 22-23,
    online: http://www.churchnewspaper.com/Get-CEN-Online.aspx. Fuller version: "Rowan Williams' Wrong Reading of Romans (... and John 14.6)," 11 pgs.
    Online: http://www.robgagnon.net/articles/homosexRowanWilliamsResp.pdf.

"Did Jesus Approve of a Homosexual Couple in the Story of the Centurion at Capernaum?" 8 pages (2007).
    Online: http://www.robgagnon.net/articles/homosexCenturionStory.pdf.

See also

'Reason, Faith and Homosexual Acts' by Dr John Finnis;
    http://www.catholicsocialscientists.org/Symposium2--Finnis--mss.htm

'The New Testament Speaks on Same-Sex Eroticism' by Professor Edith M Humphrey;
    http://www.neac.info/talks/221915eh.pdf

'How Bad Is Homosexual Practice According to Scripture and Does Scripture's View Apply to Committed Homosexual Unions? A response to R. Milton Winter's *Perspectives* article: "Presbyterians and Separatist Evangelicals": Appendix 1: How Bad Is Homosexual Practice According to Scripture? ... Appendix 2: Does Scripture's Indictment of Homosexual Practice Apply to Committed Homosexual Unions?' by Professor Robert Gagnon;
    http://www.robgagnon.net/articles/homosexWinterResponse.pdf.

Homosexuality and the Bible by Mark Bonnington and Bob Fyall (Grove Books, 1998).

12. 'One of These Things is Not Like the Others':[1] Women's Ordination, Homoeroticism and Faithfulness

Professor Edith M. Humphrey

Throughout the recent turmoil in the Anglican communion, we have seen, on both sides of the same-sex debate, a hasty and visceral correlation of this hot topic with one that preceded it in the life of the Church—the appropriateness of women's ordination. The current, and frequently unreflective, collapse of these two issues is reminiscent of another area of debate in the Church and in the public arena. Consider as a parallel the topic of abortion, and its connection with the artificial prevention of conception. In the seventies, as a young evangelical of "free church" tradition, I took great exception to the polemic of pro-choicers, who depicted the entire pro-life movement as composed of hidebound and enslaved Roman Catholics, who were ridiculously committed to an ancient worldview that played off faith against the benefits of modern medicine. At that time I pointed out, to any who would listen, that there was a qualitative difference between preventing a conception and ending the life of a pre-born baby.

I am still convinced at the soundness of this distinction. However, as I became more knowledgeable concerning the subtleties of Catholic ethics and philosophy, when well articulated, I came to be more appreciative of the subtle connection between the two topics. Clearly, there is a radical difference in *kind* between the prevention of pregnancy and abortion: yet, in the public imagination, a radical transformation has taken place over the past century, so that what was once considered an unqualified good, and a natural correlative of marriage (the blessing of children) is now seen as a potential liability, and a matter of individual preference. Connecting the question of abortion and the prevention of pregnancy is our understanding of *rights*, our attitude towards autonomous choice, and the way in which the contemporary West views inter-personal relations. On the instinctive level, it is easy to see why someone who has

---

[1] Theme song for a children's game of differentiation in the North American television programme, *Sesame Street.*

tried to prevent pregnancy, and had an "accident", might plead their "right" to a second recourse—the removal of the offending "mistake." This does mean not that birth-control is killing (though some methods combine prevention with active early abortion). But what if the *presuppositions* and *motives* for birth-control are sufficiently strong to move the mother to a second action of more clear moral consequence? It is, then, at the level of the heart that these questions need to be addressed: why is the prevention of pregnancy so prevalent, and now unreflective, even among Christians today? Why is there a trend to drop prayers for children from the marriage liturgy? What is the conceptual framework that supports birth-control as a norm and abortion as a right? Finally, what is the difference between the act of prevention and killing?

A good deal more could be said about this topic, but that is not our concern here. Let me simply remark on the shock that I now register in thinking about the phenomenon of the seventies: numerous faithful young women who were married in that decade, young women from (Protestant) pious and educated backgrounds, simply "went on the pill" or had an IUD inserted as a matter of course, as the wedding day neared. We bowed, without thinking, to the wisdom of the day—that we had to have time with our husbands, and finish our education, that we had to establish our career, before the encumbrance of children. It never occurred to any of us to ask about the mentality behind this, about the safety of what we were doing to our bodies, about the way that the method of choice worked (true prevention, or abortifacient?), or about the nature of marriage, and whether the early "surprise" of a child might not in fact cement the marriage in the way that it had done for generations before our enlightened age. All that thinking was for the rigid Catholics, and we were children of the apostle of freedom, Paul (over against Peter and James). As a result, some of us ended up paying a price, physical or emotional, for our unreflective tinkering: this hit close to home when I ended up with a "high risk" first pregnancy, threatened by the presence of a "deep vein thrombosis" directly related to side effects of the pill. It may well be that the easy connection made in the popular mind between birth control and abortion is wrong-headed—but there are deep questions concerning these matters that need to be probed, and not merely dismissed as "Roman."

The parallels with the current hot-button issues are remarkable. Recently, I attended a meeting of the American Academy of Religion, and heard a paper offered in the Eastern Orthodox group. I was dismayed to note that the argument that the young woman was offering in favour of a female priesthood was identical to the rhetoric we are hearing in our own communion concerning the ordination of practicing homosexuals—the freedom of the Holy Spirit to do "a new thing," the right of individuals to exercise their gifts, the increasing awareness of the Church regarding the liberty that the gospel offers, the radical democratization of a Church that must totally reject hierarchy, God's action in history in "drawing the circle wider" from Jew, to Gentile, to slave, to woman, to.... Those listening, who opposed the ordination of women, might easily have muttered "this is where it all begins"—if you question tradition in terms of women's ministry, the next inevitable step is the questioning of moral issues. But was this young woman's paper flawed specifically because it was questioning a tradition of the Church? And was the real issue as presented by her really the question of women in ministry? Or was the paper flawed in a deeper way, wrong in its understanding of the contours of the Gospel and the shape of our freedom in Christ? Those listening, who were in favour of women's ordination, might have been compelled to applaud the courage of this young woman to speak prophetically to a "traditionalist" Church. But was she in fact speaking prophetically, that is *for* God? Or was she offering the perspective of the world, alien arguments that do not come from the mind of Christ?

I would hope that listeners on either side of the debate regarding women's ordination, and those undecided as well, would have listened to the level of the paper that was deeper than the issue at hand—how was this woman representing the mind of Christ? I fear that many in the room, however, stayed at the surface, and were unable, given the emotive nature of the topic, to probe behind the arguments to their foundations.

If there is such an easy psychological and sociological connection between the issues of women's ordination and the debate concerning homosexuality, why is it that those who affirm the classical position against homoerotic behaviour do not necessarily agree on the question of women in ministry? Why, for example, can the Kenyan and the Nigerian provinces agree to disagree on the one question, but speak clearly and with one voice on the other? Why can an Anglo-Catholic network such as Forward in Faith, and the charismatic evangelical network New Wine, come together in common cause for purity, but continue in rigorous debate over the role of women in the Church? It would seem that this is because, especially for a Church that exhibits both Protestant and Catholic qualities, the question of women in ministry is a more complex question than that of same-sex erotic behaviour, about which the Scriptures (along with Tradition) are very clear. It is also because same-sex erotic behaviour is about morality, whereas the ordination of women is about ecclesiology: however, both are also concerned with the nature of humanity (theological "anthropology"), and this is where the "slide" from one category into another can so easily occur.

There are several reasons why the question of homosexuality may be clearly answered, whereas the question of women in ministry must continue to be posed. Those who have championed the acceptance of homoeroticism in the Church must disregard or neutralize the entire and unambiguous witness of Scripture across temporal and generic distinctions, from the Genesis view of marriage (Gen 1:27; 2:23-24), through the disapproving narratives and prescripts of Torah (Gen 18:16-19:29; Lev 20:13), to the clear statements of Romans 1:18-32, 1 Cor 6:9-11, 1 Timothy 1:9-11. They must also ignore the clear and unequivocal voice of the Church through the ages in this regard, until the past generation. Advocates of homoeroticism who remain in the Church must therefore reconstruct the passages of Scripture, engaging in special pleading so that words or phrases are reinterpreted against their clear meaning—for example, Paul was only speaking in Romans 1 about those who were not "by nature" homosexual or about those who passionately abused one another, not about loving and committed homosexual acts.[2] Again, they must tinker with the tradition, as do some scholars, who try to suggest that the ceremony of *adelphopoeisis* ("the making of brothers") found in mediaeval Christian communities legitimized homosexual physical activity[3]—though the ceremony itself emphasizes purity and the avoidance of scandal. Those who plead for same-sex unions must also revise God's very creation, suggesting that God did not create them male and female, and assigning to the Biblical books a primitive psychological understanding of humanity that cannot recognize human ambiguity. They thus exhibit what C. S. Lewis calls "chronological snobbery"—we know better than the ancients did, and St. Paul would have had a different opinion of the matter, had he been privy to the discussions of twenty-first century theologians[4], psychologists and

---

[2] For example, Robin Scroggs, *The New Testament and Homosexuality: Contextual Background for the Contemporary Debate* (Philadelphia: Fortress Press, 1983) who reduces the Biblical proscription to a critique of pederasty, or John Boswell, *Christianity, Social Tolerance and Homosexuality* (Chicago: University of Chicago Press, 1980), pp. 344-345, who limits the word *arsenokoitai* to male prostitutes.

[3] See Virginia Mollenkott, "Overcoming Heterosexism", in ed. J. S. Siker, *Homosexuality in the Church: Both Sides of the Debate* (Louisville: Westminster/John Knox Press, 1994), who on pp. 145-149 credits John Boswell with discovering an ancient fourth century liturgical document of this sort. In fact, Boswell tendentiously cites a twelfth or thirteenth century liturgy in his *Same-Sex Unions in PreModern Europe* (New York: Villard, 1994).

[4] A brilliant, but wrong-headed argument of this sort has been mounted by Eugene F. Rogers, Jr. In his *Sexuality and the Christian Body* (Oxford; Malden, MA; Blackwell Press, 1999), Rogers argues that Paul did not fully understand the counter-natural moves of an inclusive God. In his most recent *After the Spirit: A Constructive Pneumatology from Resources outside the Modern West* (Grand Rapids: Eerdmans, 2005), he argues

law-makers. Finally, they must revise the shape of the Christian gospel, rendering it a simple picture of God's "drawing the circle wider," or of increased human recognition of God's beneficence, rather than a shocking story of the willing sacrifice and humility of God, who assumes humanity, even to the point of death, and pulls us through death to resurrection and for the purpose of a new life of holiness.

The problem of women in ministry is different than this, though the polemic that has been pursued by advocates of women's ordination (unfortunately) has followed patterns analogous to the tendentious revising seen in the same-sex debate. In approaching the topic of women's ministry, it is not merely a matter of "going against" the natural readings of Scripture and the completely unified witness of the Church. Indeed, there are *two* questions involved in the issue of women's ordination, and not simply one—first, what is the structure of the Church, and how her ministers are ordered within it; second, what is one's view of the role of women in the Church? Unfortunately, while the New Testament touches upon the latter question from time to time, its teaching on Church order is not worked out as comprehensively. Thus, there has been a division of opinion among denominations that stress the priority of the Scriptures—must Churches follow the three-fold order (of episcopacy, priesthood and diaconate) or is this a matter of development, not essential to the being of the church? Connected with this is our understanding of ordination *per se,* something that also is not worked through in the Scriptures, but that depends upon the later reflection of the Church. Is ordination simply a functional thing, a setting aside of some of the congregation to various tasks for the benefit of the whole, or is ordination sacramental, effecting a change or conferring a charism upon the one so set aside? Anglicans, while following the three-fold order, and while practising an imposition of hands at the time of consecration and ordination, have not been united in their understanding of the nature of these practices. Thus, some consider the three-fold order to be an ecclesial necessity, and plead the importance of apostolic succession, while others speak of the three-fold order as merely convenient, and consider apostolicity a matter of conformity in doctrine rather than the formation of the Church around the episcopate. To put the matter in classical terms, Anglicans do not agree as to whether these ecclesial distinctions are functional, of the *bene esse* (for the "best state") of the Church, or of the actual *esse* (a matter of the "very nature") of the Church.

(distressingly) from Trinitarian inner relations and mystic intimacy towards the approval of alternate sexualities.

Finally, Anglicans (and indeed theologians from other apostolic expressions of the Church) do not agree on the relationship between bishop and priest, given the fact that the presbyterate or priesthood was a development of the Church, which originally had only two offices –presbyterate-episcopate and the diaconate. Now that the priesthood has been separated from the episcopate, we must ask, is the priest an extension of the bishop, acting with his own authority in celebrating communion, and leading the congregation? Or is the priest a delegate of the bishop, acting under the bishop's authority and simply offering "hands" to get these things done?

These are questions that have not been answered clearly in a unified voice throughout Anglican centuries. In unquiet times they have been the matter of debate, and lately they have been placed on the back-burner as we "agree to disagree." However, how we answer these questions is bound up with our consideration of whether women may be ordained, and if so, to which office(s). Before we can consider intelligently whether a woman may be set aside as a deacon, or a priest, or a bishop, we must set out our understanding of these offices. It is lamentable that this important stage of discussion has often been avoided, probably because of our disagreement concerning the ecclesial questions. More frequently, discussion has focused upon the relationship between men and women (hierarchy or complementarity), and on contrasting examples and precepts in Scripture (Deborah ruled; only male apostles were appointed; Prisca taught males; Paul silenced women teachers in the assembly; Junia was an apostle; there are different meanings of the word "apostle").

These details are significant, but they must be accompanied by a careful reflection upon the nature of ministry, and by disclosure concerning one's view of the structure of the Church. Anglican ecclesiology, given its ambiguities, cannot by itself guide us to a univocal answer concerning women in ministry, since Anglicans maintain numerous positions concerning the nature and shape of ministry in general. Some would indeed say that this plurality is desirable, and that the tradition can faithfully sustain different expressions of ministry, as it has sustained different views of the Eucharist. It would seem, however, that Anglicans often have preferred not to clarify their differences in the matters of ecclesiology, for fear of division. Such reserve has led us to confused and disjointed presentations of one position or another with regards to women's ministry, because one or more of the major ecclesiological premises has been either suppressed or assumed.

If the Anglican tradition does not provide secure ecclesial underpinnings for a decision concerning women's ministry, it does provide its members with a strong foundation for the *approach* that Christians should adopt when probing the question. Our attention to the Scriptures, our worship, our hymnody, and our embrace of the salvation story in the ecumenical creeds, are sure guides as to the nature of the questions that a faithful community may pose. Perhaps we may be tempted to think that "rights" language can be used to advantage in a discussion of women's ministry, where it is clearly inappropriate in the matter of homoeroticism. We are clear that homoerotic activity cannot be approved on the basis of "human rights" in the Church, because it is not defensible by Scripture or in the ongoing tradition of the Church. We cannot acknowledge a human "right" to immorality or to act in a manner that contradicts human nature. However, it is sometimes not noticed that "rights" language is, in itself, not in accordance with the mind of Christ, where inner-Church life is concerned. (Acts 16:37 shows Paul making use of legal rights for the furtherance of the gospel, but his manner of conduct in the Christian community, for example, in conversation with Philemon or the Corinthians, was on the basis of common affection, and aimed towards mutual edification.) The adoration of our liturgies, by which we enter into a ceaseless worship not of our own making, and the clear focus of Scripture upon our Lord, who was servant of all (Philippians 2:5-11), forbid us from following the mindset of the contemporary world, which is uncompromising, and often shrill, in the demand for rights, and jealous in the guarding of such.

Connected with this is the complex picture that Scripture presents of the way in which human beings, indeed, all sentient beings, are inter-related: at the foot of the cross, and before the Holy Trinity, there is a radical equalization, and we all cry, "Holy!" Yet, there is, as part of communion with each other, a "holy order" in which we find ourselves—husband and wife, archangel and angel, parent and child, human and beast. Part of the wonder of that order is that it can be overturned in the economy of the God who assumed humanity to himself. The one who was highest became least for our sakes, and so the head may often be called to serve, or the humble raised up to lead. This dynamic overturning, or "surprise" in order, does not mean that we are part of a homogeneous and undifferentiated group, however. Indeed, the mystery of the Holy Trinity indicates to us that order and "equality of honour" are not mutually contradictory. Christians tell a story that is infinitely more complicated and more interesting than either rigid hierarchalism or banal (and patently impossible) democratization. We must therefore resist the impulse to capitulate to the world's way of framing reality, whether we are speaking of its fondness of human rights, or its allergic reaction to order, or "holy headship" (the literal meaning of "hierarchy").

Anglicans who are intent on obedience to the Christian Way, as illuminated in the Scriptures and kept intact in the catholic tradition of the living Church, more naturally will come to agreement in the debate over homoeroticism; with regards to women's ministry, the debate may continue. But faithfulness will dictate the terms of that second debate, its approach, its parameters, and the spirit in which it is conducted. Short of a universally held view of ecclesial orders and the structure of the Church as *adiaphora* or essential, Anglicans must agree to disagree about where women fit. Short of more careful discernment concerning the nature of humanity, and the nature of man and women, in the order of creation, the fallen state, and the dawning new creation, Anglicans will continue to debate what is appropriate, good and useful in the Church so far as the service and leadership of women is concerned. It is my prayer that this disagreement can continue without rancour, without fear, without intimidation or dismissiveness, without name calling, and with a view to our final clarity together in this matter. We might do well to look outside again, but to our past and to our ecumenical partners,[5] rather than to the contemporary secular world. It may be helpful to entertain the possibility of revitalizing or fostering distinct orders of ministry; it may also be helpful to consider the suggestion that the female charism tends to the prophetic, while the male charism tends to the priestly, even while we are all called to be prophets (Acts 2:17) and priests (Rev. 1:6) within the household of God. How this mystery (our common nature and our specific roles) is to be expressed structurally is the question before us. It is my opinion that the question has been answered prematurely in many Anglican quarters, without attention to the rest of the faithful Church, and sometimes by recourse to dubious arguments and the shaky underpinning of "rights" language. (This is not to belittle the wonderful and God-directed service of many faithful female clergy who, given the present circumstances, are being used by the Lord). This question continues to raise its head among us, though it is often suppressed and declared to be "answered." Provinces disagree with each other on the question, as there continues to be conflict within those provinces that have given a clear institutional answer in the affirmative to the ordination (and the consecration) of women. Yet the

---

[5] Careful reading from other catholic traditions might include attention to works as varied as Alexander Schmemann, *For the Life of the World: Sacraments and Orthodoxy* (Crestwood: N. Y.: St. Vladimir's Press, 1973), Paul Evdokimov, *Woman and the Salvation of the World: A Christian Anthropology on the Charisms of Women*, tr. A. P. Gythiel (Crestwood, N. Y.: St. Vladimir's Press, 1994), and Michele M. Schumacher, ed. *Women in Christ: Toward a New Feminism* (Grand Rapids: Eerdmans, 2004).

questions remain, for we still have ground work to do on the underlying ecclesial concepts.

By contrast, I would plead that all the theological questions concerning homoeroticism have been asked and answered—and thoroughly too, in many volumes and with much patience.[6] What remains for those who are obedient to Christ is the formation of practical and pastoral questions and strategies regarding how best to serve those who call themselves gay, lesbian, or bisexual, whom Christ invites (as he does all of us) to repentance and to fullness of life. To continue to ask how best men and women can be set aside for God's purposes in the Church is a godly pursuit, so long as it is not predicated on worldly grounds, or framed in resentful and slanderous terms, as we address those with whom we disagree. To continue to ask whether homoerotic partners may be sanctified by the Church, or to urge the ordination of those who pursue this lifestyle, is to echo with disingenuous subtlety the ancient rebel, "Did God *really* say?"

---

[6] See, as examples of thorough dialogue with the issues: J. S. Siker, *Homosexuality in the Church: Both Sides of the Debate* (Louisville: KY: Westminster/John Knox, 1994); Catherine Sider Hamilton, ed., *The Homosexuality Debate: Faith Seeking Understanding* (Toronto, ABC Press, 2003); Timothy Bradshaw, ed., *The Way Forward?: Christian Voices on Homosexuality and the Church* (London: SCM Press, 2003) and RobertGagnon, *The Bible and Homosexual Practice: Texts and Hermeneutics* (Nashville, Abingdon Press, 2001). These are soon to be joined by another volume of essays written by specialists, edited by Andrew Goddard and scheduled for publication by SPCK in 2008. See also the four discussion papers written by Edith M. Humphrey during the debate on same-sex eroticism in New Westminster Diocese, Vancouver, available at http://edithhumphrey.net/articles.htm

Professor Edith M. Humphrey, Ph.D is William F. Orr Professor of New Testament at Pittsburgh Theological Seminary, and a member of the Commission on Ministry in the Pittsburgh Diocese. She is a Canadian expatriate, a musician, a wife to Chris, a mother of three girls and a grandmother of three babies under a year, all of whom reside in the Pittsburgh area. Nurtured in the Salvation Army, Edith has been an Anglican concerned for 'generous orthodoxy' in the Communion for over twenty years, and has close ties with evangelical, Roman Catholic and Eastern Orthodox friends. An author of popular as well as academic books, in the areas of Bible, theology and spirituality, she has most recently written *Ecstasy and Intimacy: When the Holy Spirit Meets the Human Spirit* (Eerdmans), and *And I Turned to See the Voice: The Rhetoric of Vision in the New Testament* (Baker Academic). Currently she is doing research for a book on worship in the Christian tradition, as a response to the 'worship wars' of the western church. http://www.edithhumphrey.net/ehumphrey@pts.edu

See also

Slaves, Women & Homosexuals: Exploring the Hermeneutics of Cultural Analysis by William J. Webb, InterVarsity Press, 2001.

A Slippery Slope? The Ordination of Women and Homosexual Practice - a Case Study in Biblical Interpretation by R.T. France (Grove Books, 2000).

'Why The Disagreement Over The Biblical Witness On Homosexual Practice?: A Response to Myers and Scanzoni, *What God Has Joined Together.* The case against the misogyny argument', pp. 80-83, 93-94, by Professor Robert A. J. Gagnon; http://www.westernsem.edu/files/westernsem/gagnon_autm05_0.pdf

13. Pastoral Considerations For Homosexuality

The Revd Mario Bergner

'Lord Jesus Christ, you stretched out your arms of love on the hard wood of the cross that everyone might come within the reach of your saving embrace.' (Third Prayer for Mission, *1979 American Prayer Book*, p. 101) This prayer alludes to the universal outreach of Jesus Christ which encompasses all, including people with homosexual attractions. In an attempt to apply prayers such as this, the question has been asked, 'How should the Church engage in mission to and with gay and lesbian people?' But the Holy Scripture never identifies people according to their sexual attractions (i.e. gay, lesbian, transgender, straight, etc.). The Bible divides people into two groups, male and female (Genesis 1:27) with redemption offered equally to each. Therefore, to subdivide humanity further, such as into the categories of gay, lesbian and transgender, is an extra-biblical concept. Yet, paragraph 146 of *The Windsor Report* identifies persons with same-sex attractions as 'persons of homosexual orientation.' But what is meant by this?

The compound noun 'homosexual orientation' is an idea that has gained popularity in the last fifty years. It may be defined in at least four different ways.

- o First, biologically understood, homosexual orientation is viewed as an innate, genetically determined, essential part of personhood, although there is no scientific evidence proving this.

- o Second, psychologically understood, homosexual orientation is a combination of thoughts and feelings leading to behaviors.

- o Third, sociologically understood, homosexual orientation is a category akin to race or sex, with little concern for causation.

- o Fourth, Biblically, homosexuality is never understood as an orientation, but as a behavior.

The reason I have spelled out these various definitions of 'homosexual orientation' is to show that even the language we use to address the issue of homosexuality is fraught with ambiguities, which makes discussing this matter all the more difficult. However, in today's parlance, homosexual orientation implies that attractions for the same-sex cannot be resisted, yielded to the grace of God, or changed. For the sake of clarity, I have chosen in all my publications to use 'same-sex attractions' instead of 'homosexual orientation.' Therefore, I do not view self-identified homosexuals as *gay* or *lesbian*, but as *men* and *women* with same-sex attractions. Consequently, since we at Redeemed Lives never identify people as gay or lesbian, nor do we identify them as 'ex-gay.'

I, the Rev. Mario Bergner, arrived at this understanding of homosexuality as same-sex attractions after experiencing such attractions in my own life, identifying as a gay man for seven years and then renouncing that as a personal identification. As I found my sense of belonging in the saving embrace of Jesus Christ, I came to view my same-sex attractions not only as passions and desires emanating from my sinful nature, but also as opportunities for the Holy Spirit to manifest His grace. The Lord's words to St. Paul in 2 Corinthians 12:9 capture my experience here, 'My grace is sufficient for you, for my power is made perfect in weakness.' Of great encouragement to me was the study of the Book of Galatians under Dr. Stephen Noll at Trinity Episcopal School for Ministry. It was under his tutelage that I came to contextualize my same-sex attractions as one possible example of desires and passions alluded to in Galatians 5:24-25, "Those who belong to Christ Jesus have crucified the sinful nature with its passions and desires. Since we live by the Spirit, let us keep in step with the Spirit." That was over twenty years ago. During that time, I also took graduate coursework in the physiology of behavior and in professional psychology to better understand why same-sex attractions grow in an individual. Twenty years later, scientific research has yet to prove that homosexuality is an innate biologically based orientation. Dr. Jeffery Satinover's book, *Homosexuality and the Politics of Truth*[1] shows how the goal of scientific studies attempting to find a single biological feature to account for homosexuality, such as a gay gene, are quickly brought into question by other scientists. Most researchers agree that human sexual behavior with its many expressions is complex and multiply determined. They stress that a single biological feature cannot determine or cause sexual behavior of any sort.[2]

In studying professional psychology, all the studies I read pointed clearly in the direction of a common history of relational patterns found in persons with same-sex attractions. One pattern is a sense of detachment

---

[1] Dr. Jeffrey Satinover, *Homosexuality and the Politics of Truth* (Michigan: Baker, 1996).
[2] Dr. W. Byne and Dr. B. Parsons, 'Human sexual orientation: the biological theories reappraised', *Archives of General Psychiatry*, 50, 1993, pp. 228-259.

early in life from members of the same-sex resulting in an unmet need to attach, which becomes eroticized.[3] (Moberly, 1983). Another is a feeling of inferiority regarding one's manliness or womanliness[4] (van den Aardweg, 1986). Yet, 'all psychoanalytical theories assume that adult homosexuality is psychopathologic and assign differing weights to constitutional and experiential determinants'[5] (Bieber, 1988). Psychology provides us with a variety of models for the understanding and treatment of homosexuality. Dr. Jeffrey Satinover (mentioned above) documents the various degrees of success psychoanalysts and psychiatrists have had in treating people seeking to change their same-sex attractions. According to Satinover, most therapists report a success rate of between 50% and 70% 'where success is defined as considerable to complete change' (p. 186).

Pastoral care for homosexuality can utilize science and psychology. Both scientific research and psychological treatment have provided encouragement for people seeking to change their same-sex attractions. Recent scientific research shows homosexuality can be changed. In May 2001, at the annual meeting of the American Psychiatric Association, Dr. Robert Spitzer, of Columbia University in New York City, announced the findings of his study of over 200 people who had successfully overcome homosexuality. In an article posted on the website for the National Association for the Research and Treatment of Homosexuality, he is quoted, 'Like most psychiatrists, I thought that homosexual behavior could be resisted, but sexual orientation could not be changed. I now believe that's untrue. Some people can and do change.'[6] Back in 1973, Dr. Spitzer was instrumental in removing homosexuality from the American Psychiatric Association's *Diagnostic and Statistical Manual*, also known as the *DSM*. Thirty years later he changed his viewpoint after meeting hundreds of people who, like myself, once self-identified as gay, but left that behind to marry and have families.

In my theological studies, I found comfort that the Bible identifies at least four expressions of homosexuality.

o First, there is homosexual practice of male cult prostitutes

---

[3] Elizabeth R. Moberly, *Homosexuality: A New Christian Ethic* (Cambridge: James Clarke & Co., Ltd, 1983).
[4] Gerard van den Aardweg, *On the Origins and Treatments of Homosexuality: A Psychoanalytical Reinterpretation* (New York: Praeger Publishers, 1986).
[5] Irving Bieber, *Homosexuality: A Psychoanalytic Study* (New Jersey: Jason Aronson Inc, 1988), p. 18.
[6] http://narth.com/doc/spitzer2.html

associated with pagan religions mentioned in the Old Testament (Deut. 23:17-18, 1 Kings 14:24; 15:12, 22:46; 2 Kings 23:7).

- o Second, there is the exchange of heterosexual behavior for homosexual behavior (Romans 1:27).

- o Third and fourth, in 1 Corinthians 6:9-10 (NIV), St. Paul gives a catalogue list of sins common to the human condition including two forms of homosexual behavior listed in verse 9, malakoi (μαλακοί) translated *male prostitutes* and arsenokoitai (ἀρσενοκοῖται) translated *homosexual offenders*.

For a full treatment of the Biblical texts about homosexuality, see Robert Gagnon's, *The Bible and Homosexual Practice*[7]. The Bible does not place all people who engage in homosexual activities in the same box. The comfort I find here is that the Holy Scripture takes into account various contexts within which homosexuality may manifest without labeling individuals as 'gay'.

How should the Church treat people with same-sex attractions?

The Church must treat people with same-sex attractions with sensitive pastoral care integrated with good moral theology. Pastorally, same-sex attractions may be understood in part as:

- o expressions of our sinful nature, which may include a lust wherein *natural relations are exchanged for unnatural ones* (Romans 1:27);

- o a reaction to sins done against us[8] (Payne, 1981);

- o anger and envy, which may generate into homosexual feelings[9] (Bergner, 1995);

- o demonic influences on the soul[10] (Payne, Bergner and Comiskey 1989).

However, in 1 Corinthians 6:11 St. Paul wrote these encouraging words to a Christian community whose sins included homosexual practices: 'And such were some of you, but you were washed, you were justified, you were

---

[7] Dr. Robert A. J. Gagnon, *The Bible And Homosexual Practice* (Nashville, Abingdon Press, 2001).
[8] Leanne Payne, *The Broken Image* (Grand Rapids: Baker Books, 1981, 1996).
[9] Mario Bergner, *Setting Love In Order* (Grand Rapids: Baker Books, 1995).
[10] Andrew Comiskey, *Pursuing Sexual Wholeness* (Lake Mary: Creation House, 1989).

sanctified in the name of the Lord Jesus, and by the Spirit of our God.' Notice the use of the past tense, *were*. St. Paul is clearly stating that some of the Corinthians (mentioned earlier in verse 9) came free from homosexuality by a three-fold process. First, through being *washed* – baptismal imagery implying the forgiveness of sins. Second, through being *justified* – being declared not guilty of our sin before God through the atoning work of Christ. Third, through *sanctification* – the ongoing gracious work of the Holy Spirit to grow us in holiness. This three-fold process, coupled with sound psychological insights, is integrated into pastoral courses such as *Living Waters* and *Redeemed Lives*, both of which are used to help people overcome same-sex attractions as well as other sexual and relational issues. Therefore, the Church should treat same-sex attractions with the same grace it treats all passions and desires that emanate from the sinful nature. Namely, through *sensitive pastoral care* that provides a safe place where men and women with same sex attractions can yield their passions and desires to the waters of baptism, the grace of guilt-free living through justification in Jesus Christ and *the empowerment of the Holy Spirit* in progressive sanctification.

But in today's Anglican/Episcopal churches, the topic of homosexuality is so polarizing that few parishes are willing to offer pastoral care to persons who desire to yield their same-sex attractions to the grace of Jesus Christ. I am grateful, however, for those parishes that have consistently done so, such as The Falls Church in Virginia, St. Luke's Church in Akron, Ohio, Church of the Resurrection in Wheaton, Illinois and a handful of others. Sadly, the overwhelming majority of conservative Anglican/Episcopal churches, as well as Church of England parishes, have fallen into quietism in addressing same-sex attractions from a pastoral care perspective offering transformation. This has, for decades, left a vacuum in applying the Good News of Jesus Christ to people with unwanted same-sex attractions, as well as to those who self-identify as gay or lesbian. Anglicans/Episcopalians who identify as Liberal or Progressive filled that vacuum with the Gospel of Inclusion, which opened wide the doors of their parishes to people who self-identify as gay or lesbian. For many men and women with same-sex attractions, the only places that welcomed them were such churches. Although I did attend one such parish when I lived in New York City in the early 1980's, I found their interpretation of the Gospel to be lacking in objectivity. Rather than preaching what was actually written in the Biblical texts, everything was viewed through a social justice lens that equated the rights of gays and lesbians with the struggles of African Americans and women. It was like attending a civil rights meeting cloaked in liturgy and Christian words. At the same time, these liberal and progressive Anglicans/Episcopalians announced to society that within their walls there was a safe place for people who self-identified as gay or lesbian. But for people like myself, who came to understand their same-sex attractions as unwanted passions and desires, the quietism of conservative, evangelical, catholic and charismatic parishes was a deafening silence that seemed to say, "There is no place for you here." Had it not been for the intervention of Jesus Christ, who personally visited me on my sick bed in 1983 (see my book *Setting Love In Order* for this account), I would have never believed that the Church had any answers for me. He called me to help Him deliver men and women from a life of being identified by their same-sex attractions.

It is now 24 years later and I have, as best as I could, done all in my power to fulfill that call by becoming a Priest and founding Redeemed Lives. Over 2,000 people have gone through our Redeemed Lives pastoral course in the Chicago area alone. About 20% of those who have attended struggled with unwanted same-sex attractions (about 400 people). The greater Chicago area has a population of just over seven million people. A conservative estimate of the percentage of people with same-sex attractions ranges between 1% and 3% of the overall population. That means the Chicago area alone has between 70,000 and 210,000 men and women with same-sex attractions. Yet, the Episcopal Diocese of Chicago does not have one parish that offers ministry to people with unwanted same-sex attractions. It cannot claim to be an inclusive church for that reason alone. There are, however, three churches in the Chicago area that offer help through *Redeemed Lives* and one church that offers help through *Living Waters*. These churches are members of the Anglican Mission In America, The Evangelical Free Church, The Covenant Evangelical Church or the Vineyard Christian Fellowship.

The same can be said of the Episcopal Diocese of Massachusetts, where I am licensed as a Priest. My canonical residency is under the Episcopal Diocese of Quincy, Illinois under The Right Rev. Keith Ackerman. In order to be licensed here I was required to pass through two interviews. The first was a two hour meeting with Bishop Bud Cederholm, a lesbian priest, a gay priest, the president of the standing committee and my future Rector, the Rev. Jurgen Liias. During that time, I was questioned about the nature of my work as director of *Redeemed Lives*. That meeting, even though it began in great tension, ended in a surprising peace. About one month later, I was asked to meet with Bishop Cederholm again, about my license to officiate here in the Diocese of Massachusetts. At that time I was told that my license would include a restriction, which is currently printed on the back of my license. It reads as follows:

You are Licensed to Officiate in the Diocese of Massachusetts solely as an Assistant Priest at Christ Church, Hamilton & Wenham. This License does not extend to any activities you conduct on behalf or under the auspices of Redeemed Life Ministries ("RLM"). Additionally, in conducting any activities relating to RLM, including, without limitation, programs, conferences, or publications, you may not use the name the "Episcopal Diocese of Massachusetts" or in any way state or imply that the Diocese supports or condones RLM or that your activities with RLM have any connection with the Diocese.

Failure to adhere to these conditions could result in the immediate withdrawal of your license by the Diocese pursuant to Canon III.9.6. (a).

My license to officiate here is renewed every year during Advent. Therefore, in compliance with the restrictions of my License to Officiate in the Episcopal Diocese of Massachusetts, my submission of this paper to the Listening Process is in no way connected to the Episcopal Diocese of Massachusetts, nor do I want to imply that the Episcopal Diocese of Massachusetts supports or condones anything that I have written here.

Moreover, I have submitted this paper to the Listening Process with the assurance of the full support of the Episcopal Diocese of Quincy, Illinois and the blessing of my bishop, The Right Rev. Keith Ackerman.

How *Redeemed Lives* helps people with unwanted same-sex attractions

Our most commonly asked question at *Redeemed Lives* is, 'How can I help someone who is struggling with homosexuality?' My first response is to ask a few questions: 'Is the person struggling a Christian? Has he or she been baptized, regenerated and converted in Jesus Christ?' If the answer is, 'No, they are not a Christian', then the primary need is not to address their homosexuality, but to introduce them to the Great Physician himself, Jesus. The message of the Gospel is *not*, 'Jesus loves you and wants to change your homosexuality.' It is John 3:16, 'For God so loved the world that he gave his only begotten Son, that whosoever believes in him should not perish but have eternal life.' If available, I suggest they attend the nearest Alpha course or I evangelize them myself. If the answer is, 'Yes, they are a Christian', then I ask, 'Do they *want* to change their homosexuality?' They may have wanted to change their homosexuality, but searched for help, found none and lost hope. Some may want to change their homosexuality, but have not bothered looking for help because they did not know such help was available. Others do not want to change their same-sex attractions and believe they can marry homosexuality with Christianity. Still others have self-identified as gay or lesbian for many years, even decades, but have come to the conviction that Jesus does not see them as gay or lesbian, and want to enter into a dynamic process of change.

Our starting point at *Redeemed Lives* for helping people overcome same-sex attractions is to ascertain the unique construction of their homosexuality. Answers to certain questions help understand what unmet need their same-sex attractions are attempting to fill. These questions include: Are they over-identified with the other-sex? Are they under-identified with the same-sex? Were they abused in the home environment or the school environment? Was there an early pattern of gender non-conformity? Additionally, there are at least five features about the individual's life that will influence the course their journey out of homosexuality will take.

(*i*)   Have they crossed the moral boundary of acting out?

(*ii*)   How do they identify their same-sex attractions?

(*iii*)   What is their age?

(*iv*)   Are they part of a supportive local church?

(*v*)   Would they benefit from professional psychological or psychiatric care?

(i)   *Have they crossed the moral boundary of acting out?*

Someone who has never acted out homosexually does not have to deal with the added issues of processing past homosexual experiences. Nor do they need to rebuild the moral boundary line they crossed in order to act out that first time. I have known many men and women who never acted on their homosexual thoughts and feelings because they were raised in Christian homes, resulting in strong moral boundaries against homosexual activity. However, if someone seeks help after acting out, then rebuilding the moral boundary against future homosexual activity is greatly aided by confession, repentance, reception of forgiveness and empowerment from the Holy Spirit.

(ii)   *How do they identify their same-sex attractions?*

For the person seeking help, how they identify their same-sex attractions is central to their finding freedom. Are their same-sex attractions simply the bothersome content of their temptations, but otherwise they identify as heterosexual? Do they identify themselves as gay? Are they somewhere in between, having times of self-identification as gay, and other times as straight? If they self-identify as gay, they usually employ the terminology of orientation to describe their same-sex attractions. Do they understand their orientation as biological or psychological or neither? Do they not want to put a label on their homosexuality? A growing number of teenagers choose to self-identify as gay because they are exploring all sexual attractions. Plus in some circles being gay is cool. Here the declaration of being gay is a sociological statement and sometimes a way of stating solidarity with a minority. In such cases, same-sex attractions are not the primary content of their sexual attractions. However, if they should enter into a same-sex relationship the content of their sexuality can become primarily homo-erotic. I have come to call this *transitional* homosexuality, because the majority of young people in this situation eventually partner with members of the other-sex. This is not bi-sexuality, since once they are out of their same-sex partnership, the content of their sexual behavior and desire is exclusively heterosexual.

(iii) *What is their age?*

Those seeking help from homosexuality by their early twenties seem to progress more quickly out of homoeroticism and toward heterosexual relating. One reason for this may be that puberty seems to extend into the early twenties these days, which allows for more plasticity in sexual desire and formation. I began seeking help for changing homosexuality at age twenty-four. Surprisingly, within months I experienced the first sparks of sexual attraction for women. Those seeking help between their late-twenties and mid-thirties often do so only after they have come to some dissatisfaction with homosexuality. Until then, people in this age range seem to have a determination to make homosexuality work for them. For some this means searching for a homosexual partner. But by their mid- to late-thirties many have lost hope of finding a long-term homosexual partner. Consequently, they are open to the possibility of leaving homosexuality. Sometimes they reason, 'I am still young enough that I could meet the right person, get married and have a family.' For some, the possibility of marriage and family is a strong motivation for change. Still, many people come for help well after the age when having a family is probable. Many of these folks have been involved in homosexuality for decades. They desire freedom from immoral sexual activity and freedom for holy living expressed in holy celibacy. One such man came to *Redeemed Lives* (RL) when he was fifty-eight years old. He was quite successful in his profession and accepted by most of his colleagues as a confirmed bachelor. No one knew he was living a double life. By day he was "Joe Professional" but on the nights and weekends he was the model of the well-adjusted successful gay man. Then he met the Lord Jesus through the friendship evangelism of one of his co-workers. As his desire to follow the Lord Jesus grew, he noticed a growing dissatisfaction with the gay community of Chicago. He joined a supportive church, entered into the RL program and happily settled into a celibate life. While it is possible he could marry, he has no desire for marriage.

(iv) Are they part of a supportive local church?

Integration into the body of Christ where we can know others and be known by others is key to overcoming homosexuality. This is not to say that everyone in the church needs to be informed of the ones who struggle with homosexual attractions.   But a supportive environment with plenty of outwardly directed opportunities for fellowship such as Bible studies, small groups and a shared common life is necessary to healthy growth. Some churches actually have programs specifically aimed at helping people overcome sexual brokenness. While this is a great benefit, I have known many men and women who successfully came out of homosexuality simply through integrating into a loving church family and becoming a disciple of Jesus Christ.

(v) Would they benefit from professional psychological or psychiatric care?

Proper diagnosis of psychological disorders can be a critical factor influencing change from homosexuality and other sexual struggles. Over the last twenty years, I have observed how clinical psychological and psychiatric needs can interlock with a sexual struggle. Once these are properly treated, healing is greatly advanced. Until these are properly treated there may be a discouraging pattern of reverting into sinful behavior in an attempt to medicate untreated psychological disorders.   The successful treatment of depression, anxiety, bi-polar, obsessive-compulsive disorders, paranoia and substance abuse is central to recovery for people with homosexual attractions who also suffer from these disorders.

The first time my eyes were opened to see the benefits of psychological and psychiatric care for people overcoming homosexual attractions was fifteen years ago. At the time I was studying diagnosis of psychological disorders as a graduate student in professional psychology. Johan (not his real name), a Lutheran pastor, came to me for help at the recommendation of his superintendent. Johan was married and the father of three teenage sons. For the duration of his twenty-year marriage he had been involved in anonymous homosexual encounters. Early on, in the late 1960's, he was so desperate for help he moved his entire family to New

York City, stating he wanted to earn a PhD at a theological college there. But his real motivation for the move was to receive help from a psychoanalyst in Manhattan well known for his successful treatment of homosexuality. Through this doctor's care, Johan came alive to his sexual need for his wife, and although sexual attraction toward men lessened, he still acted out homosexually several times each year. He told me it was as if he were under an uncontrollable sexual compulsion. After we met several times, I thought he might be a good candidate for a psychiatric evaluation. So I asked him if he would consider seeing a psychiatrist. He was hesitant to do this, as he had traveled the road of professional care before. But I assured him of the considerable advancement in psychiatry in the ten years since he had been in psychoanalysis. Johan was not aware that only recently had psychologists and psychiatrists begun working together to help their shared clients. He agreed to be evaluated and saw a good psychiatrist who diagnosed him with depression, anxiety and a form of clinical paranoia responsive to medication. This psychiatrist was also a psychologist and Johan entered into a second round of therapy with this skilled doctor. Within a few months I witnessed one of the most remarkable transformations I have ever seen. He reported that the love he had long held for his dear wife was continually on the surface of his heart. Moreover, his homosexual struggle was now nothing more than occasional bothersome thoughts that eventually went away if he did not pay them too much attention. Eventually, he went off the medication for the anxiety and the paranoia but remained on a low dosage of an antidepressant. For five years we remained in contact. He never acted out homosexually again and his marriage grew stronger and stronger.

When Has *Redeemed Lives* Failed?

In the many years that we have been in existence we have cared for some people who, after coming to us for help, returned to self-identifying as gay or to embrace other passions of the sinful nature. How did we fail them?

Our early failures at helping people with same-sex attraction were due in part to inexperience. We learned over the years that when people say they want help, we have to help them ascertain exactly what they mean by help. Some want an instant fix, thinking that a magical cure exists out there. People who come to *Redeemed Lives* unwilling to embrace the arduous process of progressive sanctification in Jesus Christ generally do not do very well. Also, we found that anyone who had an addiction to a substance, such as to alcohol or to drugs, did not do well in *Redeemed Lives*. Usually, half way through the pastoral course, as personal struggles surfaced, they would medicate their pain with the substance. Once under the influence of the alcohol or the drugs, this sometimes led them to return to homosexual activity, sometimes to simply embrace it all over again. Others who came to us were not part of a supportive church, and made *Redeemed Lives* their only source of Christian fellowship. However, once the course was over, they no longer had the support needed to continue walking in the light of Jesus Christ, and returned to homosexual activity. Still others had clinical levels of depression, anxiety and other disorders that required medical treatment, but refused to see their doctors for ongoing medical care.

Therefore, we learned over the years to have people fill out a detailed application form, where they are asked to commit to the process of sanctification in Jesus Christ, disclose any alcohol or drug abuse, show membership in a supportive local church, and disclose any diagnosis of medical conditions such as clinical depression and bi-polar disorders. When such disclosures are made, we require them to seek medical attention and follow the directives of their physicians. We also learned to ask people if they were living with someone with whom they once had a sexual relationship. We learned that if people were living with former lovers, that this was counter- productive to receiving help. Therefore, in order to be part of *Redeemed Lives*, all these concerns must be satisfactorily addressed before a person is admitted into the course. For some this has meant entering into drug and alcohol rehabilitation prior to going through *Redeemed Lives*. For others it has meant they needed to see a physician to adequately deal with their psychiatric needs. For still others, it has meant selling the home they bought with their former gay partners and moving out before being part of *Redeemed Lives*.

Still, even with all these requirements met, there have been a relatively small number of people who have returned to homosexuality, or embraced other life-controlling conditions of the sinful nature. We have always kept open the doors of love to them. For a number of such folks, I have personally remained in contact with them. On several occasions I have challenged people who have gone on to embrace gay and lesbian self-identification after going through *Redeemed Lives* to meet with me once a week for lunch at my expense. My challenge to them is this, 'I will meet with you as long as you will meet with me. And my conviction is that as long as you stay connected to me in Christian love, one day you will come to see the emptiness of self-identification as gay. Then I will be there for you to help you to once again embrace the arduous process of sanctification.' On two occasions this has already happened.

The Mission of the Church is to Teach, Preach and Heal.

The Church can effectively minister to the person struggling with homosexual attractions through preaching, teaching and healing. The Bible attests to this three-fold call to mission in Matthew 9:35, *"Then Jesus went through all the towns and villages, teaching in their synagogues, and preaching the good news of the kingdom, and healing every disease and sickness."* This verse bridges the first and second halves of Matthew's Gospel. The first half is about Jesus *teaching, preaching, and healing.* The second half is about Jesus' disciples teaching, preaching and healing.

As the Church we are to *teach* and practice a moral and pastoral theology that actually believes living in abstinence, holy celibacy or change leading to heterosexual marriage are viable options for Christians struggling with same-sex attractions. Our message about homosexuality needs to state it is but one of the many sins Jesus died to redeem us from, and that in the majority of cases same-sex attractions can be changed. As the Church we are to evangelistically *preach* the Good News leading to regeneration through baptism and deeper conversion to Jesus Christ. As the Church we are to equip pastoral leaders to minister sexual redemption and *healing* in Christ to all people, not only to those with same-sex attractions.

Finally, as the Church we need to be encouraged, strengthened and empowered with the truth that we have had success in ministering to people with homosexual attractions since the days of the Apostles. As stated earlier in this paper, St. Paul clearly writes that some of the Corinthians came free from life-controlling sins including homosexuality through a three-fold process of being washed, justified and sanctified. (1 Corinthians 6:9-11) When St. Paul's three-fold process combines with St. Matthew's three-fold mission of teaching, preaching and healing, the Church becomes a safe place where men and women with same-sex attractions find transformation.

In this time when every branch of Christianity is being rocked by sexual scandals, it is essential to equip both lay and ordained pastoral caregivers to minister effectively to all people in their sexuality. *Living Waters Trainings (LWT)* and *Redeemed Lives Equipping Seminars (RLES)* exist to equip lay and professional pastoral workers in this ministry. Log on to the *Desert Stream* web page www.desertstream.org for more information about the next *LWT.* For information about the next *RLES* log on to the *RLM* web page at www.redeemedlives.org.

Some of my journey out of homosexuality

My own journey out of homosexuality and into heterosexuality included addressing both spiritual dynamics and psychological issues. Spiritually, my healing from homosexuality came as my conversion to Jesus deepened and I learned to repent of my sin. I first met the love of Jesus at age six in the care of Roman Catholic nuns who lived in my neighborhood. When I met Jesus personally at age 14 through the evangelical preaching of Leighton Ford, I was also experiencing the emergence of same-sex attraction. I searched for help for overcoming homosexuality, but was unsuccessful. By the time I was eighteen, I lost all hope of finding help for healing, went to university and entered into the gay lifestyle in New York City.

By my early twenties, I had several immunity breakdowns and landed in a hospital room in Boston with the possible diagnosis of AIDS looming over my head. While on my hospital bed in fear and despair, I prayed to the Lord Jesus. He appeared to me saying, 'I want to heal your whole person, not just your sexuality. Choose.' In response to his initiative, I chose him. I recovered fully from my symptoms and was never diagnosed with AIDS and later tested HIV negative. The turning point in my life came when, a few months later, I repented of homosexuality and received the forgiveness of sins. My spiritual healing from homosexuality continued as I learned to forgive others and resist temptation. I needed to forgive others for how their sins had negatively shaped me. Additionally, I had to learn how to suffer like a Christian in order to resist the temptations to take back homosexual sin.

The Lord used psychological insights to address my lack of affirmation in my identity as a man and fears related to men and women. I came to see how I misperceived manhood in myself. I grew to accept the unique ways God has created me to be a man and masculine. Through healthy friendships with men, I began to accept myself as a man among men. I had to press through my fear of relating to both men and women. The many godly men and women I met in my local church showed me a new model for male and female relationships. Also helpful was the love and acceptance of fellow students, faculty and staff at Trinity Episcopal School For Ministry in Pennsylvania where I studied for the priesthood. Of special help was the prayerful counsel of Leanne Payne and the many Christian leaders who have served alongside her at *Pastoral Care Ministries*.

As I continued growing in the Lord, so did my desire for marriage and family. Concurrently, so did my attraction to women. I was abstinent for twelve years before I married. In 1996 I married Nancy and since then we have had five children. Today, my growth into manhood includes growing as a husband and father. Through the Lord's grace and the loving input of faithful Christians, I have learned of the many areas of weakness in my soul that continually requires His healing presence. These weaknesses are not limited to occasional homosexual thoughts and feelings, but include pernicious sins such as pride. Along with St. Paul, I have had to face a thorn in my flesh. Although he asked the Lord to remove it three times, three times the Lord refused to remove it. Instead the Lord said to St. Paul, 'My grace is sufficient for you, for my power is made perfect in weakness.' (2 Corinthians 12:9). I may always be weak and vulnerable in my sexuality. But through His power working in me, I can be obedient. Even though same-sex attractions occasionally revisit me, they no longer have the power to define who I am. In reality, I was never gay, therefore I cannot be ex-gay, for these both are misnomers that find no support in the Holy Scriptures for identifying men and women. I am a Christian, a husband, father and a priest. Most importantly, I am a child of God. 'Yet to all who received Him, to those who believed in His name, He gave the right to become children of God – children born not of natural descent, nor of human decision or a husband's will, but born of God.' (John 1:12-13).

The Revd Mario Bergner is husband to Nancy and father to their five children. He is an Episcopal Priest canonically resident in the Diocese of Quincy in Illinois, and the Associate Rector of Christ Church in South Hamilton, Massachusetts. He is the author of *Setting Love in Order* (Baker 1995), and was a contributing author for *The Christian Educator's Handbook on Family Life Education* (Baker 1996). He has published articles on pastoral care for Leadership Journal, Good News Magazine and Cornerstone Magazine, and he is the author of five DVD pastoral courses, which are used in over sixty venues worldwide.

Twenty years ago, Mario founded *Redeemed Lives* (RL), located in Ipswich, MA. (www.redeemedlives.org). RL has given pastoral conferences in North America, Europe, Asia and Africa. The mission of RL is to bring *all people into the healing and saving embrace of Jesus Christ.*

Mario has also enjoyed a career in the professional theater that has included working in television and on stage, as well as serving on the drama faculties at Boston University, Wright State University in Dayton, Ohio, Carnegie-Mellon University in Pittsburgh, Pa. and Roosevelt University in Chicago.

He holds a degree in Theater from the University of Wisconsin at Milwaukee, and that of Master of Divinity from Trinity Episcopal School for Ministry in Ambridge, Pa.

See also

'How Jesus Heals Us Through His Church' by Andrew Comiskey;
    http://www.desertstream.org/healing%20ohomosexuality.htm
'Risen with Christ, Our Wounds Yet Visible' by Andrew Comiskey;
    http://www.desertstream.org/weakness.htm
'Cold Turkey or the Gradual Way ?' by Alan Medinger;
    http://www.ldolphin.org/coldturkey.com

14. Civil Partnerships – Advice to UK Parishes and Clergy

The Revd Paul Perkin and Mrs Christine Perkin

1. Introduction

On 25 July 2005 the Church of England's House of Bishops issued a Pastoral Statement on Civil Partnerships "to help the Church as it addresses the pastoral and other implications of the new legislation". This came into force with the Civil Partnership Act of 5 December of the same year. However, in the light of subsequent developments in church and society, a number of concerns have come into sharper focus, and these have brought into question the adequacy of the bishops' advice. The House of Bishops offered its pastoral guidelines to the church, but there has been little opportunity since then to discuss their meaning or explore their consequences. However, it has come to light, now that the guidelines have filtered down through the bishops to individual dioceses, that the bishops are offering to their clergy variant interpretations of the Statement, or even substantially different advice between themselves. The pastoral practice the clergy are being expected to follow has become a post-code lottery. Moreover, reflection on the Pastoral Statement has helped people to see certain ambiguities, and perhaps even inconsistencies, either within the statement itself or between the Statement's requirements and other responsibilities laid upon the clergy.

2. Concerns

(i) *When it comes to specific concerns, the first is about the status of marriage itself.*

The Christian biblical understanding of marriage is that it is the union between one man and one woman (legally recognised in the UK as over 16 years old), who are neither already married to a person still living, nor previously closely related to each other. This union is to be personally and freely undertaken in love, publicly declared, and sexually consummated, in faithfulness to each other. It is to be monogamous during the lifetime of both partners, expressed in the sharing of all material goods, through an example of sacrificial devotion, taking precedence over other familial relationships. In the case of Christian believers the Bible urges them to marry only another believer, and to see the ideal of marriage as an expression of Christ's union with his bride the church.

The Civil Partnership Act desires to remedy injustice and remove discrimination - but it does so at the expense of undermining marriage, on account of "two indisputable facts: the Act radically alters family law and redefines family within UK law by allowing family ties to be established and widened by a means other than marriage ... [and] The Act redefines marriage in statute law by creating new legal impediments to marriage" (Grove Ethics booklet E141, p.10). For example, entering a civil partnership creates bonds of affinity that may prevent other individuals from subsequently marrying due to the relationship established by a civil partnership. And an existing civil partnership is now a just cause and impediment to marriage. This is significant because the House of Bishops' Pastoral Statement claims: "The new legislation makes no change to the law of the land in relation to marriage". This is incorrect – and a serious flaw in its account.

More worrying still, the new legislation does necessitate two changes to church law: Canon B31, recognising the new impediments, and Church Measures by Orders in Council, giving government ministers authority to add the phrase "or civil partner" wherever Measures refer to "spouse". The statutory granting of authority to ministers to "amend, repeal or (as the case may be) revoke any church legislation" represents an unprecedented surrender of the Church's self-government, the right to define herself, if necessary, over and against the state. None of these amendments has been debated, let alone approved, by the Church, whose government has been seriously undermined.

Moreover, on marriage registers, a couple registering their marriage at a registry office are asked if they have been previously in 'any form of marriage'. An undissolved civil partnership is a bar to marriage. In this way the Church is forced to recognize an undissolved civil partnership as having the same status as a marriage.

(ii)   *The second concern is the nature of civil partnership as quasi-marriage.*

The Pastoral Statement helpfully reiterates in outline the church's understanding of marriage. However, the Statement also claims that "Civil partnerships are not a form of marriage", and it is on account of *this* that it has now clearly come to be recognised, with hindsight, that the bishops were deceived by parliament. The government website, and the utterances of government proponents in both houses of parliament, all use the language of 'Gay Marriage'. Civil partnership mimics marriage, in practice, but it is inconsistent with Christian teaching. The initial Church of England response by the Archbishops' Council to the legislation pointed this out in September 2003: "As they stand these proposals risk being seen as introducing a form of same-sex marriage with almost all of the same rights as marriage". The House of Bishops, it seems, was unwise to ignore the Archbishops' Council's warning, but it has now admitted this in its amendment to the Civil Partnerships motion debated in General Synod in February 2007, acknowledging "the diversity of views within the Church of England on whether Parliament might better have addressed the injustices affecting persons of the same sex wishing to share a common life had it done so in a way that avoided creating a legal framework with many similarities to marriage".

Subsequently, the Guide to Civil Partnership produced by Stonewall, supported by Barclays Bank, and distributed by the Citizens Advice Bureau, announces: "You're gay, you're in love, you want to be together forever ... Get hitched!". It continues: "So, civil partnership, is this marriage or not? To all intents and purposes, yes. With civil partnerships you get every right and every privilege and every responsibility straight couples get when they marry. It's the same thing .... Is that what we become, civil partners? Yeah, but no one can stop you calling each other what you like - husband, wife, husbear, her indoors - though not on official documents. If you want to take your partner's name on your driver's licence say, or your passport, proof of identity and your civil partnership certificate will be enough to sort that out .... So presumably, we'd have to get a divorce if it all went wrong? It's called a 'dissolution' but yes, you would .... And can we tie the knot in church? You can have a blessing in church with your favourite gay-friendly vicar (or equivalent gay-friendly religious leader), the same as straight couples who marry in a register office, but there can be no religious service during the registration itself, just as with straight couples in a civil wedding." So the government's and the bishops' claim that a Civil Partnership is not a marriage is now refuted by reality.

There are at least six central ethical issues that render civil partnerships unwise, at best, and perhaps altogether inappropriate, as a way of life for a disciple of Christ:

- they are exclusive to one person

- they are an impediment to marriage

- they create family ties

- they require the intention of a life-long bond with someone of the same sex

- they are viewed as same-sex marriages in wider society

- they (at least) imply a sexual relationship and suggest a bad witness, as happens, for example, when an unmarried Christian man and an unmarried Christian woman live together; even if their relationship is chaste, the reputation and witness of the church is at stake

The Pastoral Statement is unclear on all these vital points, and leaves pastoral guidance confused.

(iii)   The third concern focuses on the teaching role of the clergy.

It is the bishops' responsibility to ensure their clergy adhere to the church's teaching. This is, according to the November 1987 General Synod motion (still in force), that "homosexual genital acts ... are to be met by a call to repentance", and that "holiness of life is particularly required of Christian leaders". Also, according to the December 1991 House of Bishops' report, *Issues in Human Sexuality*, the church's teaching is that "the clergy cannot claim the liberty to enter into sexually active homophile relationships". And then, in the wider Anglican Communion, the church's teaching is expressed in Resolution 1.10, passed at the Lambeth Conference in 1998: "This Conference ... cannot advise the legitimising or blessing of same sex unions nor ordaining those involved in same gender unions."

All this the House of Bishops affirms, but it has made a rod for its own back. The Pastoral Statement declares that:

> The House of Bishops does not regard entering into a civil partnership as intrinsically incompatible with holy orders, provided the person concerned is willing to give assurances to his or her bishop that the relationship is consistent with the standards for the clergy set out in *Issues in Human Sexuality.*

But there is no clear statement as to how assurances are to be sought, or what is to happen if they are not forthcoming. It has been suggested that it is debatable whether the pastoral guidelines *could* have provided a clear means of ensuring that its teaching was enforced – however, this should have been foreseen and addressed. As it stands, the bishops are left with the responsibility of clergy discipline. However, as the confidentiality of the confessional and the cumbersome Clergy Discipline Measure may both cause hindrances, they are unable to do anything about it.

Moreover, the acceptance in principle of civil partnerships, albeit with certain unrealistic attempts at obtaining assurances, makes it much more uncertain as to the outcome of any legal challenge to the implementation of discipline, if those assurances are not given. (This is because an appeal could be made to Article 8 of the Human Rights Act.) It has been claimed that had the Church of England *not* acknowledged civil partnerships in principle, clergy might have been open to legal challenge. Even if they had been so challenged, they could have appealed to Article 13 which allows religious exemption on grounds of matters of faith, and the government would have accepted it. The Roman Catholic Church did not recognise civil partnerships, and have not been challenged. Even if the church were subject to legal challenge, Christians have not historically rejected that as an unthinkable option, in view of the enormously greater consequences for the church when it has stood for truth against the state in other periods of history, and in most other parts of the world today. Ultimately, the over-riding biblical precept in such matters of conscience is: "We must obey God rather than men."

(iv) *The fourth concern focuses on the clergy's pastoral responsibility at the local level.*

Church leaders should be as the apostle Paul was to the Thessalonian Christians, "gentle among you, as a mother caring for her little children", and "as a father deals with his own children, encouraging, comforting and urging you to lead lives worthy of God" (1 Thessalonians 2:7,11f). They should respond in compassion towards all those in their care, whether members of their congregations or enquirers seeking the church's help.

However, the Pastoral Statement is ambiguous. On the one hand it argues that "it would not be right to produce an authorised public liturgy in connection with the registering of civil partnerships", and indeed that "clergy of the Church of England should not provide services of blessing for those who register a civil partnership". On the other hand, clergy are urged to "respond pastorally and sensitively" to requests for prayer in relation to entering into a civil partnership. While the distinction between public services and private prayers is real and valid, some will be encouraged to take advantage of the ambiguity in order effectively to bless civil partnerships.

Similarly, the House of Bishops "considers that lay people who have registered civil partnerships ought not to be asked to give assurances about the nature of their relationship before being admitted to baptism, confirmation and communion". Despite a possible quibble over the difference between 'asking about the nature of the relationship' and 'asking for assurances about the nature of the relationship' (after all, why would one be asking at all, if not to ask for assurances?), the key issue is: if this, as it appears, prevents the exercise of church discipline in such cases, then it does represent a significant and dubious shift in what has been understood for centuries to be the Church of England's pastoral practice. How can sacramental discipline in relation to "open sin without repentance", demanded by Canon B16 with regard to Holy Communion, and in relation to "fitness" for confirmation, demanded by Canon C24, be exercised if the nature of relationships cannot be raised? Even Canons B22 and B23 on baptism insist on the appropriateness of delay, in the event of pastoral concerns, for the purpose of necessary instruction, and also on the necessity, for godparents, of "the example of their own godly living". These too are set aside. Is any sacramental discipline left?

3. *Questions*

Question: If church teaching is now being dictated by statutory authorities, what should parishes teach about marriage?

Answer: Church leaders should be encouraged to continue to teach and uphold the Christian view of marriage, its place and importance, and to teach about the wrongness of all sexual activity outside the marriage bond. In all cultures marriage is privileged – for the propagation of society, for the protection and safe nurture of children, and for the maintenance of secure homes as the basis of a stable society.

We also need to explain the nature of the Civil Partnership contract. A contract cannot be about that contract itself; it will always point to something. The registration of a civil partnership consists solely of two signatures on a register. It is not a signed witness to a pledge – but rather, and tautologously, it is a witness to itself. There are rights and implications that follow from the partnership, but there is no declaration of any vows, nor any undertaking which implies vows – indeed the spoken word has no necessary place in the formation. This was quite deliberate – there is to be no commitment of love or sexual faithfulness to a Civil Partnership, although there will be some contractual agreements over "tax, social security, inheritance and workplace benefits" (DTI, *Civil Partnerships* September 2005). But as a contract this is nowhere near equivalent to the covenant of marriage. This may have repercussions back into the perceived understanding of marriage, which is definitively a covenant between two people, stemming in its origin from the biblical concept of God's covenant with his people.

Question: What response should churches give to those asking advice about entering a civil partnership?

Answer: The clergy are rightly called upon by their ordination vows, by the canons of the Church, and by the bishops' Statement, to be pastorally sensitive. They should respond in compassion and care when dealing with those with homosexual inclinations. However, it would be unwise to encourage Christians to enter civil partnerships because they are a counterfeit of marriage and they undermine marriage. They should instead provide resources, both of literature and of pastoral ministries, such as Living Waters (PO Box 1530, London SWlW OWF, 0207 630 1044); (www.living-waters-uk.org/), The True Freedom Trust; (www.truefreedomtrust.co.uk), and The Healing Prayer School (www.healingprayerschool.org).

Question: What response should be given to those requesting prayer in relation to a civil partnership?

Answer: Churches are not legally allowed to "bless" civil partnerships, and there is no rite of blessing allowed by Canon law for doing so. Clergy who do conduct such blessings are acting illegally. Attempts to get around the law by holding a communion service for the couple, or by offering prayer privately and informally rather than publicly and formally, are disingenuous. When asked to pray for people, clergy should always be pastoral and sensitive, but they should not appear to endorse a civil partnership by praying for a same-sex couple in a way that affirms the relationship. It would, of course, be uncontroversial to offer prayer for any two friends.

Question: What direction should be given to congregational members on baptism and Holy Communion?

Answer: Clergy have Scripture, the Articles of the Church of England, and Canon law on their side in exercising discipline in their churches, providing they do so within the limits of the law. However, they need to be consistent, exercising discipline not just on one issue, but evenly with regard to heterosexual and other sin as well as homosexual sin. Discipline with regard to baptism may involve delay, but not outright refusal: in the case of children adopted or born by *in vitro* fertilization to a same-sex couple, it would be possible to offer the Service of Thanksgiving for the birth of a child. However, clergy are required by law to ask of baptismal candidates whether they reject all rebellion against God, renounce the corruption of evil, and repent of the sins that separate us from God and neighbour. In the same way, the exhortation to Holy Communion in the Book of Common Prayer warns against coming to the Lord's table until specific sins, including sexual sins, are renounced. These are serious questions concerning genuine repentance and turning to Christ, and they have real meaning.

Question: What advice could be given to parents over the choice of godparents?

Answer: The Church of England Canons require parents, in the choice of godparents, and clergy in the conduct of baptism, to be thoughtful about the example of godparents to the child as he or she grows up. Godparents are also often given guardian responsibilities in the event of the death of the parents. If Christians believe that God's order for marriage and the family is one man and one woman in faithful monogamy, as the marriage service urges for the nurture of children, they should be reluctant to encourage a same-sex couple to take on a role that is in any way *in loco parentis*. This consideration will also, inevitably, affect parents' concerns about the ethos of their children's schools and the teaching and example of their teachers.

Question: What advice can be given to church members invited to attend Civil Partnership ceremonies, or the celebrations following them?

Answer: Christians invited to a ceremony, or celebration following a civil partnership, will want to weigh up carefully what their attendance will say to those present. On the one hand, they may desire to retain the attitude: "While we don't believe a civil partnership is God's will for the greatest happiness of individuals or for the health of society, we want to keep lines of communication and friendship open." On the other hand, church members will be well advised to ask whether there are to be any formal vows or prayers, and whether they themselves will be expected to participate in any ceremony. They should beware of giving any potential signal that they approve of same-sex partnerships.

Question: How should churches handle requests to use church premises to celebrate civil partnerships?

Answer: Churches have been concerned about their vulnerability to the Sexual Orientation Regulations and the Single Equality Bill. However, a Northern Ireland High Court judge has ruled that Christians can make use of Article 9, rights to religious liberty, when defending themselves against actions brought under the regulations (Mr.Justice Weatherup, 11 September 2007). He opined that the belief that the practice of homosexuality is sinful is a "belief worthy of recognition". Moreover, this belief is a long established part of orthodox Christian belief and of the world's major religions. Moreover, until put to the test it is uncertain whether churches' freedom of conscience is preserved in the hiring out of churches and church halls, but legal advice at present is optimistic that parishes are protected in this matter.

Question: How should churches offer pastoral care to those already in a civil partnership?

Answer: Churches might suggest that civil partners reconsider their decision to enter such a partnership. If they made no vows in the forming of the civil partnership, and subsequently withdraw from it within the terms of the regulations, they will be legally terminating a commitment in material terms, but they need not be breaking a declared moral obligation, and so can withdraw from their signature to registration with a clear conscience.

It is important to distinguish this from the breaking of marriage vows which, although legal, will usually involve a moral lapse needing a pastoral ministry of repentance, absolution and, if possible, restitution. Indeed the normal pastoral approach to a marriage in danger of breaking down will be to help the couple towards reconciliation, whereas the normal pastoral approach to a civil partnership under pressure may be to help the partners to mediate the most painless separation. A married couple, in the event of separation, may need help to repent of the breakdown of the relationship, rather than repenting of the relationship itself, whereas civil partners may need help to repent of the relationship rather than its breakdown.

Question: What communion might churches be encouraged to maintain with neighbouring churches and clergy whose teaching or practice are outside those allowed by the church's permission?

Answer: If bishops cannot or will not exercise discipline, it is all the more important that the local church does. Congregations and their leaders have no responsibility of oversight of other congregations, but they do have responsibility with regard to their example and witness. Inevitably fractures in fellowship will result from innovations in doctrine, and even if Church of England congregations wanted to insulate themselves from these, wider fractures in the Anglican Communion will force them to stand on one side or the other of the divide. The Primates are in the present situation, unable to take Holy Communion together. Church of England congregations may similarly come to the deeply sad conclusion that they can no longer enjoy the luxury of sitting on the fence of a superficial unity.

Question: Given the discrepancies, whose advice should we take, the local bishop's or others'?

Answer: There is indeed a serious risk of impairing the unity of the Church of England nationally and of the Anglican Communion worldwide. Bishops' responses have been inconsistent, but some of them could helpfully be used to defend an orthodox practice. The advice given to clergy in some dioceses – Winchester, Durham and London, and in particular the *Ad Clerum* letter sent to all the clergy in the diocese of Rochester – is widely available and might be found most helpful.

Question: What approach should the parish make to the bishop in the light of the general shift in perception ?

Answer: There now appear to be strong grounds for writing to the local bishop, requesting and expecting him not to allow his clergy to enter a civil partnership. This is the stance of the Roman Catholic and other churches, and there is no reason why the Church of England could not have taken a similar one.

Question: Should we encourage our own bishop to re-visit the Statement, or to urge the House of Bishops to review it?

Answer: The bishops have already been called upon to revisit the Statement. They did not respond at first, but the pressure is now mounting. As a result, the February 2007 General Synod noted "the intention of the House [of Bishops] to keep their Pastoral Statement under review", and bishops are more likely actively to review their advice if encouraged to do so by local churches.

Moreover, "keeping under review" implies a provisionality about the Statement, and some bishops have candidly gone further, suggesting that their Statement has no greater status than that of advice. This may not help clarity, but it does imply a certain flexibility – which is, of course, two-edged. Bishops have been unclear as to the status of what they have said – can it be the basis of discipline?   Can it be used as a means of interpreting the legislation? Some churches will want to ask their own bishop to clarify his understanding of the Statement.

The Revd Paul Perkin and Mrs Christine Perkin together pastor St.Mark's Battersea Rise, a church plant from Holy Trinity Brompton in London. Among the responsibilities of a growing and planting congregation, they lead *Marriage and Family Ministries*. As part of the leadership team of *New Wine*, they have encouraged the growth of the *Family Time* courses, developing the *Parenting Teenagers Course* with the help of their three now-grown-up children who have monitored every reference to themselves! Paul is a keen motor-biker and gardener, and still keeps his previous interest in theoretical physics, while Christine continues to teach the violin which she studied at the Royal College of Music.

See also

'The Church of England, Civil Partnerships and the House of Bishops' by the Revd John P. Richardson; http://www.anglican-mainstream.net/downloads/CPLeaflet.PDF

'Church Policy as Regards Homosexual Practice: Membership and Ordained Ministry' by Professor Robert A. J. Gagnon; http://www.robgagnon.net/articles/homosexChurchPolicy.pdf

15.   Gay Wednesday's 'Gay Pain'

Dr Lisa Severine Nolland

As Gay Wednesday's debate revealed, the issue of 'gay pain' is vitally important. I fully agree. Though I have spent years relating to gay issues, any sensitive person would be troubled. However, I also note the apparent monopoly on pain claimed by the lesbian/ gay/ bisexual / transgendered (LGBT) community, with the corresponding imperative upon the rest of us to 'do something about it'. Besides reiterating the obvious, where can we go from here?

In fundamentally important ways, of course, LGBT people have no monopoly on pain. Which of us does not carry burdens of one sort or another from the past, wounds, frailties, sometimes even forgiven sins as well, which have darkened and oppressed, even irretrievably damaged, us? Sometimes these plagues are apparent; often they are invisible. The more one listens to people's 'real' stories, however, the worse it gets. And though sometimes the individual finds a kindred spirit along the way, often he or she remains alone in a Stygian underworld. Few know, fewer care and no one really understands. If the imperative to attend to gay pain encourages us to attend to other hitherto closeted types and modes of pain, well and good. Although those in the LGBT community may not realize that they have *lots* of company – and reading their websites indicates as much – they are far from alone in navigating the minefields of sexuality, marriage and family.

What other types of personal pain remain covert, and thus without psycho-social legitimacy, within the church context? There is the difficult lot of the single Christian woman in her 30s (and older) who has negligible chance of marriage and motherhood because of the paucity of eligible Christian men. With her biological clock ticking inexorably – and this is a female-only phenomenon: males can father children well into old age – she can either marry outside the faith or remain single 'for the Lord'. This cross is all the heavier because society neglects or ridicules her, or else is profoundly ambivalent towards her as a 'spinster' – a pejorative term, unlike the male equivalent, 'bachelor' – while the church, ostrich-like, simply pretends the situation is not there. (So what's new?)

And what of the Christian adolescent, the widow or widower, the divorced, other singles? What of *their* pain, passion, loneliness, libido? Some may later find a suitable mate but presently sleep alone, while increasing numbers will always do so. I include here those with unwanted same-sex attraction issues who appear unable to realign their sexual orientation. Married people too can carry heavy but invisible burdens. Some believe they have found the man or woman of their dreams only after marrying someone else. For others, the marriage which began so promisingly somehow loses its grip and withers away. And finally, others have appallingly bad circumstances thrown at them – the illness or death of a child, say – and their relationship bites the dust.

However, 'gay pain' is now the pain that counts. I began reading auto/biographical gay narrative, gay theology and theory, along with second-wave feminist theology and thought, in the 1980s, and have followed the trajectories of both the gay and the feminist movements. Without doubt gays have been dreadfully marginalized and excluded (and sometimes worse), and been forbidden to own what they consider to be their true identity. Many of them insist that on 'coming out' they have 'come alive' for the first time in their entire life – they had not *known* they could feel this good! – and naturally they view the orthodox Christian position on sexual morality as positively Draconian, something of a living death sentence. The authenticity and desperation of these experiences, and their illumination of 'the actual, lived, embodied, existences of real [gay] people'[1], cannot be doubted. Who would *not* empathize? But more pressingly, what can be done?

The Christian LGBT community wants us to respond to 'gay pain' by legitimizing their 'relationships' – a step that is easier to take because the relationships we keep being told about are presented as, apparently, mirror-images of heterosexual marital relationships. Fair enough – this seems a sensible, rational response. However, I would argue that it is also profoundly misguided, serving the best interests of no one.

Why? To reconfigure the essential paradigms of sexuality, gender and marriage, in order to benefit the LGBT community, cannot alter transcendent truths of morality and the created order. In concrete terms, for us as a post-modern, post-Christian society to liberate sex from the domain of heterosexual marriage does not change the ethical dimension. It simply says that we want to expand the range of our sexual options, and need to feel virtuous about ourselves while we do so. But in fact, redefining the parameters of morally legitimate sexual expression is not a small step:

---

[1] William Lindsey, 'The AIDS Crisis and the Church: ...', *Christian Perspectives on Sexuality and Gender*, eds. Elizabeth Stuart and Adrian Thatcher (1996), p. 355.

it is an absolutely massive one, with profound repercussions for us all. However, the Christian LGBT community would have us celebrate and sanctify LGBT relationships, which include LGBT sex.

As such, this is deeply worrying. Christians maintain that God can *not* bless sin in any form. He knows that, though the sweets taste wonderful, they have been poisoned. My besetting sins – a unique cocktail of noxious attitudes, habits and behaviours aggravated by psychological vulnerability and need – are as toxic to my welfare as yours are to you. For Victorian Christians, a man did not break the commandments but broke himself upon them. Today's motto could be, '"Take what you want", God says, "and pay for it"'.[2] If not now, then later. Sin is never 'free', and people do not 'get away with it'. Life simply does not play out like this. Hence God's warnings to flee the virulent, but often powerfully strong, ensnarement of transgression; it may feel good, but this will only be temporary.

However, for the LGBT community and its allies, these views are unwelcome, irrelevant and even semi-incomprehensible. I say 'sin' and they hear 'relationships' – and what can be wrong with them? On 'Gay Wednesday', the Revd Mary Gilbert pleaded for 'lesbian and gay Christians [whose relationships] ... exhibit fidelity, commitment, self-sacrifice'. The Revd Canon Professor Marilyn McCord Adams eulogized 'partners, faithful to God and to one another for 30 and 40 years', while the Revd Canon Jane Fraser praised 'loving, faithful, committed and exclusive' lesbian and gay relationships.[3]

I have no doubt that lesbian and gay sexually monogamous or exclusive (abbreviated to 'exclusive'), closed, binary relationships do exist! However, many other types exist as well, and these are presently kept well below the radar. They are not good PR material. However, despite emotive anecdotal evidence to the contrary, the broader gay movement, even in its Christian manifestation, allows for but does not demand exclusivity from those in lesbian and gay relationships. This is apparent from the websites of gay Christian organizations such as the Lesbian and Gay Christian Movement (LGCM) and, even more importantly, Changing Attitude (CA). Courage Trust (CT) maintains a different position, coming close to Canon Dr Jeffrey John's views (see below). CT upholds either celibacy or a same-sex partnership characterized by 'mutual commitment, equality, respect and

---

[2] Quotation, Noreen Riols/Maureen Long.
[3] Proceedings of General Synod, Third Day, 28 February 2007.

faithfulness'; immorality is forbidden.[4] This probably translates into an imperative to be exclusive. However, CT is clearly out of step with the broader movements within gay activism, religious or secular, and has little to say to the emerging bisexual community. For this group the 'Noah's Ark' principle – pair bonding – is inapplicable; they consider it to be based on nothing stronger than prejudice and stereotype – indeed, they view it as positively discriminatory.

Established over 30 years ago, the LGCM affirms that 'human sexuality in all its richness is a gift of God, gladly to be accepted, enjoyed and honoured', and that a 'personal sexual relationship' between people of the same sex is 'entirely compatible with the Christian faith'.[5] The website has much on exclusive lesbian or gay relationships. However, I could locate no imperative to be exclusive. Non-exclusive lesbian or gay relationships were discussed positively but briefly; bisexuality received little mention.

In fact, however, the action lies elsewhere. The premier gay Christian organization in the UK today is CA. It is trendier, edgier, more powerful than the LGCM, both nationally and globally, and it can boast of impressive ecclesiastical patronage and also grassroots involvement and ownership. CA also highlights the presence of the bisexual and transgender communities – now out and proud – an indication of how our culture has morphed and moved on.

CA's ethical position has recently been radicalized. Compare its two primary documents (both on its website), the first written in 2003 and the second (far longer) in 2004. According to 'A guide to ... lesbian and gay people in the Anglican church', 9 October 2003:

> In the West ... we have begun to create relationships in exactly the same way as adult heterosexuals. We flirt and date, fall in love, commit ourselves to partners in faithful, loving, monogamous relationships. We also fail in exactly the same way as heterosexuals. Partners are sometimes unfaithful, and relationships can break down.

> Partnered lesbian and gay people who are practising Christians have heartfelt, strongly held, theologically grounded beliefs about our calling to live in a loving, faithful relationship. Such a relationship of commitment between two men or two women, no less than a

---

[4] http://www.courage.org.uk/basis/faith.shtml
[5] http://www.lgcm.org.uk

heterosexual Christian marriage, is a reflection of [p.1] Christ's love for his Church. It is no less a vehicle of grace [p.2]. [6]

Though exclusivity is not mandated, these relationships resonate far more with those described by, say, CT or Jeffrey John. When such 'vehicles of grace' are presented, permanence is implied, commitment is affirmed, and infidelity is discouraged; such relationships are treasured icons of the relationship between Christ and his Bride.

But then, something changed.

In 2004 the document, *Sexual Ethics: A Report of the Lesbian and Gay Clergy Consultation Working Group*, ed. by Andrew Henderson, was published. In it, the sexually 'open' ethical views of leading theologians like James Nelson, Elizabeth Stuart and (the now deceased) Michael Vasey are promoted. Exclusivity in relationships is presented as neither an ethical requisite nor, necessarily, a desirable aspiration for those in the LGBT community, or even for heterosexuals (though that is less certain). 'This approach to relational ethics [the love ethic] is probably valid generally for everyone, not just LGBTs; and the recovery of provisional (eschatological) thinking in sexual ethics may be part of our contribution to the church' [p.8]. Heterosexuals can thus be tutored in how to 'do' relationships by members of the LGBT community. Professor McCord Adams pleaded with her listeners 'to learn what gay and lesbian partnerships have learnt about intimacy and modelling God's love'. One wonders if this is what she had in mind.

Indeed, in *Sexual Ethics* there is not the slightest hint of an exclusive imperative! I offer a series of excerpts from the document so that its readers may 'hear' exactly what is said.

> The ideal outcome may be for mature adults to live in covenantal relationships that are stable, sexually exclusive/monogamous and permanent. This ideal is in tension with our common inheritance of genetic predispositions and developmental damage that compromise our capacity for relating, and often make serial commitments, and serial faithfulness, a more realistic aspiration. [p.9]

Exclusivity is held up as a fine ideal, but not as a realistic aspiration for most.

---

[6] http://www.changingattitude.org.uk/publications/AllGodsChildren.asp

Even harder to cater for and to evaluate is the degree to which any committed relationship may actually inhibit one or both partners from realising their full potential in some respects. [p.9]

Infidelity at this point may wound the partner: it can be destructive of trust and relationships – not just between the two partners, but in social networks and wider society ... Yet to leave a failing relationship can be a creative move towards allowing oneself to discover in another relationship new experiences and a new phase of growth. [p.10]

Exclusivity is seen as potentially restrictive of, even harmful to, personal growth and development.

It seems to be axiomatic that from the individual's point of view respect for the communal norms of sexual behaviour will always be in tension not only with the realities of the human condition, but also with the radical gospel challenge to remain open to a possible call to 'forsake all' to follow the Way. The role of the individual conscience comes to the fore. Here we encounter the ethical value of personal growth and creativity, the commitment to risk change in allowing one's personal identity to expand and develop. This can lead to relational failure or conflict, where one partner grows beyond the capacity of the relationship to sustain further intimacy and growth. [pp.9-10]

The suggestion is made that the Christian gospel challenge may be to move beyond exclusivity.

Thus while it is clear to us as LGBTs when we survey the gay scene, and indeed much of contemporary social life, that casual sex can often be addictive and destructive, we think it is important to remain open to the possibility that brief and loving sexual engagement between mature adults in special circumstances can be occasions of grace. Risky, but then as Paul Tillich said, 'A Christian is safest taking risks!' [p.11]

'Brief and loving' sexual encounters can be a means of grace.

The exploration of our sexual selves can be something which benefits from involvement with more than one person. Sexual involvement does not necessarily involve any greater psychic risk to a person than does emotional involvement (though the two are deeply intertwined). [p.11]

Our sexual lives may be enriched by having sex with more than one person.

Ethical sexual relations should involve: – [Among other considerations] Respect for the integrity of self and others, i.e. free consent to sex; no *serious physical hurt or harm*; understand and use of safe sex. [p.14, italics mine]

BDSM (bondage, domination, sadomasochism), or other rough forms of sex, is no bad thing, provided there is no serious physical pain or damage.[7]

So much for the 'mirror-image' of marriage! What we are dealing with here is simply light years removed from it. Now, we have blue-sky thinking on serial relationships, concessionary infidelity legitimated by the therapeutic, even Christian, imperative for self-actualization and 'personal growth' (what a boon for all those trapped in boring, dead-end marriages, or even those who just need a little 'on the side'!); and 'brief and loving sexual engagement between mature adults in special circumstances' as 'occasions of grace'. Just how brief, one mentally queries? In addition, we are warned against inflicting *'serious physical hurt or harm'* [italics mine] upon a partner. (And in fact, BDSM is enjoying unprecedented popularity in 'alternative sexuality' spheres.[8])

Hmmm. More than a dozen Church of England VIPs, the Archbishop of Mexico and the Primus of the Scottish Episcopalian Church are publicly known as CA patrons; they are in sympathy with, and endorse the views of, CA. One wonders whether they are aware of the exact nature of these views. Moreover, if these are *Christian* sexual ethics, which the document clearly claims they are, what would non-Christian ones look like?

But let me return to the issue of exclusivity. Some relationships well may be exclusive, as in Jeffrey John's eloquently-written *'Permanent, Faithful, Stable'* (1993/2000).[9] Dr John spends considerable time challenging '"difficult" conservative' opponents on the right – no surprise there – and also – and this is even more telling, on the left.[10] His more radical conversation partners are none other than Elizabeth Stuart and, to a lesser extent, Michael Vasey, both of whom he considers 'the two best known Christian gay writers in Britain in recent years' [p.32]. Marcella Althaus-Reid, a theologian at the Edinburgh School of Divinity, takes Ms

---

[7] http://www.changingattitude.org.uk/publications/PDF/booklets/Sexual-Ethics.pdf
[8] BDSM is sympathetically written-up in Wikipedia and elicits much cyberspace interest, with 91,403,777 entries under 'BDSM' alone (18 June 2007).
[9] Jeffrey John, *'Permanent, Faithful, Stable': Christian Same-Sex Partnerships* (1993/2000), p. 32.
[10] John, op. cit. p. 47.

Stuart's argument to new and far more subversive 'transgressive' levels in her highly acclaimed *Indecent Theology* (2000) and *The Queer God* (2003).[11] Apart from the obviously pornographic terminus, where will this end? Though it is hard to say, it is indubitable that the notion of mandatory exclusivity in lesbian and gay relationships is being neither bought nor sold by leading LGBT advocacy – except Dr John and probably CT.

A poll commissioned in 2006 by the prestigious gay US magazine, *Advocate*, of just under 3,000 lesbian and gay people found that only 45.5% '*currently*' in a relationship' [italics mine] ticked the 'completely monogamous' box. Moreover, it is important to note that the 'completely monogamous' category represents the status of the present relationship, and fails to take into account the person's past or future. In broader terms, the survey asked for numbers of *different* [italics mine] same-sex partners had over a lifetime. 5.6% ticked the 'none' (number of sexual partners) box; 6.7%, the 1 box; 20.2%, 2-5; 12.7%, 6-10; 12.2%, 11-20; 14.4%, 21-50; 9.9%, 51-100; 9.6%, 101-300; and 8.4%, 300+. 82.0% claimed they would like to marry or were already married. Also, the editors positively noted the 'adventurous histories' many of their readers reported: over half claimed a same-sex encounter with three or more people. Interestingly enough, also, though 41.7% had never had sex with a person of the opposite sex, the remainder had. Of the total number, 19.4% ticked the 1 box; 26.7%, 2-5; 6.0%, 6-10; while the rest were much smaller in number. [12]

Though these statistics may seem a little high, they are not incongruent with one of CA's ideological tenets, that one's sexual self can be developed through sexual connections with other people. And in fact, the notion that sexual development occurs in this manner surfaces not infrequently in LGBT literature. As the UK gay men's health charity, the GMFA, explains, 'Generally we're not taught how to be a fantastic lover, but the more sex you have – the more you learn.'[13]

This is not the end of the matter, however. According to Evan

---

[11] From Marcella Althaus-Reid's, *Indecent Theology* (2000), back cover: 'All theology is sexual theology. Indecent theology is sexier than most. What can sexual stories from fetishism and sadomasochism tell us about our relationship with God, Jesus and Mary?' A great deal, apparently, much of it couched in soft – or not so soft – pornographic terms. Paul Tillich's SM predilection 'for photographs of crucified young naked women' (pp. 88-89) was news to me, as well.

[12] http://www.advocate.com/2006.com/2006_sex_survey_results_02.asp; also *The Advocate*, 15 August 2006, p.66.

[13] http://www.gmfa.org.uk/sex/bettersex/index

Wolfson of Freedom to Marry (an organization which campaigns for gay marriage in the US), the gay community differentiates between 'monogamy' and 'exclusivity'.[14] The former refers to emotional fidelity while the latter describes sexual behaviour. So, in fact, the claim that 45.5% of those interviewed were 'completely monogamous' may mean completely *emotionally* monogamous. As the *Advocate* did not specify, it is difficult to be certain.

Finally, in terms of the American gay marriage scene, it is important to listen to the voice of the 'conservative' gay RC pundit, Andrew Sullivan, 'arguably the nation's most visible proponent of gay marriage' (David Blankenhorn).[15] Though Mr Sullivan is known for his more traditional cultural views, he is no exclusivist, as can be seen from last year's blog entry (May 2006) describing a public discussion on sexuality in New York City.

> For me the interesting point came when Dan [Savage] and I agreed that moderate hypocrisy – especially in marriages – is often the best policy. Momogamy [sic] is very hard for men, straight or gay, and if one partner falters occasionally (and I don't mean regularly), sometimes discretion is perfectly acceptable ... An acceptance of mild hypocrisy as essential social and marital glue is not a revolutionary statement. It's a post-revolutionary one.[16]

Perhaps Jeffrey John is unaware of this new development in Andrew Sullivan's thought. According to Dr John, who published a second edition of his book '*Permanent, Faithful, Stable*', in 2000, Andrew Sullivan is 'one of the most intellectually substantial of contemporary gay writers' who 'argues powerfully for gay – and straight – monogamy on psychological, social and political grounds'.[17] Mr John would have had to be defining monogamy in terms of exclusivity in order for his moral argument to make sense and have any force or credibility. So what changed, other than Mr Sullivan's defection from the exclusive camp, because he realized that exclusivity placed too great a demand upon male sexuality? The real loser here, of course, is Jeffrey John's adherence to an iconic exclusivity for gay marriage.

---

[14] David Blankenhorn, *The Future of Marriage* (2007), p. 149.
[15] Blankenhorn, op. cit. p. 161.
[16] Andrew Sullivan, 'Two Generations', 31 May 2006;
http://andrewsullivan.theatlantic.com/the_daily_dish/2006/week22/index.html
[17] John, op. cit., p. 3.

James Parker was, until recently, the ministry coordinator of Living Waters, in London, having spent a number of years in the gay scene himself. He has invested heavily in the lives of those who are trying to exit this realm, and says that he is aware of two gay couples – possibly – who are sexually exclusive. Otherwise, the gay couples he has known over the years have all, at some time of other, had 'sex friends' on the side. The Revd Mario Bergner, founder of Redeemed Lives in the US, confirms this view; he has never met a gay couple who have remained each other's exclusive sexual partner. All the gay couples he knew when in the gay lifestyle (even those who had been together for decades), and in the 23 years since he came out of homosexuality, have had an agreement for 'sex-buddies' outside the gay partnership.

But there is even more going on here. Of course, the really significant, almost iconic, figure whose moment has finally arrived is the bisexual, the woman or man who connects emotionally and sexually with members of both sexes, sometimes sequentially, at other times simultaneously. In the General Synod debate, it was fascinating to notice what was left unspoken. CA specifically includes members of the bisexual community: but where was the bisexual voice on Gay Wednesday? And of course, what happens to the binary principle when bisexuals 'come out'? Even more recessive are the self-identified 'polys'– the polyamorists, literally, those of 'many loves' who are ethical, intentionally non-monogamists. Outside the church, they are beginning to make their presence felt in the UK. Poly relationships – which are committed, non-sexually promiscuous (theoretically) – can be bi, straight or gay: the material point is that two won't do. As one reads poly narrative, the structural role of bisexuality, especially female bisexuality, frequently comes to the fore. Will polys be encouraged to share their experiences of being disempowered, silenced and marginalized by the binary majority?

'Polyamory Uk' on Microsoft's own search engine provides 20,000 entries. Recently the *Sunday Times* wrote up a fairly positive interview with poly people.[18] According to Victoria Gill's 'I got you, you, you, you and you, babe' (04 March 2007), there are over 5,000 UK poly practitioners. One poly activist moderates on-line poly communities with 1,000 members. As with lesbians and gays, you probably know poly people – though you are not aware of it. Further advanced in the US, poly activists are working hard for government recognition of their – and other – types of

---

[18] http://polyamoryonline.org/smf/index.php?board=27;topic=1322.0#msg7328

'alternative' lifestyles, though conservative views still maintain a cultural and legal hegemony for the moment. A milestone was reached last summer with the publication of *beyondmarriage.org*, a social justice manifesto signed by over 300 leading North American LGBT activists, academics, artists and their supporters and allies. For them, 'The struggle for same-sex marriage rights is only one part of a larger effort to strengthen the security and stability of diverse households and families. LGBT communities have ample reason to recognize that families and relationships know no borders and will never slot narrowly into a single existing template.'[19] How expansive are these borders? Well, they specifically include 'households in which there is more than one conjugal partner'.[20]

Gay pain? Unquestionably there, alas. Exclusivity in gay relationships? Far less certain. In the long run, where will this socio-sexual revolution terminate? Even now it is leading to the public demand for greater choice, freedom and fluidity – the cultural and now, increasingly, the legal, affirmation of various types of 'relationships' and family structures, aided in no small part by advanced reproductive techniques. It is also leading to increased public awareness, acceptance and practice of a plethora of alternative 'sex style' practices also emerging from the closet: ('"vanilla" (boring "old fashioned" sex) is fine but have you tried ...?').[21] And in the process, what has happened to exclusivity in marriage, and even to marriage itself? David Blankenhorn argues that if the present trajectory continues, marriage will be significantly weakened, marginalized, privatized and deinstitutionalized – with the real losers, the real victims, being the children. However, as many view marriage as inherently patriarchal, oppressive and dyadic, its demise can not happen a moment too soon.[22] For those of us concerned about the future welfare of marriage, and of children, the outlook is increasingly bleak.

---

[19] http://beyondmarriage.org/full_statement.html
[20] http://beyondmarriage.org/
[21] Althaus-Reid, op. cit. pp. 87-89, also pp. 51-57.
[22] Blankenhorn, op. cit. pp. 127-169.

Lisa Severine Nolland's doctoral dissertation (University of Bristol) has recently been published as *A Victorian Feminist Christian: Josephine Butler, the Prostitutes and God* (Paternoster) and she currently works as a lay chaplain. She has taught in North America and the UK at primary, secondary and tertiary levels and is website consultant for Anglican Mainstream.net. She lives in Bristol with her husband, John, their teenage daughter, Elisabeth and, until his death, a beautiful Golden Retriever, Shem – and is step-mother to David, whose mother died when he was seven. For more than twenty years she and John have been connected with Trinity College, Bristol, where John is Vice Principal. To help her cope with 2008, she regularly escapes into the realms of the English historical and literary past, *Just William*, architecture and botany. Her claim to fame is that of being related to a *Titanic* steerage survivor, Oscar Hedman, her irascible great-uncle, ironically known as Uncle Happy.

See also

'Same-Sex Unions: Personal experience, social convention and scriptural witness' by Revd Dr Will Strange;
http://www.churchinwales.org.uk/theologywales/samesexunions.html

16. Unexpected Consequences: The Sexualisation of Youth

Dr Lisa Severine Nolland

> 'We believe everything is OK
> As long as you don't hurt anyone
> To the best of your definition of hurt,
> And to the best of your knowledge ...
> We believe that taboos are taboo'[1]

Various factors are presently contributing to the sexualisation of older prepubescent children and youth: hedonism, secularism, materialism, the erosion of socially conservative values, the breakdown of the family, and the fact that there is money, vast amounts of it, to be made from sexually aware and/or active kids – think the whole 'body beautiful' cult, the fashion, media and music 'cults', and the burgeoning sexual 'health' industry.

At the moment, government youth enterprises (educational establishments, groups and organizations) increasingly see their *raison d'être* in terms of preparing kids to meet the challenges of life. Of course, sex is a part of life, so kids need to know about sex. According to the experts of the Family Planning Association (UK), 'Sexual health means enjoying the sexual activity *you want* without causing yourself or anyone else suffering or physical or mental harm.'[2] In fact, the nomenclature has been vital; sex 'education', though sounding thoroughly respectable, has proved to be the perfect Trojan Horse for implementing and legitimizing a massive social engineering project, that of sexually liberating the ignorant, inhibited and repressed youth of today.

Prior to the heightened awareness of LGBT lifestyles ('sex' styles), kids were taught about 'vanilla' (bog standard, old fashioned, binary) sex and practised unrolling condoms on carrots. Prior to that they learned the basics of the body's anatomy and physiology, where babies came from and not a great deal more. However, as Dylan's 1960s hit reminds us, 'The times, they are a changin''. Now it is assumed that kids will be sexually

---

[1] Steve Turner, 'Creed', excerpt;
http://www.apuritansmind.com/Apologetics/SteveTurnerCreed.htm
[2] Italics mine; http://www.fpa.org.uk/guide/index.htm

active and consequently in need of 'information', which is presented in terms of 'how-to-do-it' tips about sexual practices that their parents have never even heard of, never mind experimented with or become proficient at.

Let's start with the curriculum in schools. I begin with the easy-to-read, popular British publication, *Key Stage Four PSHE* (2001), for 14-16 year olds – and for the record, having sex under 16 is still illegal in this country, though there is increasing pressure to lower the age of consent (AOC) in the West. Pedophiles – though they reject this term as pejorative – in the Netherlands and child rights advocates in Canada both sponsor this agenda, as does the leading British gay rights campaigner, Peter Tatchell, who argues for the AOC to be lowered to 14.[3] Potential new legislation in Northern Ireland would drop it even further, to 13, if there was no more than a three year hiatus between partners.[4] However, back to this book: though there are some very good qualities inherent in it, some insidiously bad ones exist as well. I will quote from its pages, even though its breezy tone and 'value-free' approach may be offensive. In fact, the book is not value-free at all; it is underpinned by a very strong set of moralistic values, which just happen to be trendy, radically-individualistic, PC ones.

As a lead-in to the first quote, the author actively discourages what s/he considers to be 'early' sex. I believe this means for those under 13: we read that having sex with a girl under 13 is something society 'really doesn't like'. S/he goes on to warn those between 13 and 16 that having sex is risky: one might end up in trouble with the law. Underlining is in the original.

<u>Waiting is Usually Worth It</u>

A lot of people who have sex <u>early</u> can really <u>regret</u> it. Not being <u>ready</u> for your first time makes it <u>rubbish</u>. It's <u>not</u> worth having sex if you aren't going to <u>enjoy</u> it.

---

[3] Given all the sexually active lesbian and gay kids under 16, Peter claims it is 'more realistic ... and much fairer' for the AOC to be 14: http://www.petertatchell.net:80/. For an eye-opening account of gay life in the fast lane, see 'I'm 14, I'm Gay & I want a Boyfriend'. 'Lee', a young gay teen, had his initial sex experience – at 8 – with 8 year-old John, anal sex at 11 and graduated to having sex with men at the age of 12;
http://www/petertatchell.net/age%20of%20consent/14%20gay%20boyfriend.htm.
According to the recent poll (2006) done by the prestigious US gay periodical, *The Advocate*, of almost 3,000 readers, in answer to the question, 'At what age did you have your first same-sex sexual experience?', 16.66% answered 'Before the age of 12'. 18.58% ticked the 12-14 box and 16.05% ticked the 15-17 box;
http://www.advocate.com/2006_sex_survey_results.asp
[4] http://www.christian.org.uk/pressreleases/2006/october_10_2006.htm

...

<u>Oh My---They do...That?</u>

There's no accounting for taste. People's <u>likes</u> and <u>dislikes</u> in sex are <u>varied</u>. Not <u>everyone</u> likes oral sex. Not <u>everyone</u> likes ham and cheese sarnies, either. A lot of people are <u>really grossed out</u> by the idea of <u>anal sex</u>. Some people like it, and here's a reason why: men have a gland called the <u>prostate</u>, near the rectum. If they're on the receiving end of anal sex, this gland is stimulated, causing <u>sexual pleasure</u>. Some <u>women</u> enjoy it too.

Decisions to engage in sexual activity are solely the youngster's. Advice is given on handling the disapproval of parents: 'It's <u>natural</u> that your <u>parents</u> will feel, at the least, a bit "<u>icky</u>" about the idea of you having sex. But it is <u>up to you</u>'. Kids are informed that the wisest way to have oral sex is 'to use a condom on a man, and clingfilm on a woman'. From the workbook, kids are questioned about how they should avoid getting diseases from oral sex, what should always happen if they opt for anal sex, and ideas for getting 'sexy' with another individual without having full penetrative sex (yet).[5]

The websites available to kids – even that of the trusted BBC – are even more sexually graphic, and though there may be helpful, common-sense information there, it will be cheek by jowl to what is essentially soft porn. For example,

http://www.bbc.co.uk/slink/sexlovelife/index.shtml?page=body –
BBC's Slink – under the entry, Oral Sex, shows a photo of a cute brunette holding a large peeled banana up to her open mouth. Kids are informed of the protocol, etiquette and procedures: 'you're up close and personal with each other's genitals – seeing, smelling and tasting them at the same time'; 'it's one of the most intimate things you can do with someone'; 'it's normal to feel vulnerable, especially with someone new'; and 'have a wash beforehand'. Kids find out about fingering and masturbation, and are encouraged only to have sex when they feel ready, and not because of peer pressure. Gay-identified kids are given lots of helpful information as well. And,

http://www.ruthinking.co.uk/about_sex/glossary/index.aspx – RU Thinking About It? – is even more explicit. Kids can learn about dildoes

---

[5] *Key Stage Four PSHE*, (Coordination Group Publications, Ltd, 2001): *The Study Guide*, pp. 4-8; *The Workbook*, p. 7.

and using a dental dam as well as definitions of 'licking out', 'doggy styles' and 'rimming' ('a person uses their mouth and tongue to stimulate or pleasure another person's anus'). There is a warning about catching hepatitis and 'serious gut infections' from rimming, to give slight pause.

Local authorities are also encouraging such explicit approaches. In sexual terms, it is all Blue Sky Thinking. In *Taking Sex Seriously* (for kids 11+), 'Sexual Activities: What do people actually do?', the sexual menu is a positive cornucopia, inclusive of sex toys; SM – pain, and BD – 'tying up'; simultaneous, multiple partners; partner exchanges; 'kissing/licking' clitorises, penises, bottoms, ears, body parts (in general); fingering, anal sex and of course, just boring old 'vanilla'. According to its authors, 'Some examples of sexual activities are given below. You may need to give a few examples to get the group thinking on the right lines.'[6] Brighton & Hove and East Sussex County Council 'strongly recommended' this curriculum in 2000; Croydon Council recommended it in 2003, as did Hampshire County Council from 1995-2003 and the Metropolitan Borough of Wirral in 2003.[7] Evidently, its Blue Sky Thinking was too 'blue', and the less controversial content from *Taking Sex Seriously* has become incorporated into *Safe and Sound* which abbreviated it and placed it within a 'Safer Sex' context. Jettisoned from the listing was any mention of sex toys, SMBD, and plural partnerships, among other things.[8] Richmond-upon-Thames Council asked kids to 'think of three sexy things you can do with fruit without any risk of infection or pregnancy' – and, for your information, bananas did not count. An Avon Health Promotion Service video (2001) encouraged kids to explore their sexuality from a bi-friendly vantage point: 'Try experimenting with other boys and girls and see who you feel most comfortable with'.[9]

And more recently, the government has recommended Michael Willhoite's *Daddy's Roommate* for primary schools and Paul Magrs' *Strange Boy* for secondary schools. The former normalizes gay family structure for little children, while the latter validates (very) young gay sexuality through its positive description of the liaison of two boys – aged 10

---

[6] Julian Cohen and Pam Wilson, *Taking sex seriously: practical sex education activities for young people* (Healthwise, 1995), p. 31.
[7] *Sex lessons for kids* (The Christian Institute, 2003), p. 6
[8] Julian Cohen, *Safe and Sound: 11-16 Sex and Relationships (SRE) Education Pack* (Healthwise, 2004), p. 101.
[9] *Sex lessons for kids* (The Christian Institute, 2003).

and 14.[10]   The insidious process of the sexualisation of younger kids is evident here – so much for age of consent concerns!

This phenomenon, of course, has received considerable media approval in North America through the recent groundbreaking Canadian film, *Breakfast with Scot*. Scot, 'a budding queen [slang for effeminate homosexual] of an 11-year old', turns the lives of a 'straight' gay couple upside down, and in so doing, endears himself to all and stimulates fresh thinking on issues of gender, self-acceptance, social conformity and family structure. That the prestigious Toronto Maple Leafs have associated themselves with the film – one of the gay men is a former Leafs player while the other is the lawyer for the team – is of equal significance; this is the first time a major sports team has provided such high-profile endorsement.[11]

The critical point here is that sex is now divorced from life-long commitment, marriage, family, babies and generational ties. Indeed, it actually has been divorced from love and 'relationships' in the process as well: the latter are good but so is enjoying a great orgasm in countless hitherto unthought-of modes. Developing the personal identity of kids has come to mean developing their sexual identity – gay, bi or straight – and sexual identity has come to mean having sex – gay, bi or straight – with the goal of having great sex. This approach is understood and advanced by the LGBT community. The Christian gay organization, Changing Attitude, described how people's sexual selves are developed through relating sexually with more than one person.[12]   According to the UK gay men's health charity, the GMFA, 'Generally we're not taught how to be a fantastic lover, but the more sex you have – the more you learn.'[13] Echoes of *Taking Sex Seriously* can be heard – and here too there is a lot one can learn!

The GMFA's sexual smorgasbord includes (and I use their terms) fisting, fucking, oral sex, rimming, wanking, sex toys and watersports (the erotic use of urine). If one applies a Venn diagram technique, there would be a not insignificant overlap between the recreational activities and techniques in the 'educational' *Taking Sex Seriously* and the GMFA's

[10] Ibid. See Paul Magrs, *Strange Boy* (2003).
[11] 'Inside Out Toronto Lesbian and Gay Film and Video Festival', May 17-27, 2007; http://www.insideout.on.ca/17Annual/programme_details.cfm?program_id=10
[12] Andrew Henderson, ed., *Sexual Ethics*, (2004), p. 11; http://www.changingattitude.org.uk/publications/PDF/booklets/Sexual-Ethics.pdf;
[13] http://www.gmfa.org.uk/sex/bettersex/index

offerings.[14] The impressive US website, GayHealth.com, provides information on a similar plethora of gay sexual activity: oral and anal sex, toys and fisting, water sports, rimming and scat (the erotic use of faeces).[15] Some readers may wonder about the background of this website, especially given the final item in the list, but in fact GayHealth.com appears quite respectable and mainstream. 'Staffed by professionals from within our own community', it claims to be 'the first health and wellness site dedicated to Lesbian, Gay, Bisexual and Transgender men and women'. It aims to offer 'accurate, current and vital health information' within a context of strong personal identification with and care for its LGBT readership. Though some might feel its content is beyond the pale, such practices obviously score sexually for many. The gay advocates Marshall Kirk and Hunter Madsen render them more psychologically comprehensible, if any of my readers want additional information.[16]

I have worked with kids for over 30 years now, both in North America and in the UK. It is my impression that youth culture is more explicitly, actively, aggressively sexual than it used to be. Though there is still lots of 'just-talk', there is also more 'not-just-talk-but-doing-it'. I have checked this out with others who work with kids and they agree. This phenomenon is showing up among 13-14 years olds, even; what used to be the terrain of the middle-teen is now creeping up to those in year 9, say. It is also becoming a more public phenomenon. Oral sex – girls giving boys 'blow jobs' – seems quite popular and also easy to do in semi-public places. The girl just covers her head with a coat, unzips his trousers and nuzzles in the boy's lap. She can write off her reputation as she heads into the fast lane, but for her it is worth it. She won't be with any one boy for long – or so kids tell me.

Church or religious kids are not immune, either, though they might hold out longer, or place more emphasis upon the uniqueness of their 'relationship', by which they hope to legitimize their sexual activity. Alcohol, of course, plays a huge role here in lowering levels of resistance. Condoms are believed to be almost 100% effective across the board – or so I

---

[14] Compare http://www.tht.org.uk/informationresources/publications/ gaymengerneralinformation/bottomlinethirdedition124.pdf, Terrence Higgins Trust (2006) material which describes in detail fisting, rimming, scat, fingering, sex toys and various positions for sex.
[15] http://www.gayhealth.com/templates/sex/how/index.html
[16] Marshall Kirk and Hunter Madsen, *After the Ball: How America Will Conquer Its Fear and Hatred of Gays in the '90s* (Doubleday, 1989), pp. 302-12.

am told. As long as they slip on a condom before things get 'out of hand', young people assume that they will be 'safe'. There is no awareness that condoms, even when used successfully, do not protect one from all STDs.

I recently attended a sexual health clinic and did a little study on the posters pinned up around the waiting room. One proclaimed that it was okay not to be sexually active while the other eight or nine described how to do 'it' safely. This general sentiment is replicated on the websites mentioned above: it was quite acceptable not to be sexually active, but all the emphasis, interest, attention and airtime was given to those who were.

In conclusion, what is presently occurring in our post-modern, post-Christian society is an unequivocal advocacy of alternative practices and sexualities, with the only proviso that things be 'safe and consensual'. The target audience is not the adults, who are far too inhibited and 'Victorian', busy and tired, for 'all that'. Rather, it is their offspring, who are often more open-minded and adventurous, and who have the libido, time and energy and possibly the inclination. Even more critically, they have been conditioned to think that as long as no one gets 'hurt', what is the problem?

Lisa Severine Nolland's doctoral dissertation (University of Bristol) has recently been published as *A Victorian Feminist Christian: Josephine Butler, the Prostitutes and God* (Paternoster) and she currently works as a lay chaplain. She has taught in North America and the UK at primary, secondary and tertiary levels and is website consultant for Anglican Mainstream.net. She lives in Bristol with her husband, John, their teenage daughter, Elisabeth and, until his death, a beautiful Golden Retriever, Shem – and is step-mother to David, whose mother died when he was seven. For more than twenty years she and John have been connected with Trinity College, Bristol, where John is Vice Principal. To help her cope with 2008, she regularly escapes into the realms of the English historical and literary past, *Just William*, architecture and botany. Her claim to fame is that of being related to a *Titanic* steerage survivor, Oscar Hedman, her irascible great-uncle, ironically known as Uncle Happy.

See also

'But What do I Say?' by Dr J. Budziszewski;
    http://catholiceducation.org/articles/homosexuality/ho0035.html
'The truth about same-sex attractions' by Dr Warren Throckmorton;
    http://catholiceducation.org/articles/homosexuality/ho0077.html

Epilogue

The General Synod debates in February 2007 and these responses have only covered the central issues of this discussion. Far more evidence is relevant and available on the following six related topics which are covered below.

Why present this material? Many of us would much prefer to know nothing about it. The point is that a warning must be given: the ideas presented in the following appendices will soon be in circulation in everyday life. They are 'just around the corner'; they are 'coming down the street', as one might say in America. Please contact us (via the publisher) if, after reading these appendices, you would like to discuss issues arising from this material.[1]

Warning: Some of this material is explicit in the extreme. If you find male sexually graphic images offensive, upsetting, or a source of sexual temptation, please don't look. (Lisa Nolland).

---

[1] All, or almost all, of the websites mentioned in this book were accessed in November or December 2007. If you have difficulty in accessing any of the material, please contact me. (LSN)

Appendix 1: Gay health, sex and culture

John R. Diggs, Jr., 'The Health Risks of Gay Sex', 2002;
http://www.corporateresourcecouncil.org/white_papers/Health_Risks.pdf

Five major distinctions between gay and heterosexual relationships: levels of promiscuity, physical and mental health, life span and monogamy.

A. Dean Byrd, 'The American Journal of Public Health Highlights Risks of Homosexual Practices', updated 20 April 2006;
http://narth.com/docs/risks.html, which includes a powerful exposé of the sex guru, Alfred Kinsey.

From the 'leading' UK gay men's health site, the GMFA;
http://www.gmfa.org.uk/aboutgmfa/index

Entries under 'fisting, frottage, fucking, kissing, oral sex, rimming, sex toys, wanking, watersports'; http://www.gmfa.org.uk/sex/howriskyis/index

'Generally we're not taught how to be a fantastic lover, but the more sex you have – the more you learn. At GMFA we get the chance to talk to lots of gay men about the things that can make for great sex and we've gathered some of their best advice here, as well as some tips that help keep the sex you have safe. We've also taken the time to really learn about how the arse works and how you can increase your pleasure and reduce your pain when you're getting fucked. We can guarantee that the section on your arse will teach you things that they never taught you in sex education at school. We know that not everybody is going to like the same thing, but whether you've just come out or you've been around the block a few times, we hope that there will be something here that you can use. The more confident you are in sexual situations, the easier it is for you to stay in control of the sex you're having'; http://www.gmfa.org.uk/sex/bettersex/index

See also Terrence Higgins Trust's highly informative
http://www.tht.org.uk/informationresources/publications/gaymengernerali
nformation/bottomlinethirdedition124.pdf. This publication uses plastic male dolls to 'show and tell'; all sorts of gay sexual matters are visually depicted [warning: graphic imagery].

From the US Gay and Lesbian Medical Association (GLMA), 'the world's largest and oldest association of lesbian, gay, bisexual and transgender (GLBT) health care professionals':
http://www.glma.org/index.cfm?fuseaction=Page.viewPage&pageId=532

Ten Things Gay Men Should Discuss with Their Health Care Providers: HIV/AIDS; Safe Sex; Substance Use; Depression/Anxiety; Hepatitis Immunization; STDs; Prostate, Testicular, and Colon Cancer; Alcohol; Tobacco; Fitness (Diet and Exercise), and Anal Papilloma;
http://www.glma.org/index.cfm?fuseaction=Page.viewPage&pageID=690

From US GayHealth.com, the 'first health and wellness site dedicated to Lesbian, Gay, Bisexual and Transgender men and women [and] staffed by professionals from within our own community':
http://www.gayhealth.com/templates/aboutus/index.html

'Facts you should know about our favorite recreational activity'; Entries are as follows: Oral Sex and Using a Condom (MSM – men who have sex with men); Water Sports (erotic use of urine), Toys and Fisting, and Anal Sex for both MSM and lesbians; Oral Sex (lesbians); Scat (erotic use of human faeces) and Rimming (the tongue stimulates the area around and inside the anus) for both MSM and lesbians;
http://www.gayhealth.com/templates/sex/how/index.html

For one of the most illuminating sets of Q&A on Anal Sex (I counted 150 or so entries) see
http://www.gayhealth.com/templates/sex/faq/index.html?record=123

Robert Hogg *et al,* 'HIV infection and risk behaviours among young gay and bisexual men in Vancouver', *Canadian Medical Association Journal,* 162 (1), 11 January 2000.

Esther Addley, 'Let's Talk About Sex', *The Guardian,* 17 February 2007;
http://www.guardian.co.uk/gayrights/story/0,,2015220,00.html
http://gaydar.com/90.0.html [warning: extremely graphic imagery]

Stephen Fry, 'HIV and Me', BBC 2, 2 October 2007; includes the notoriously 'unsafe' practices of British youth: Manchester's Dr Ed Wilkins' comment about anonymous sauna/bathhouse sex (one of his patients admitted having 200 partners in one weekend), and Mark Thomas' description of an HIV negative 19 year-old who wished to receive 'The Gift' (HIV) and so had sex with five HIV positive lads – 'Gift Givers' – who then inserted a 'butt plug' to ensure that the HIV-infected semen would not seep out. Stephen Fry was horrified by both the 'active weekend' and 'The Gift'/'Gift Givers' accounts.

http://www.pinknews.co.uk/news/articles/2005-5608.html gives a rather censored account of the programme.

For more see 'Last rites for the man who chose Aids', *Daily Telegraph*, 15 January 2006;
http://www.telegraph.co.uk/opinion/main.jhtml?xml=/opinion/2006/01/15/do1507.xml

'Bug Chasers: The men who long to be HIV+', *Rolling Stone*, 23 January 2003; http://www.rollingstone.com/news/story/5933610/bug_chasers

'The Gift', 31 January 2003;
http://www.annoy.com/features/doc.html?DocumentID=100454   gives both sides of the 'The Gift' debate.

And finally, the wildly successful BDSM Folsom Street Fair which is heavily sponsored and supported by members of the LGBT community, and which is in the process of exporting itself to London and elsewhere around the globe;

http://en.wikipedia.org/wiki/Folsom_Street_Fair

http://www.pinknews.co.uk/news/articles/2005-5622.html

http://www.catholic.org/adv/catholicleague/folsom1.php [warning: graphic imagery]

http://zombietime.com/folsom_sf_2007_part_1/index.php [warning: extremely graphic imagery]

Appendix 2: Why children need mothers and fathers

'Who is not necessary to raise a child, the father or the mother?'
Jordan Lorence (American Author)

'Dr. Byrd Provides Testimony In English Court Case Regarding Same-Sex Adoption', 2007; http://www.narth.com/docs/byrdtestimony.pdf

> The gender-specific and gender-complementary contributions of mothers and fathers to their children's development.

> The various methodological limitations and flaws in the major studies on gay parenting.

'The Revolution in Parenthood: The Emerging Global Clash Between Adult Rights and Children's Needs: An International Appeal from the Commission on Parenthood's Future' by Elizabeth Marquardt, Principal Investigator, 2006;
http://www.marriagedebate.com/reg/pdf_download.php

> The significant body of evidence which demonstrates that children do better when they are raised by the parents who made them and love them, and love each other, and why.

> The increasingly intrusive role of government in issues of reproduction, parenting and family.

> The perspectives of the first generation of children whose father is 'donor'.

'Do Mothers and Fathers Matter? The Social Science Evidence on Marriage and Child Well-Being' by Maggie Gallagher and Joshua K. Baker, iMAPP, 2004; http://www.marriagedebate.com/pdf/MothersFathersMatter.pdf

> The problematic apples-and-oranges methodology and, in particular, how 'the vast majority of these studies compare single lesbian mothers to single heterosexual mothers' (p. 3).

'Top 10 Social Scientific Arguments Against Same Sex Marriage (SSM)', 2006; http://saveelca.blogspot.com/2006/05/top-10-social-scientific-arguments.html

> The needs of children both to know and to be known by the two people who created them; good summary.

'Changing marriage, regardless of why we do it, changes marriage for *everyone*. In particular, it changes parenthood for everyone. When Canada, by way of implementing same-sex marriage, erased the concept of natural parent from basic Canadian law, there was no asterisk saying "for gay and lesbian couples only." The idea of the natural parent got wiped out in law for every child and every couple in Canada. Changing a public meaning is a collective event; the meaning changes for everyone. If the child's current right to her two natural parents goes down completely, as the proponents of the new rights claim insist that it must, then that right as a societal promise will no longer pertain to any child. When a change of this sort takes place, we as a society seldom feel an immediate impact. It's not like an earthquake, but more like the imperceptible shifting of the earth's tectonic plates. Our foundations change, as deviancy is defined down. The movement is slow, but powerful and ultimately determinative.' David Blakenhorn, *The Future of Marriage* (Encounter 2007), pp. 198-199.

Appendix 3: How can my civil partnership[1] possibly damage marriage, yours or anyone else's?

In his reply to this question, Charles (Chuck) Colson describes a plausible ideological dynamic that could be created by same-sex marriage (SSM), and which would have a negative impact upon everyone's marriage. The following is from 'Why Not Gay Marriage?', published in the magazine *Christianity Today*, 28 October 1996, with slight reordering of the material.

According to Chuck, SSM 'will exert enormous pressure throughout society to move from the Complementarity to the Choice model [or worldview] ... [In relation to the latter] marriage is [seen as] a human invention. And if people believe marriage is just an invention, then they will feel free to change it, redefine it, or even discard it. Family structure is as pliable as Play-Doh, and virtually any form is acceptable.' He then predicted that people would have less commitment to marriage as an institution and that children especially would suffer.

Charles Colson's grim forecast – written over a decade ago now – has proved to be correct. David Blankenhorn, a lifelong Democrat and 'essentially ... a liberal', demonstrates how support for traditional marriage is significantly weaker in countries which now enjoy the benefits of SSM. Blankenhorn deploys data from two recent massive surveys, the 2002 International Social Survey Programme and the 1999-2001 World Views Survey, to argue that SSM is yet one more nail in the coffin of the traditional family, along with increasing rates of non-marital heterosexual cohabitation, intentional single motherhood, divorce and so forth.[2][3] And most crucially, those with the greatest vulnerability and the most to lose are not the already-formed, this-works-just-fine-for-me adults, but the children, who have little if any choice in the matter.

The results from this World Values Survey are remarkably similar to those from the International Social Survey Programme. The

---

[1] In the UK; in Scandinavia, the Netherlands, Canada and South Africa the term is same-sex marriage (SSM)

[2] David Blankenhorn, *The Future of Marriage* (Spence, 2007), p. 2.

[3] David Blankenhorn describes marriage as 'society's most pro-child institution', in 'Defining Marriage Down ... *is no way to save it*', *Weekly Standard*, 2 April 2007;
http://www.weeklystandard.com/Content/Public/Articles/000/000/013/451noxve.asp.
Above all else children need and desire 'the mother and the father who together made the child, who love the child, and who love each other' (Blankenhorn, *Future*, p. 3).

weakest support for marriage as an institution is in those countries with same-sex marriage. Countries with same-sex civil unions [e.g. the UK] show more support, and countries with only regional recognition [i.e. the USA and Australia] show still more support. By significant margins, the most support for marriage is in countries without same-sex unions. These correlations do not prove that gay marriage causes marriage to get weaker. I am not trying to prove causation.[4] I am only trying to prove correlation. But correlation is important   Correlation shows that certain things tend naturally to cluster together... We know that any one [factor] increases exposure to the others.   It's the same with marriage. A rise in unwed childbearing and a decline in the belief that people who want to have children should get married. High divorce rates and less belief in marital permanence. The embrace of gay marriage and of the belief that marriage itself is a personal private relationship. The acceptance of collaborative reproduction and of the casual effacing of the child's double origin. *These things go together.*[5]

How else will SSM harm marriage? I argue below that public gay culture is even now damaging marriage, through its successful re-working of what the concept of personal commitment in a partnership actually entails. In particular, the meaning of commitment is being broadened out to include the acceptance of a partnered individual having sex with others, while

---

[4] Stanley Kurtz has done some interesting work in terms of SSM/family dissolution issues in Scandinavia and the Netherlands (the first country to have full SSM) and deploys theories of causation. See for example, 'Here Come the Brides: Plural marriage is waiting in the wings', *Weekly Standard,* 26 December 2005;

http://www.weeklystandard.com/Content/Public/Articles/000/000/006/494pqobc.asp
'Standing Out: The sharp increase of non-marital births in the Netherlands needs some explaining', *National Review,* 23 February 2006;

http://article.nationalreview.com/?q=ODcyNzgxNGNkMzEwMDZhNmQzYzhjZDU4MDcw
OWRmODA=
'No Nordic Bliss: There's no refuting the claim that same-sex partnerships harm marriage', *National Review,* 28 February 2006;

http://article.nationalreview.com/?q=NmNlNWYxNmZjMjVjNjEzYjdhODAwYmFiYTUwM
WQyMTM=
'Smoking Gun: The Netherlands shows the effect of same-sex marriage', *National Review,* 2 June 2006;

http://article.nationalreview.com/?q=MDFhMjkoYjI4NzgyZGM4NjMxZmY4NTQwZWNjY
zkzYjg=
[5] Blankenhorn, *Future,* excerpt from pp. 231-233. See also Blankenhorn, 'Defining Marriage Down'.

remaining happily, solidly, 'commitedly' within the relational dyad (or duo). In fact, verbal engineering has managed to shift the technical definition of monogamy – previously, it meant 'sex-with-only-one' – to its present definition of emotional 'commitment-to-one'.[6] Yesterday's monogamy has been re-invented and sold as today's exclusivity, but as many heterosexuals do not keep up with the evolution of the terminology, they work with outdated definitions and reach correspondingly inaccurate conclusions.

With same-sex (SS) couples, each couple must decide what will work best for them: monogamy, exclusivity or something in-between, even as they present their relationship to the world as a 'loving committed stable partnership' – which, for them, is most probably true. This is how they experience their partnership. However, the rest of us assume 'exclusive' when we hear 'loving, committed and stable' – and now even 'monogamous' – hence the catch. I realise that alarm bells will be ringing wildly for those who keep assuring the world that the partnered SS couples they know are as devoted and 'married' to each other as any heterosexual couple, perhaps more so. Fair enough! However, in terms of broader gay sexual norms, culture and political agendas, gay partnerships fall under a different rubric. Why do I make such a claim? My evidence is as follows.

I listen to those who analyze gay phenomena, and advance the gay cause, in the West and around the world, and I study the research and surveys. This information I correlate with broader movements and developments within Western culture. I will begin with the influential British sociologist, Anthony Giddens, whose seminal work on the sex revolution is congruent with what is encountered on a regular basis in the culture, with the odd surprise here and there. For Anthony, the sexual revolution of the past few decades in the West has not been fundamentally about sexual promiscuity – and yes, that was news to me too. Rather, its engine has been fuelled, first of all, by the liberation of female libido and sexuality (largely thanks to birth control) and secondly, and more to our purposes, 'the flourishing of homosexuality, male and female. Homosexuals of both sexes have staked out new sexual ground well in advance of the more sexually "orthodox"'.[7] Later, Anthony proceeds to explain how, 'since marriage "in the traditional sense" is disappearing, it is the gays who are pioneers [in doing relationships] ... – the prime everyday experimenters. They have for some while experienced what is becoming

[6] Blankenhorn, *Future*, pp. 149-150.
[7] Anthony Giddens, *The Transformation of Intimacy* (Polity, 1992), p. 28.

more and more commonplace for heterosexual couples'.[8] The latter could learn a thing or two from the former about 'pure relationships' ('a relationship of sexual and emotional equality') and 'plastic sexuality' ('decentred sexuality, freed from the needs of reproduction', inclusive of various sexual tastes and practices hitherto labelled and tabooed as 'pathology' and/or 'perversion').[9] Though many 'straights' have further to go on the pathology/ perversion fronts – they are making progress there too, though (see below) – the working concepts of the 'pure relationship' and 'plastic sexuality' are now prevalent in the collective psyche, value systems and lifestyle options of heterosexuals as well.

Anthony describes gay men's relationships as markedly non-exclusive. With equanimity he describes various studies of gay men who have literally hundreds of partners (plus a live-in one at home!), while even among the lesbians interviewed, relationships are by no means necessarily exclusive (two-thirds were exclusive, according to one of his primary studies).[10] He is able to give non-addictive 'impersonal, fleeting contacts' and 'episodic gay sexuality' a positive press because of their capacity to detach sex from 'differential power' (i.e. rigid forms of oppressive traditional-gendered sexuality), a supreme value which seems to trump every other moral, social or religious consideration.[11]

Gay marriage's most eloquent spokesman, Andrew Sullivan, echoes aspects of Anthony Giddens' thought here, though he comes from a more conservative ideological stable. In *Gay Wednesday's Gay Pain (GWGP)* above, I have quoted Andrew as saying that he feels no moral obligation to the concept of exclusivity for either gay or straight married men, though sexual 'lapses' are to be seen more as natural by-products – *c'est la vie!* - than anticipated, desired results. For Andrew, exclusivity 'is very hard for men, straight or gay, and if one partner falters occasionally (and I don't mean regularly), sometimes discretion is perfectly acceptable'.[12] It would

---

[8] Giddens, *Transformation*, p. 135, see also p. 15.

[9] Giddens, *Transformation*, pp. 2, 13-16, 32-34, 134-147. He describes how certain forms of BDSM, bathhouse and other types of sexual exchange could be enlisted to liberate heterosexual couples stuck in cul-de-sacs of rigid, hierarchical tradition.

[10] Giddens, *Transformation*, pp. 14-15, 140-148. The social value of the committed partnership has increased since Civil Partnerships etc. and thus one could expect to find less promiscuity, though this must be balanced against contra-indicators like the wildly successful gay get-a-sex-date site, Gaydar. See the survey materials below for current statistics.

[11] Giddens, *Transformation*, p. 147.

[12] Andrew Sullivan, 'Two Generations', 31 May 2006;

seem we have turned the hands of the clock back to the time of the Victorians! In *Virtually Normal*, Andrew promotes a more sexually-open relational dynamic:

> There is more likely to be greater understanding of the need for extramarital outlets between two men than between a man and a woman .... Something of the gay relationship's necessary honesty, its flexibility, and its equality could undoubtedly help strengthen and inform many heterosexual bonds .... There is something baleful about the attempt of some gay conservatives to educate homosexuals and lesbians into an uncritical acceptance of a stifling model of heterosexual normality.[13]

Well, it appears that Andrew need not have worried. Various indicators reveal that a corporate exclusive norm until death (or divorce or even separation)-us-do-part is nowhere on the gay radar.

In *GWGP* I quote the fairly alarming statistics from the very recent (2006) Advocate survey of almost 3,000 people on sexual lifestyles and practice in the US gay community, even more interesting because of the editor's comment about the survey results revealing 'surprisingly conservative values'.[14] A few years earlier, a massive survey of the inaugural (2000-2001) same-sex couples joined in civil unions indicate that, at least for the men involved, sexual non-exclusivity was deemed 'inappropriate' by only fifty per cent – and these are the 'newly-weds'![15] The fascinating study by Gretchen Stiers, *From this Day Forward: Commitment, Marriage, and Family in Lesbian and Gay Relationships* (2000), concedes a far lower figure for committed-for-life lesbian and gay couples.[16]

---

http://andrewsullivan.theatlantic.com/the_daily_dish/2006/week22/index.html

[13] Andrew Sullivan, *Virtually Normal* (Picador, orig. pub. 1995), pp. 202-203.

[14] http://www.advocate.com/2006_sex_survey_results.asp

[15] 'Look to Vermont for Civil Union History, Statistics'; 2004; http://www.newswise.com/articles/view/503346/

[16] Gretchen Stiers, *From this Day Forward: Commitment, Marriage, and Family in Lesbian and Gay Relationships* (Palgrave MacMillan, 2000), p. 50. In answering a questionnaire on 'Meanings of Commitment', 32% of lesbians and 10% of gay men ticked the 'Exclusivity/monogamy' box (other options were: Permanence, Working on problems, Personal growth (under Beliefs) and Buying a house, Living together and Raising children, (under Investments)). During the discussion of this questionnaire, these embarrassing statistics were given a miss. Gretchen later adds that 'when respondents for this book were asked in their interviews what type of agreement they had with their partners concerning sex outside their relationship', another set of much higher, more respectable statistics emerged. 92% of the women and 81% of the men had 'agreed to be monogamous or assumed the

In what is one of the world's largest surveys ever carried out among GLBTI (I is for 'intersex') people in Australia ('Private Lives: A report on the health and wellbeing of GLBTI Australians', 2006), almost 5,500 individuals between the ages of 16 and 92 were interviewed on matters ranging from pets, discrimination, home ownership, education and BMI (body mass index) to commitment, marriage and optimal frequency of sex. Interestingly, few interviewees desired to formalize their relationship (5% of the males and 10% of the females ticked the box marked 'interest in a commitment ceremony'), while even more interesting was the complete absence of questions about total numbers of 'relationships' and sexual partners.[17] Why this glaring omission? I imagine PC censorship has something to do with it. We were told, however, that 37% of the men had known their most recent sexual partner for less than 24 hours before having sex with him; that 80+% of men and 55+% of women had had sex with someone they had met on the internet; that sex at least daily was the right frequency for a quarter of all respondents, and that over three quarters of the women had enjoyed an orgasm in their most recent lesbian tryst.[18] If nothing else, sex is crucial!

In 2003 the gay sociologist, Barry Adam, from the University of Windsor, Canada, described the results of a limited study in terms of open sexual relationships being the norm, rather than the exception. 'Three-quarters of Canadian gay men in relationships lasting longer than one year are not monogamous' (exclusive). Moreover, the ones who were exclusive tended to be younger and from a Latino or Asian background, with an emphasis upon romance. According to Barry,

> One of the reasons I think younger men tend to start with the vision of monogamy is because they are coming with a heterosexual script in their head and are applying it to relationships with men ... What they don't see is that the gay community has their [sic] own order and own ways that seem to work better.[19]

---

relationship was monogamous' (p. 53). You can almost hear her sigh of relief. What cannot be doubted is that, in theory at least, exclusivity is not only not a high priority, but rather, a very modest one.

[17] http://www.latrobe.edu.au/arcshs/assets/downloads/reports/private_lives_report.pdf; pp. 26-27, 44-47.

[18] http://www.latrobe.edu.au/arcshs/assets/downloads/reports/private_lives_report.pdf, pp. 26, 45, 47

[19] http://www.washblade.com/2003/8-22/news/national/nonmonog.cfm

And does this impact heterosexuals, married heterosexuals? According to a 2005 *New Yorker Magazine* article, 'The New Monogamy', it does and this is one of the dynamics involved.

> Many straight couples struggling with these issues look to gay male friends, for whom a more fluid notion of commitment is practically the norm ... 'Talking about my sexual adventures outside my relationship shocks my straight friends, then titillates them,' says William. 'Until finally they recognize the permanence of my relationship and begin to reinterpret it all as healthy and evolved.' Exhibit A is William's married friend Nick, who took notice and took action. 'Being a spectator of Will's easy-come-easy-go escapades, though recognizably self-destructive at times, inspired me to bring some casual lust to a vagina not belonging to my wife,' he explains over e-mail. He was able to finagle a swinging episode with another couple. 'I can't say that my wife and I would never try it again. Her getting off turns me on.'[20]

Type in Swinging, Polyamoury and BDSM (Bondage, Domination, Sadism, Masochism) to Google and there are literally millions of entries. Alternative sexuality/ies for all – equal opportunities, you know! – is a growth industry, no doubt of it. Of course the LGBT community cannot be blamed (or, for some, commended) for the entirety of this phenomenally successful sexual liberation project. However, as Anthony Giddens reminds us, our lesbians and gays blazed the trail; they showed the rest of us how it could be done by doing it themselves and doing so unapologetically and openly in the public sphere.[21] And where they have gone, culture has followed – as have many of us as individuals, as networks and sub-groups within communities and regions, and now as churches and denominations.

One other aspect in relation to SSM in the US needs to be noted. Many of those advocating SSM in the public arena are unequivocally hostile

---

[20]http://nymag.com/lifestyle/sex/annual/2005/15063/

[21]A close connection between BDSM and local public figures and active members of the LGBT community can be seen at, say, the recent 'leather' S&M Folsom Street Fair, the largest event of its kind in the world which welcomed 400,000 (according to its official website) from around the globe on 30 September 2007.
http://www.folsomstreetfair.org/fair-faq.php
http://en.wikipedia.org/wiki/Folsom_Street_Fair;
http://www.pinknews.co.uk/news/articles/2005-5622.html
http://www.catholic.org/adv/catholicleague/folsom1.php (warning: graphic images)
http://zombietime.com/folsom_sf_2007_part_1/index.php (warning: graphic in the extreme)

to notions of marital exclusivity. For David Blankenhorn, 'People who professionally dislike marriage almost always favour gay marriage ... Ideas that have long been used to attack marriage are now commonly used to support same-sex marriage.'[22] One of many gay advocates whose views are presented in David's book is Yale University's Jonathan Katz, who claims that SSM could topple 'one of the pillars of heterosexual marriage, and perhaps its key source of trauma', sexual exclusivity – and really, for Jonathan, the sooner the better.[23] This view of marriage as archaic, oppressive, indeed positively foul, is reiterated by leading gay rights activists and academics who are agitating to promote SSM in the US.[24]

The culmination of SSM, of course, could be seen in the beyondmarriage.org manifesto, 2006, which has been signed by over 300 US political and cultural elites and their allies (and in a brief search, I found that half a dozen SSM advocates/marriage revolutionizers from David Blankenhorn's chapter on the topic crop up here too). This manifesto has resonances of a Brave New World, with its insistence on the social and legal legitimacy of, and justice due to, various modes of relationship, kinship and family life, including 'households in which there is more than one conjugal partner'.[25] Though he did not sign the document, Evan Wolfson, founder and executive director of the powerful Freedom to Marry (for SS couples), admitted that 'ninety percent of what's in that document could have been signed onto by virtually every person working in the gay movement today'.[26] Elsewhere Evan has described SSM as 'conservatively subversive'.[27]

A fascinating peek into the fissures which exist in the SSM/beyond marriage/LGBT communities and their allies, in terms of the all-important issues of strategy and timing, is found in Stanley Kurtz's commentary on the beyondmarriage.org statement. When will the real agenda be owned

---

[22] Blankenhorn, *Future*, p. 128.
[23] Jonathan Katz, as quoted by Blankenhorn, *Future*, p. 149.
[24] Blankenhorn, *Future*, pp. 127-169; for a broader sociological view which includes Europe see Stanley Kurtz, 'Zombie Killers: A.K.A., "Queering the Social"', *National Review,* 25 May 2006; http://article.nationalreview.com/?q=MTU4NDEzNTY5ODNmOWU4M2YiMGIw MTcyODdjZGQxOTk=
[25] http://beyondmarriage.org/
[26] Evan Wolfson as quoted by Stanley Kurtz, 'The Confession II: "Conservative" proponents of same-sex marriage are about to [be] overtaken by radicals', *National Review,* 1 November 2006; http://article.nationalreview.com/?q=MmRhNTdlNDNkOGQxOGFhNDE3ODdlOGI4ODU5 ZDljOGE=. The link to Evan's quotation which Stanley provided was not working the various times I tried to link directly.
[27] Blakenhorn, *Future*, p. 136.

publicly, be able to come out and take its place in the civil realm? Indeed, when will family radicals stop being perceived as 'skunks at a garden party'? Stanley writes,

> Take Michael Bronski, a radical academic, popular New England columnist, and long-time proponent of same-sex marriage. Bronski favors same-sex marriage for its potential to destabilize the traditional organizing principles of Western culture. In a piece explaining why he'd signed the Beyond Gay Marriage manifesto, Bronski said that he and his fellow family radicals were tired of being treated like 'skunks at a garden party' for honestly owning up to their radical reasons for supporting gay marriage. Bronski then told the story of a radio appearance in which his conservative opponent had claimed that gay marriage would 'change society as we know it.' Instead of denying it, Bronski agreed with this family traditionalist that gay marriage would indeed provoke a broader cultural transformation, adding that this was a good thing. 'That afternoon,' Bronski recalled, 'I received a barrage of e-mails from marriage equality supporters complaining that I had committed a major faux pas and should not do media on the issue of marriage again unless I was willing to state the "official" marriage equality line, which is that gay marriage is about nothing more than equal rights for couples who love one another.'[28]

SSM as a vehicle by which 'traditional' marriage is buttressed, affirmed, valued, bequeathed to the next generation? I think not.

One final comment on the impact of SSM on heterosexual marriage. Stanley Kurtz wrote the following a few years ago now, and, as with Charles Colson's article, it has proved prophetic. And I predict that as SMM as a cultural and legal phenomenon reaches to hitherto untouched parts of the globe, we will have even greater cause to be worried. 'Change happens', as a recent television advertisement claims. And yet so often we are behind the times and the last to figure it out. In terms of, say, the less controversial but still profoundly disturbing phenomena of soaring rates of divorce and of illegitimacy (which now, of course, is described and experienced according

---

[28] Stanley Kurtz, 'The Confession: Have same-sex-marriage advocates said too much?', *National Review*, 31 October 2006; http://article.nationalreview.com/?q=ZDY4Y2U4MGJkO DRlZTFhNj k2MjZhZTZlMGMyNmUzZWE=

to the 'kinder', less pejorative 'single motherhood'), change *has* happened, and that on an immense scale over our lifetime – yet for many of us the penny has *still* not properly dropped. We have not realised what has actually been diminished, lost, or forfeited, in terms of social norms. It is the old tale of how to boil a frog with her consent. Or, if we do realise, we believe that we and those we love will be immune from its noxious impact – that though such tarnished thinking might corrode others' worlds, we are safe. As Stanley observes, social norms do not operate like that. No-one is exempt: ultimately this will get at us all, if not now then within the next decade or so. This is why some continue the fight.

> The libertarian [who wishes to get the state out of matters of consensual adult sex] asks, *Just because two married gay men live next door, is that going to make me leave my wife?* In a way, the answer is 'Yes.' For one thing, as a new generation grows up exposed to gay couples who openly define their marriages in non-monogamous [exclusive] terms, the concept of marriage itself will gradually change. No doubt, movies and television in a post-gay-marriage world will be filled with stories of the 'cutting edge' understandings of open marriage being pioneered by the new gay couples, even if the actual number of such married gay couples is relatively small.

Then Stanley describes the dynamic which we have already noted in David Blankenhorn's research, that SSM advocates are pressing for SSM because they feel that marriage as we now know it is a *bête noire*, irredeemably flawed (and so forth) and that SSM could prove its salvation. Plural marriage – presently being advocated in cutting-edge Canadian academic and government circuits – will destroy the concept of dyadic exclusivity in marriage.[29]

> Still, the libertarian asks, *Would the group marriage next door really make me leave my wife?* Maybe not. Of course, the married commune next door might invite the two of you over for some fun, with potentially problematic results for your marriage. But even that is not the real problem. The deeper difficulty is simply the breaking of the taboo on adultery ...

> So the mere social statement that marriage does not mean

---

[29] Stanley Kurtz, 'Dissolving Marriage: If everything is marriage, then nothing is', *National Review*, 3 February, 2006; http://article.nationalreview.com/?q=YTVjMzA5NzNkZmUoYW MxMjQ4NDk1YjFkZGQ4YjQ5NzQ=

monogamy [exclusivity] is where the real danger of legalized gay-marriage and polyamory lie. And the collapse of consensus about shared social institutions really does affect us as individuals. *Once we as a society no longer take it for granted that marriage means monogamy, you may not decide to leave your wife. But you may be more likely to give in to the temptation of an affair. And that could mean the end of your marriage, whether that's what you wanted going into the affair or not* [italics mine] ...

As with the taboos on incest and sodomy, society can't enforce the taboo on adultery with laws. Laws on matters of sexual conduct do make a difference, but less as enforcement mechanisms than as embodiments of common values. Precisely because the state cannot monitor and prosecute adultery, society writes a taboo against the practice into our hearts. The laws of marriage as currently constituted embody and express that taboo. Transform those laws, and the taboo will disappear.[30]

[30] Stanley Kurtz, 'The Libertarian Question: Incest, homosexuality, and adultery', *National Review*, 30 April 2003; http://www.nationalreview.com/kurtz/kurtz043003.asp

Appendix 4: Culture War Casualties

A free society is one where it is safe to be unpopular.

Adlai Stevenson

It is seldom that liberty of any kind is lost all at once.

David Hume

Evil people exploit good people by persuading them that it is wrong to call evil by its name.

James Hitchcock, *Touchstone*, April 2006.

There will never be a problem if one keeps clear of where the problem is.

John Nolland

As man forgets God, the noose on the neck of mankind grows tighter.

Alexander Solzenitsyn

Soft 'coercion' produces no martyrs to disturb anyone's conscience, yet it is highly effective in chilling the speech of ordinary people.

Maggie Gallagher, 'Banned in Boston: The coming conflict between same-sex marriage and religious liberty', 15 May 2006;
http://www.weeklystandard.com/Content/Public/Articles/000/000/012/191kgwg h.asp

It is now no longer enough for the apostate to be able to live undisturbed according to his convictions, as he calls them; to him there is no well-being and no peace as long as his convictions have not become the only ones recognized as right and valid.

Samuel Silver, 'Some of My Best Friends are Gay', *Toward Tradition*, 'A Guide to Same-Sex Marriage From the Manufacturer's Instruction Manual', 19 April 2004;
http://www.intellectualconservative.com/article3337.html

They do not want to ban hatred. They want to ban dissent. Freedom of speech, if it means anything at all, must include freedom to offend.

UK Black Church Leader, 2007, quoted by Don Horrocks, Evangelical Alliance, House of Commons General Committee, Criminal Justice and Immigration Bill, 18 October 2007.

People who favour gay rights face no penalty for speaking their views, but can inflict a risk of litigation, investigation, and formal and informal career penalties on others whose views they dislike. Meanwhile, people who think gay marriage is wrong cannot know for sure where the line is now, or where it will be redrawn in the future.

Maggie Gallagher, 'Banned in Boston'.

Many other teachers I know don't like what's being put forward for the schools either. The difference is, these teachers are afraid to speak up [while Chris Kempling is not].

J. Fraser Field (Catholic Educator's Resource Centre). 'Chris Kempling and the BCCT', 2003; http://catholiceducation.org/articles/education/ed0167.html

We should also consider the fact that in just over one generation we have been shifted from a society in which homosexual acts were a crime under the then existing law, to a society in which homosexual acts have become a government-protected and fostered activity, while voicing criticism of it 'publicly' has become the crime.

Michael D. O'Brien, 'Same-Sex "Marriage", "Hate Crimes," and the New Totalitarianism', 28 February 2005; http://www.lifesite.net/ldn/2005/feb/050228a.html

Those who torment us for our own good will torment us without end for they do so with the approval of their own conscience.

CS Lewis

[Totalitarianism]: What [the tyrant] really means by the word 'unity' is uniformity, sameness. He cannot remain content with a pacified populace, because there always lurks beneath the surface of even the passive a potential for dissent, the threat of revolt against his power. Thus the pacified must be re-educated, so that at the core of their thinking no virus of resistance remains ... More difficult to identify is the idealistic tyrant who expands his power in a sincere effort to protect what he considers to be the good of his subjects ... Of course, he will find that basic human nature is rather difficult to remold, and as time goes on he will need to continuously expand his power until his control approaches the level of totality ... [However, many concede that] somebody at last is doing something about the human condition! ... Why shouldn't a 'dysfunctional' people entrust itself to its sociopolitical physicians? Somewhere during the therapy there is a decisive transfer of power and responsibility. In some cases there may even be no visible dictator, only a system or a social philosophy which permeates and controls everything ... The philosopher Josef Pieper points out that this is the most dangerous form of totalitarianism of all, almost impossible to throw off, because it never appears to be what, in fact, it is.

Michael D. O'Brien, 'Same-Sex "Marriage" ... and the New Totalitarianism'.

Those on the Left regard themselves as seeking the betterment of humanity (and I would not question the sincerity of their intention). But they also regard themselves as best-equipped to decide what a better humanity should look like. Thus, in seeking to improve the rest of us, they must, necessarily, take away our freedom. And they do it with good intentions. One often hears (particularly from the religious Left) the quote from Queen Elizabeth I, 'I have no wish to make windows into men's souls.' Yet windows into our souls are precisely what the Left must make if they are to redeem humanity.

John Richardson, 'Why we should hate "hate crime"', 26 November 2007;
http://ugleyvicar.blogspot.com/2007/11/why-we-should-hate-hate-crime.html

in tyranny's domain/ you are the link in the chain, / you stink of him through and through,/ the tyranny IS you; ... because where tyranny obtains/ everything is vain,/ the song itself though fine/ is false in every line,/ for he stands over you/ at your grave, and tells you who/ you were, your every molecule/ his to dispose and rule.

Gyula Illyés, 'A Sentence About Tyranny', 1950;
http://www.hungarianquarterly.com/no139/p15.html

United Kingdom

Very recent cases include the following:
Andrew McClintock:
'Christian Magistrate Loses Freedom of Conscience Case', 31 October 2007;
    http://www.ccfon.org/latest.php?id=180

Vincent and Pauline Matherick:
'Council Accepts Christian Foster Parents should not be forced to Promote
    Homosexuality', 1 November 2007;
    http://www.ccfon.org/latest.php?id=182

Jonathan Petrie, 'Christian foster parents condemn "gay laws"', 24 October
    2007;
    http://www.telegraph.co.uk/news/main.jhtml?xml=/news/2007/10
    /24/nfoster124.xml

Dr Tammie Downes:
'GP may be struck off for her 'think twice' plea to abortion patients', 11
        November 2007; http://www.dailymail.co.uk/pages/live/articles
        /news/news.html?in_article_id=493009&in_page_id=1770

The Bishop of Hereford:
'Bigot of the Year', Stonewall
                http://news.bbc.co.uk/1/hi/wales/6904057.stm
                http://www.herefordtimes.com/mostpopular.var.1807436.0
                .stonewall_names_bishop_of_hereford_as_bigot_of_the_year.php?s
                =s

And in the past, there have the alarming situations of Harry Hammond, Stephen Green, Lynette Burrows, Brian Herbert, the Bishop of Chester, the Archbishop of Glasgow and Joe and Helen Roberts.
See http://www.christian.org.uk/rel_liberties/cases/index.htm

The ante has been upped in relation to the Civil Partnership legislation up in Scotland's Western Isles. 'The Council says it will fulfill its legal obligations to register partnerships, but will not be offering additional wedding-like ceremonies (which are not required by law) ... The Council has since received hate mail from around the world as a result of their highly principled decision. Emails included a death threat saying that councillors should be "hanged from the nearest tree".'
http://www.christian.org.uk/rel_liberties/cases/western_isles.htm

North America

The stakes are even higher in other parts of the world. In Canada 'soft coercion' has been slowly extinguishing civil and religious liberties – and oddly, very few have seemed to notice and even fewer have seemed to care. It is far more dangerous to speak up *in public* about the 'red-button' issues (abortion and homosexuality being two of the top ones) and for most people this carries too high a price. This self-censorship pertains especially to engagement with the secular realm, but is also present in a somewhat modified form across the wider Christian sub-culture. Not only is nothing heard from them personally or collectively on these matters, outside the safety of the organization or church (if that), but they keep their distance from the few brave souls who do venture onto the battlefield. Public expressions or acts of solidarity are too costly.

Various psychological, sociological and theological factors coalesce to form this unfortunate response by the leadership of the Christian community, it seems to me. There is denial – at least *my* flock is still relatively intact and 'sound' and we can operate as a church with relative immunity: it is business as usual for now. After all, we are not legally required to do same-sex marriage ceremonies (yet?). Denial is compounded by a notable lack of awareness, an almost blissful ignorance of how bad things actually are 'out there', because accurate soundings of the cultural situation are never taken – minefields are avoided on principle. To denial and ignorance is added what some see as the ultimate priority – 'Preaching the Gospel', with the imperative to stay clear of negative, divisive, often messy political and cultural issues, which some argue are secondary in any case. Who are *we* to judge, after all? We simply live our lives as those who love Jesus and we leave the rest to God. Moreover, we all have different callings, you know. And even if these issues *are* valid and important, there are so many other issues too, and they are far less tangled and explosive, no bad thing. Fear also plays a conscious or subconscious role: who desires the dreadful publicity of nasty lawsuits, or heavy fines? What would happen to our building programme or the organ fund? And finally, given the normal exhausting round of life for many Christian leaders, with members of their flock facing dire personal circumstances of illness, unemployment, family breakdown or death, say and with the various church programmes which must be kept ticking over on a shoestring budget, and with all the internal friction and clash of personality, perspective and priority – who needs additional stress? Because so few are willing to 'go there', it is a far more onerous task for the lone rangers who do – and who then, in the process, often become more assertive and even strident in order to survive. They feel abandoned – even betrayed – by those whom they know share their convictions but who do so on the quiet, and without cost.

At this point, then, it appears that Christians are still busily doing their Christian 'thing' – personally, collectively and denominationally – in their sequestered Christian spheres. Of course, there is some interaction – perhaps a great deal – with the outside PC world, but not in relation to the minefields. Subjects like Two-Thirds World poverty and hunger, the homeless and the elderly, the environment, Christianity and the arts, Christianity and business, our spiritual traditions and journeys etc. are perfectly safe. Stick to them! You won't be hauled before the Human Rights Tribunal.

See Michael D. O'Brien's alarming 'Same-Sex "Marriage"' (from above). A broad overview of the slow dissolution of freedom of speech is found in Fr Alphonse de Valk's 'Canadians' right to speak freely'[1]. For Fr Alphonse, 'The real issue is the right to publicly oppose the homosexual lifestyle in speech and writing, and even the right to not want to be involved in promoting this lifestyle – in business, schools, and as owners or employees of companies of any size.' And then he gives a lengthy casualty list of Christian people and organizations punished because they did not support gay rights at work, in their unions, businesses or educational establishments (even private Christian schools are not immune). See also Dr Chris Kempling's 'Religious Freedom in Canada' (below). As Maggie Gallagher ('Banned in Boston') rightly perceives, first the state determines what certain types of religious people can and cannot do out in the public square; then the state determines what can happen on the border where the church and state interface – in the plethora of organizations which bridge between the two (i.e. Christian schools, camps, adoption agencies, local community groups, etc.). What comes next, you ask? The state will be determining what can and cannot be said and done in the sanctuary, of course. The privacy of the home will then be targeted; the individual conscience is the final stronghold.

In terms of leaders, the RC Bishop of Calgary, Alberta, Bishop Fred Henry and Dr Chris Kempling (British Columbia) are two of its bravest martyrs. Bishop Henry has been threatened by the Alberta Human Rights Tribunal and the Canadian tax department.[2]

Dr Kempling has been disciplined – formally reprimanded and suspended from his teaching position – for having the audacity to write letters to the editor and make contributions to his local newspaper in Quesnel, BC, and for giving interviews on the national CBC in his own time. The former related to his beliefs and views of homosexuality and some of the related scholarship, and the latter concerned the dynamics of reparative therapy. There had been no complaints from the public prior to this point. At one point he was driving a dump truck simply to support himself. Legal fees have been astronomical. In order to be professionally reinstated he would need to recant publicly. (*Déjà vu!*) The most recent news I could locate of Dr Kempling was that he is taking his case to the United Nations Commission on Human Rights. In relation to this he was

---

[1] Fr Alphonse de Valk: 'Canadians' right to speak freely', 24 October 2006; http://catholicinsight.com/online/editorials/printer_685.shtml
[2] For the latest on Bishop Henry see http://www.rcdiocese-calgary.ab.ca/ ; also http://catholicanada.com/web/index.php?option=com_content&task=view&id=476&Itemid=91

asked to speak at the United Nations.[3]

In the United States, one of the most recent culture war casualties relates to the African Americans, Regina Rederford and Robin Christy, who set up the Good News Employee Association. They have been threatened with dismissal by the city of Oakland CA, for placing the following sentence in the public work domain: 'Marriage is the foundation of the natural family and sustains family values.' 'Happy Coming Out Day' was legitimate, as was gay-straight bashing of the Bible and the N word (n*****), but a flier promoting 'Natural Family, Marriage and Family Values' was not, for it could offend and scare employees. The case is headed for the Supreme Court at this point.[4]

Dr Rob Gagnon has documented appalling cases of individuals humiliated or harassed at their place of employment, or fired, or stripped of their civil rights in their personal lives. It is grim reading! Again, there is never a problem as long as one goes along with the PC party line. The problem only rears its ugly head when one does not promote gay rights in the work or school environment, or even when one simply asks not to be included in those activities. This is a sackable offence! Even more worrying, though, is the almost complete ignorance of such occurrences among devout Christians. Even fairly conservative Christian media outlets just 'don't go there' – or only on the very odd occasion – because of their fear of being tarred by an 'anti-gay' brush. Shuts them up every time!

See what happened to the AT&T employee, Albert Buonanno (2001), the Eastman Kodak employee, Rolf Szabo (2002), Dr Cheryl Clark (2003), the Temple University student, Michael Marcavage (2004), the Hewlett-Packard employee, Richard Peterson (2004), Dr Michael Campion (2006 – present) – and this list is by no means exhaustive.

Perhaps the most extreme narrative that Rob Gagnon presents is the bizarre murder, in 2002, of Mary Stachowicz by Nicholas Gutierrez, who then hid her body in his apartment for two days. We have heard

---

[3] See 'Religious Freedom in Canada', 4 March 2005;
http://catholiceducation.org/articles/persecution/pch0080.html; and also his 'Against the Current: The Cost of Speaking Out for Orientation Change in Canada', 13 June 2005: http://www.narth.com/docs/current.html. Finally, 'Chris Kempling'; http://en.wilkipedia.org/wiki/Chris_Kempling.
[4] George Will, 'When marriage became a "hate crime"', 25 June 2007; http://www.jewishworldreview.com/cols/will062507.php3
Bob Unruh, 'N-word fine, but "family values" banned', 05 June 2007; http://www.worldnetdaily.com/news/article.asp?ARTICLE_ID=56013

endless concern about Matthew Shepard (the gay man tortured and killed by three heterosexuals) – and what happened to poor Matthew is dreadful! But what happened to Mary is equally dreadful. And there has been almost no media coverage of this tragedy.

According to Rod Dreher,[5]

> I reach this conclusion [of media bias] based on the deafening media silence around the savage murder of Mary Stachowicz, the middle-aged Chicago churchgoer allegedly killed by coworker Nicholas Gutierrez, a 19-year-old homosexual who reportedly snapped when the Catholic woman told him he should quit sleeping with men. According to Chicago police, Gutierrez confessed to killing Stachowicz in his apartment after arguing with her about his lifestyle. According to Chicago authorities, Gutierrez confessed that he set upon Stachowicz when she asked – are you ready for this? – "Why do you [have sex with] boys instead of girls?"
> ...
>
> As a state's attorney told the *Chicago Tribune*, "He got upset with her. The defendant punched and kicked and stabbed the victim until he was tired. He then placed a plastic garbage bag over her head and strangled her."

For Rod Dreher, the acts of torture and murder (elicited by what the victims allegedly said to their assailants) of Matthew Shepard and Mary Stachowicz were equally deplorable.

> Both were heinous, and both deserve publicity. Yet the American media made Matthew Shepard an overnight cause célèbre, and have so far said very little about Mary Stachowicz – just as the media said very little about Jesse Dirkhising, the 13-year-old Arkansas boy raped, tortured, and strangled by homosexuals in 1999. Andrew Sullivan, who is probably the most articulate gay-rights advocate in journalism, explained in a 2001 *New Republic* article how stark the media bias was in these cases.

Rod quoted Andrew Sullivan at length.

> In the month after Shepard's murder, Nexis recorded 3,007 stories about his death. In the month after Dirkhising's murder, Nexis

---

[5] Rod Dreher: 'These Victims are People, Too: What hate crimes have wrought', *National Review* 26 November 2002; http://www.nationalreview.com/dreher/dreher112602.asp

recorded 46 stories about his. In all of last year, only one article about Dirkhising appeared in a major mainstream newspaper. The Boston Globe, The New York Times, and the Los Angeles Times ignored the incident completely. In the same period, The New York Times published 45 stories about Shepard, and The Washington Post published 28. The discrepancy isn't just real. It's staggering.

...

What we are seeing, I fear, is a logical consequence of the culture that hate-crimes rhetoric promotes. Some deaths – if they affect a politically protected class – are worth more than others. Other deaths, those that do not fit a politically correct profile, are left to oblivion.

Professor Robert Gagnon's materials:
> http://www.robgagnon.net/articles/homoBalchFalseWitness.pdf, pp. 10-19.

For Dr Michael Campion see 'Smith Decries Minneapolis PD's Suspension of Christian Psychologist Due to Past Ties to IFI'; http://www.christiannewswire.com/news/48309856.html

For Jesse Dirkhising see Michelle Malkin, 'Why is trial involving marathon torture session by gays against a teen being ignored?' 16 March 2001; [warning: explicit] http://www.jewishworldreview.com/michelle/malkin031601.asp

Media absence is noted in relation to other gay-related events as well. See, for instance, the 400,000 (official site statistic) world-renown Folsom Street Fair, September 2007: http://zombietime.com/folsom_sf_2007_part_1/ [warning: very graphic imagery]

Appendix 5: Winning through the media: a strategy that has worked

From After the Ball: *How America Will Conquer Its Fear and Hatred of Gay in the '90s* by Marshall Kirk and Hunter Madsen (NY: Doubleday, 1989).

This volume is a fascinating exploration of the mental workings, views and vision of two classy, well-educated and, in many ways, very sensible, decent gay advocates. They describe fully and frankly what they have encountered over long years in gayland – reader, you are warned! – and complain bitterly about the anonymous public sex, the competition and shallowness, and the emphasis upon youth and physical attractiveness. In its final pages, the authors advance a notion of the gay family based upon their reading of Plato, a suggestion that they realise will elicit much opposition both within and without the gay community. The book is witty and urbane, ranging widely across the sexual terrain of the 90s; it's no wonder it became popular.

But perhaps more importantly, Kirk and Madsen manage to formulate, circulate and 'sell' a sophisticated strategy to 'gay-ize' the US in the 90s which has proved extraordinarily effective, though it was not completed within the time frame. But, what was advocated back then, with questionable hopes for successful implementation, has indeed virtually come to pass in many places, and done so while most of the rest of us were engaged elsewhere.[1]

Kirk and Madsen looked into their crystal ball, so to speak, and, drawing on what they knew, both about the ways straights (their term for heterosexuals) and gays tick psychologically and also about the current cultural milieu, they created a strategy which would advance a moderate, reasonable gay agenda with some chance of success. However, where they reach moments of brilliance relates to their strategy for deploying the media in this initially subterranean social revolution. The straight public is re-conditioned, gradually at first, in the process of this sexual revolution; the trick is to so manage it that no one really 'gets it' until it is too late. All is

---

[1] If Bruce Bawer had not already deployed this metaphor in his aptly-named book *While Europe Slept: How Radical Islam Is Destroying the West From Within* (2006), I could have entitled this review something along the lines of 'While We Slept: How the Radical Gay Agenda is Destroying the West From Within'.

not set adrift, however: certain notions of decency, family and even duty remain constant throughout the volume. But that we are dealing with a social-sexual revolution of first-order magnitude is beyond dispute.

It is interesting to note, though, how significantly gay culture of the past 20 years has evolved. In 1989 our authors warn against the dangers of violence and 'kink' – inclusive of BDSM – and 'fist fucking' (their terms), and firmly oppose their inclusion within mainstream gay culture.[2] Who listened?   Not very many, it would seem.   September 2007's wildly successful BDSM Folsom Street Fair of San Francisco (which is presently being exported to London and elsewhere around the globe) used models for its advertisement from the local LGTB and BDSM communities; moreover, the fair was largely patronized by the same, along with more open-minded 'straights' and others.[3] The authors' censure of 'fist f***ing' has also been ignored.[4]

Though some of Kirk and Madsen's ideas have been more effective than others, I will quote all eight, with excerpted material from each, so that

---

[2] Marshall Kirk and Hunter Madsen, *After the Ball: How America Will Conquer Its Fear and Hatred of Gays in the 90s* (Doubleday, 1989), p. 305.

[3] http://en.wikipedia.org/wiki/Folsom_Street_Fair
http://www.pinknews.co.uk/news/articles/2005-5622.html
http://zombietime.com/folsom_sf_2007_part_1/ [warning: extreme imagery]
Theoretical engagement with and affirmation of BDSM by the gay Christian movement in the US can be found in, say, the recent meetings organized by the Gay Men's Issues in Religion Group at the   prestigious American Academy of Religion's (AAR) 2004 Annual Meeting (Nov. 20-23, San Antonio, TX, USA). The theme was 'Power and Submission, Pain and Pleasure: The Religious Dynamics of Sadomasochism'.   Papers with titles such as 'Ecstatic Communion: The Spiritual Dimensions of Leathersexuality' and '"You Seduced Me, You Overpowered Me, and You Prevailed": Religious Experience and Homoerotic Sadomasochism in Jeremiah' and 'Oh, Daddy! God, Dominance/Submission, and Christian Sacramentality and Spirituality' were presented.
See http://www.robgagnon.net/AARGayMen'sGroup.htm
In the UK, one of the most prominent advocates for this innovative theology is the widely acclaimed Professor Marcella Althaus-Reid of Edinburgh's School of Divinity.   See her *Indecent Theology* (2000) and *The Queer God* (2004), a fascinating/appalling (pick your adjective) mix of liberation and feminist theology with a hefty dose of porn: if nothing else, post-Christianity at its edgiest.

[4] How to do fist f***ing safely and enjoyably is described on the premier gay American site, GayHealth.com (written and run by gay doctors for those in the LGTB community) and the London-based Gay Men's Health Charity, the GMFA, which claims to be 'the UK's leading gay men's health charity';
http://www.gayhealth.com/templates/sex/how/activity.html?record=18
http://www.gmfa.org.uk/sex/howriskyis/fisting
See also http://www.gmfa.org.uk/sex/howriskyis/index

the reader may gain an appreciation for the immensity and breadth of their project. All italics are in the original.

'The Strategy of "Waging Peace": Eight Practical Principles for the Persuasion of Straights', from pp. 172-191:

Don't just express yourself: Communicate!

Communication, then, not self-expression, is the basis of a mass-media campaign. To achieve it, every public message in the campaign should be the direct result of gays having put themselves in the public's binding high-button shoes and asked: If I were straight and felt the hostility most straights feel toward gays, *what would it take to get me to change my antigay feelings?* In other words, don't start by determining what you most ardently wish to tell straights: start by determining what they most *need* to hear from you.

It is crucial to understand and empathize with where the anti-gay Opposition is coming from emotionally so that we can woo and win them over. Remember the adage about walking in another's shoes? It has more than a little truth!

Seek ye not the saved nor the damned: Appeal to the skeptics

Ambivalent Skeptics [the undecided middle] *are our most promising target.* If we can win them over, produce a major realignment solidly in favour of gay rights, the Intransigents [the hard-line anti-gays] (like the racists twenty years ago) will eventually be effectively silenced by both law and polite society. Our Friends, on the other hand, will be emboldened to support our interests more aggressively.

It is most realistic and cost-and-energy effective to target the Undeclared Middle, who are potentially invaluable allies. As they are seen to 'convert', our Friends will be encouraged, energized and empowered. As for the unreachable, implacable Intransigents, damage-limitation is the objective: they need to be isolated, marginalized and muzzled.

Keep talking

The fastest way to convince straights that homosexuality is commonplace is to get a lot of people talking about the subject in a neutral or supportive way. Open, frank talk makes gayness seem less furtive, alien, and sinful: more aboveboard. Constant talk builds the impression that public opinion is at least divided on the subject, and that a sizable bloc– the most modern, up-to-date citizens – accept or even practice homosexuality ... The main thing is to *talk about gayness until the issue becomes thoroughly tiresome* ... In the early stages of the campaign, the public should not be shocked and repelled by premature exposure to homo*sexual* behaviour itself. Instead, the imagery of sex per se should be downplayed, and the issue of gay rights reduced, as far as possible, to an abstract social question.

'Chatting' wins the war, or helps to win this one at any rate. Casual, off-the-cuff discussion which assumes that gay is a given desensitizes, acclimatizes and normalizes the issue and moves people closer to normalization and social acceptance. The more one talks the less emotive and controversial 'gay' seems to be. Keep talking and most people will get thoroughly bored by it before long, concede defeat (if they were not already on our side) and move on to other issues. But be careful to give the actual topic of gay sex a miss.

Keep the Message Focused: You're a homosexual, not a whale

The movement should eagerly ally itself with large, mainstream groups that can actually advance our interests (e.g. the Democratic Party, the National Organization for Women, or the Presbyterian Church). But even then, we should demand to see some major public demonstration of their commitment to our cause before we rush to commit to theirs.

Though there are many sincere fringe groups endeavouring to liberate the oppressed and improve the quality of life for all, keep them at arm's length. Position the struggle for gay rights firmly within the solid, respectable centre, to gather mainstream support and respectability.

Portray gays as victims of circumstance and oppression, not as aggressive challengers

In any campaign to win over the public, gays must be portrayed as victims in need of protection so that straights will be inclined by reflex to adopt the role of protector. If gays present themselves instead, as a strong and arrogant tribe promoting a defiantly non-conformist lifestyle, they are more likely to be seen as a public menace that warrants resistance and oppression. For that reason, we must forego the temptation to strut our gay pride publicly to such an extent that we undermine our victim image ...

The purpose of victim imagery is to make straights feel very uncomfortable: that is, to jam [shut down] with shame the self-righteous pride that would ordinarily accompany and reward their antigay belligerence, and to lay groundwork for the process of conversion by helping straights identify with gays and sympathize with their underdog status ...

An effective media campaign would make use of symbols and spokespersons that reduce the straight majority's sense of threat and induce it to lower its guard ... Persons featured in the media campaign should be wholesome and admirable by straight standards, and completely unexceptional in appearance ...

One could also argue that lesbians should be featured more prominently than gay men in the early stages of the media campaign. Straights generally have fewer and cloudier preconceptions about lesbians and may feel less hostile towards them [since women are generally seen as more vulnerable] ...

The public should be persuaded that gays are *victims of circumstance*, that they no more chose their sexual orientation than they did, say, their height, skin color, talents, or limitations. (We argue that, for all practical purposes, gays should be considered to have been *born gay* – even though sexual orientation, for most humans, seems to be the product of a complex interaction between innate predispositions and environmental factors during childhood and early adolescence) ... Straights must be taught that it is as natural for some persons to be homosexual as it is for others to be heterosexual: wickedness and seduction have nothing to do with it. *And since no choice is involved, gayness can be no more blame worthy than straightness.*

In order to engage positively with straights, we must be seen to be like them. This stimulates identification with and concern and support for us. Lesbian role models are important: as females they are seen as more vulnerable, among other things. The sympathy of straights will be far easier to gain if they are convinced that our gayness is like other heritable traits, hence the importance and utility of the 'born gay' argument. If we are born like this, it is not our fault! And more significantly, they need to see that it could just as well have been them.

Give potential protectors a just cause

Few straight women, and fewer straight men, will be bold enough to defend homosexuality per se. Most would rather attach their awakened protective impulse to some principle of justice or law, some general desire for consistent and fair treatment in society. Thus our campaign should not demand explicit support for homo*sexual* practices, but should instead take *antidiscrimination* as its theme. Fundamental freedoms ... basic fairness and decency toward all of humanity – these should be the concerns brought to mind by our campaign.

We must be seen to be straightforward, sincere and vulnerable in how we present our case, but – again – keep the gay sex out of it. It is not especially agreeable to straight women, and even less so to straight men. Frame the argument in terms of rational, reasonable humanitarian rights, not what actually happens in terms of sex.

Make gays look good

In order to make a Gay Victim sympathetic to straights, you have to portray him as Everyman. But an additional theme of the campaign will be more aggressive and upbeat. To confound bigoted stereotypes and hasten the conversion of straights, strongly favourable images of gays must be set before the public. The campaign should paint gay men and lesbians as *superior* – veritable pillars of society.

Yes, yes, we know, this trick is so old it creaks. Other minorities have used it often ... But the message is vital for all those straights who still picture gays as 'queer' losers ...

By casting its violet spotlight on such revered heroes [Socrates, Alexander the Great, Leonardo da Vinci, Eleanor Roosevelt etc.], in no time a skillful media campaign could have the gay community looking like the veritable fairy godmother to Western civilization.

We have an ancient and honourable cultural heritage to claim in public, and we must begin to do so. We are not as 'good as you' – as some claim is the acronym for G-A-Y – but better, in fact. Just look at how much gays have contributed – and that in an often hostile social context. This tactic is worth a try, at any rate.

Make victimizers look bad

The objective is to make homohating beliefs and actions look so nasty that average Americans will want to dissociate themselves from them. This, of course, is a variant on the process of jamming. We also intend, by this tactic, to make the very expression of homohatred so discreditable that even Intransigents will eventually be silenced in public – much as rabid racists and anti-Semites are today.

The best way to make homohatred look bad is to vilify those who

226

victimize gays. The public should be shown images of ranting homohaters whose associated traits and attitudes appall [sic] and anger Middle America. These images might include:

Klansmen demanding that gays be slaughtered or castrated; hysterical backwoods preachers, drooling with hate to a degree that looks both comical and deranged; ... a tour of Nazi concentration camps where homosexuals were tortured and gassed.

In TV and print, images of victimizers can be combined with those of the gay victims by a method propagandists call the 'bracket technique'. For example, for several seconds an unctuous beady-eyed Southern preacher is shown pounding the pulpit in rage against 'those perverted, abominable creatures.' While his tirade continues over the soundtrack, the picture switches to heart-rending photos of badly beaten persons, or of gays who look decent, harmless, and likable; and then we cut back to the poisonous face of the preacher. The contrast speaks for itself. The effect is devastating.

This is perhaps the most interesting concept of all. It resonates with what I have read elsewhere about why people distance themselves from a previously-held ideology or belief system, which had been proudly and publicly owned and advanced over an entire lifetime. It has been contaminated by, and made repulsive to them, by association with other distasteful traits. These individuals are then left in a fluid limbo land where they are psychologically open to ideological movement and change, or 'conversion', as our authors say.

Appendix 6: Finally

I have met many ex-homosexuals – but I have never met an ex-black.
> Private communication, 2007. Dr Ken Hutcherson, Senior Pastor and Marriage
> Activist (and Black), Antioch Bible Church, Redmond, Washington, USA

But the reality is that since 1994 – for ten years – there has existed solid epidemiologic evidence, now extensively confirmed and reconfirmed, that *the most common natural course for a young person who develops a 'homosexual identity' is for it to spontaneously disappear unless that process is discouraged or interfered with by extraneous factors.* We may now say with increasing confidence that those 'extraneous' factors are primarily the 'social milieu' in which the person finds himself.
> Dr. Jeffrey B. Satinover, 'The "Trojan Couch": How the Mental Health Associations
> Misrepresent Science'; http://narth.com/docs/TheTrojanCouchSatinover.pdf

Let's differentiate between two meanings of the word *natural.* The first ... is 'what we can infer from the design of Creation.' The second is 'anything that occurs in Nature' ... It's ... obvious that penis and vagina are designed to fit together, but they undeniably get used in other ways. Whatever people do with these body parts can be termed 'natural' in that second definition, a label that appears to hallow whatever it touches. But there's a problem. If 'natural' means 'anything that happens', there are absolutely no limits. Anything that anyone can think of doing with his sex organs has to be called natural.
> Frederica Mathewes-Green, 'Bodies of Evidence', June 2005;
> http://touchstonemag.com/archives/articles.php?id=18-05-027-f

Marriage is not just about more intimacy. It is about merging with one's sexual other half or counterpart, a complementary sexual other. Erotic desire for what one is as a sexual being is sexual narcissism or sexual self-deception: an attempt at completing oneself sexually through merger with a sexual same. Most people intuit something developmentally deficient about being erotically attracted to the body parts and essential gender that one shares in common with another.
> Dr Robert A.J. Gagnon, 'How to make a valid secular case against cultural
> endorsement of homosexual behavior', 2004/2006;
> http://www.robgagnon.net/SecularCase.htm

But the Holy Scripture never identifies people according to their sexual attractions (i.e. gay, lesbian, transgender, straight, etc.). The Bible divides people into two groups, male and female (Genesis 1:27) with redemption offered equally to each. Therefore, to subdivide humanity further, such as into the categories of gay, lesbian and transgender, is an extra biblical concept.

The Revd Mario Bergner, Director of *Redeemed Lives*

[The Judeo-Christian revolution] consisted of forcing the sexual genie into the marital bottle. It ensured that sex no longer dominated society, heightened male-female love and sexuality (and thereby almost alone created the possibility of love and eroticism within marriage), and began the arduous task of elevating the status of women ...

Throughout the ancient world, and up to the recent past in many parts of the world, sexuality infused virtually all of society. Human sexuality, especially male sexuality, is polymorphous, or utterly wild (far more so than animal sexuality). Men have had sex with women and with men; with little girls and young boys; with a single partner and in large groups; with total strangers and immediate family members; and with a variety of domesticated animals. They have achieved orgasm with inanimate objects such as leather, shoes, and other pieces of clothing, through urinating and defecating on each other...; by dressing in women's garments; by watching other human beings being tortured; by fondling children of either sex; by listening to a woman's disembodied voice (e.g., 'voice sex'); and, or course, by looking at pictures of bodies or parts of bodies. There is little, animate or inanimate, that has not excited some men to orgasm. Of course, not all of these practices have been condoned by societies ... but many have, and all illustrate what the unchanneled, or in Freudian terms, the 'un-sublimated', sex drive can lead to.

Dennis Prager, 'Judaism's Sexual Revolution: Why Judaism (and then Christianity) Rejected Homosexuality', 1993;
http://catholiceducation.org/articles/homosexuality/h00003.html

As a philosopher the thing that strikes me most is the brilliant strategy of the gay marriage movement. Like Orwell in 1984 it sees that the main battlefield is language. If [gay rights advocates] can redefine a key term like 'marriage' they win. Control language and you control thought; control thought and you control action; control action and you control the world.

Peter Kreeft, *Boston College Observer*, April 2004

Social engineering is always preceded by verbal engineering.

Bill Muehlenberg, 2007;
http://www.billmuehlenberg.com/2007/05/12/motherhood-madness-why-mums-
are-not-really-mums/

Yet since marriage 'in the traditional sense' is disappearing, it is the gays who are the pioneers in this respect – the prime everyday experimenters. They have for some while experienced what is becoming more and more commonplace for heterosexual couples ... From this perspective, even in the shape of impersonal, fleeting contacts, episodic sexuality may be a positive form of everyday experiment. It reveals plastic sexuality for what it (implicitly) is: sex detached from its age-old subservience to differential power. Episodic gay sexuality of the bathhouse culture type thus expresses an equality which is absent from most heterosexual involvements ... By its very nature, it permits power only in the form of sexual practice itself: sexual taste is the sole determinant. This is surely part of the pleasure and fulfilment that episodic sexuality can provide, when shorn of its compulsive characteristics.

Anthony Giddens, *The Transformation of Intimacy* (Polity, 1992), pp. 135, 147.

Let me start by outlining the gay liberationists' vision of society. I suppose that the society to which they aspire is one in which young people, as they grow up, will become aware of a wide variety of life patterns: monogamy – multiple partnerships; partnerships for life – partnerships for a period of mutual growth; same-sex partners – opposite-sex partners – both; chastity; living in community – living in small family units; and so on. A world, furthermore, where each young person becomes aware that each of these life patterns is held in equal esteem in society. So that each will feel free to choose the partner or partners with whom they wish to share their lives.

Malcolm Macourt, ed., *Towards a Theology of Gay Liberation* (SCM, 1977) p.24

Gay and Lesbian Families Are Here; All Our Families Are Queer; Let's Get Used to It!

Judith Stacey, chapter 27, *Sexuality and Gender*, eds C. Williams and A. Stein (Blackwell Readers in Sociology, 2001/2002)

The highest estimate to date [April 2006] of the proportion of gays and lesbians who have married in any jurisdiction where it is available is 16.7% (Massachusetts). More typically, our survey of marriage statistics from various countries that legally recognise same-sex unions suggests that today between 1% and 5% of gays and lesbians have entered into a same-sex marriage. In the Netherlands, which has had same-sex marriage as a legal option for the longest period, between 2% and 6% of gays and lesbians have entered marriages in the first five years.

Maggie Gallagher and Joshua K. Baker, 'Demand for Same-Sex Marriage: Evidence from the United States, Canada, and Europe', iMAPP; Vol. 3, No. 1, 26 April 2006; http://www.marriagedebate.com/reg/pdf_download.php

It is easier to come out of the closet as gay, bi, kinky, even Republican than poly because you're challenging the foundation of everybody's relationships.

George Marvil, PolyLiving spokesperson, 2006; http://metromix.chicagotribune.com/tv/mmx-0602210332rev22,0,13159.story?coll=m

We happily accept that we can love more than one child, parent, sibling ... When you think of it like that, isn't the total exclusiveness that we expect of spousal love positively weird?

Richard Dawkins, January 2007 archives: http://polyinthemedia.blogspot.com

'What is your view of people being allowed to have more than one marital partner at a time?' Responses of the 18-34 yr old cohort: 27% Accept. 'No One Family Arrangement is Ideal': Responses of same: 52% Affirm.

Survey of 2000+ Canadians, the Vanier Institute of the Family; http://www.vifamily/ca/newsroom/press_jan_25_05.html

My life with my wives is wonderful ... Other than the fact that I have two wives (and we all have outside lovers), our lives are pretty normal. And it's our normal, everyday life that convinces others that we are not a threat – slowly, one step at a time. And that seems the only long-term answer to the opposition. Gays and lesbians gained because straight people discovered that many of the 'normal' people they knew around them were homosexual, and otherwise normal, and they became more tolerant as a result.

Black Eagle, 'Understanding Opposition to Polyamory'; http://www.polyamorysociety.org/ Understanding_Opposition_to_Polyamory.html

We are here. We live among you, and have, some of us, for many years. And you have not known us. We are among your close friends and valued parishoners, but there are essential things about who we are that you probably have never known. Unless, of course, you are one of us, yourself.

Harlan White, 'Are We Ready for This?' Unitarian Universalists for Polyamory

Pedophilia 'has all the same characteristics as homosexuality, transvestism, fetishism, etc.,' said Dan Markussen, spokesman for the 100-member [Danish Pedophile] association, which was founded in 1985. 'Sexual orientation is defined as a lifelong attraction, which pedophilia obviously is'. The assertion by pedophiles that their attraction to children is a natural sexual orientation with which they were born has done little to gain them allies. While many may disagree with the pedophiles' claim that they are born with a taste for the young, a leading American doctor on the subject of pedophilia is willing to concede they are half-right. 'I think it can be both a disorder and an orientation,' said Dr. Frederick Berlin, founder of the Sexual Disorders Clinic at Johns Hopkins Hospital in Baltimore. While he believes people who are sexually attracted to children should not feel ashamed of their condition, he also says they should not act on them [sic]. http://www.nj.com/specialprojects/expresstimes/index.ssf?/news/expresstimes/sto ries/molesters1_otherside.html. See also http://everything2.com/index.pl?node=Pedophilia

Information on:

1. *Gay pre-adolescence*:

http://www.imdb.com/title/tt0910847/plotsummary

http://queerbeacon.typepad.com/queer_beacon/2006/11/breakfast_with_.html

Paul Magrs, *Strange Boy* (Simon & Schuster, 2002).

'I'm 14, I'm Gay & I Want a Boyfriend', Lee speaks to Peter Tatchell; http://www.petertatchell.net/age%20of%20consent/14%20gay%20boyfrie nd.htm

2. *Zoos* (those psycho-sexually involved with animals): http://www.time.com/time/arts/article/0,8599,1583009,00.html for review of the highly-acclaimed US documentary, 'Zoo'.

Understanding Bestiality & Zoophilia by Hani Miletski (East-West Pub., 2002), from a doctoral dissertation at the Institute for Advanced Study of Human Sexuality, San Francisco.

3. *Inter-familial sex/incest*: http://www.boston.com/news/globe/editorial_opinion/oped/articles/2007/ 05/02/lawful_incest_may_be_on_its_way/ (father & daughter – US)

http://news.bbc.co.uk/2/hi/europe/6424937.stm (brother & sister – Germany)

http://www.guardian.co.uk/Archive/Article/0,4273,4331603,00.html
(father & daughter – UK)

http://www.slate.comid?2081904/ (sibling incest – US)

Glossary of Terms in the Gay Debate

The Revd John Richardson and Dr Lisa Severine Nolland

Introduction

This is a work-in-progress document which will, we hope, prove useful in defining and clarifying important terms and concepts from a traditional Western historical and religious perspective. We offer it as a tool in order to help comprehension, stimulate thinking, deepen understanding and promote communication.

In this glossary we are approaching terms and concepts from a distinct ideological place; the very inclusion (or exclusion) of certain terms is itself value-laden. But all who communicate do so from a distinct ideological vantage point, whether they realize it or not. The idea of there being an entirely neutral moral outlook is beginning to be seen for what it is – a myth. The issue is, how aware we are of this fact. We stand squarely in the historic orthodox stream of Christianity and perceive things accordingly. Others, from different moral or philosophical starting points, will call things differently. Let us have an honest recognition of how we are using language and what we actually mean by what we say.

Finally, it is important to be aware of the principle that, as the American philosopher, Peter Kreeft, noted recently, 'Control the language and you control thought; control thought and you control action; control action and you control the world.' (*Boston College Observer*, April 2004) In the last few decades there has been a covert emptying-out, and re-filling of certain key words with new meanings. This process subtly modifies how we perceive and deploy the original word, and also how we consider the matter to which it pertains.

The most obvious example is the term 'partner', which is now the only acceptable term in the public realm for 'wife' or 'husband'. But far more is at stake here. Referring to a wife or husband as a 'partner' in effect neuters the concepts of 'wife' and 'husband', stripping them of the whole range of traditional meanings, including those of sex, gender, permanence and sexual exclusivity. 'Partner' simply means 'my present domestic (including sexual) VIP'. However, this meaning rides on the back of the traditional meanings associated with the words 'wife' or 'husband' and, in so doing, loosens the moorings of collective meaning and value which used to be attached to them. Many of us now refuse even to use the word 'partner' because of the ideological baggage it carries; it is anything but a neutral, 'value-free' term.

Here, then, is the glossary which, for all its lack of neutrality, attempts to render accurately the meaning of some commonly-used terms.

Biological family
A person's biological mother and father and, via them, their siblings, grandparents and wider kin. These links generally provide access to family heritage and culture. See *traditional family*.

Birth-assigned gender
See *gender*.

Bisexual
A person who is sexually, and sometimes emotionally, attracted to both genders, sometimes simultaneously. Many claim this is a sexual orientation or preference.

Celibacy
Abstinence from sexual activity.

Chastity
Restraint from sexual activity outside the context of marriage. May refer specifically to the state of being a virgin.

Civil Partnership
A legally-recognized relationship between people of the same gender, involving most of the legal rights and privileges of marriage, and having legal status in the UK and elsewhere. Now often termed 'marriage' in the media etc.

Closed Relationship, Closed Marriage, 'Exclusive'
Expression frequently used, by those who support *open* relationships, to describe a relationship or marriage where there is no sexual activity other than that within the relationship. See *open relationship*.

Coming Out
The process by which a person begins to declare him- or herself as 'gay', having same-sex attraction, affirming it and being identified by it. See *outing*.

Common-law Marriage
English expression for a relationship between a woman and a man which has the long-term stability of marriage but which has not been legally enacted. In reality, no such legal entity has ever existed and there are no legal privileges attached to such a relationship. See *partnership*.

Continence
Archaic expression for celibacy, found in the Church of England's *Book of Common Prayer.*

Cross-dressing
Wearing the characteristic clothes of the opposite gender. May or may not be accompanied by same-sex attraction, and may or may not involve mimicking the mannerisms of the opposite gender. See *transvestite.*

Drag, dressing in drag
A man, or occasionally a woman, mimicking the mannerisms and dress of the opposite biological gender. Stands for DRessed As a Girl.

Drag Act
A traditional stage-act performed by someone mimicking the mannerisms and dress of the opposite biological gender.

Ex-gay/post-gay
A person (of either gender) who formerly experienced same-sex attraction and who now declares that he or she has left a homosexual lifestyle. This may include people who, in addition, experience an increased emotional and sexual attraction to the opposite biological gender and also, possibly, a reduction in or loss of same-sex attraction.

Ex-Gay Movement
Individuals, groups of individuals, organizations and networks which promote the possibility of change in sexual orientation, and facilitate the processes by which this change may occur. There are two primary approaches which, though different, are equally valid and important; they can operate in overlapping, complementary ways. The first is the overtly Christian/psychological realm of 'inner healing' developed by Mario Bergner, Leanne Payne, Exodus and Living Waters *et al.* The second is the scientific, secular psychotherapeutic realm of 'reparative therapy' developed by Dr Joseph Nicolosi, the (American) National Association for Research & Therapy of Homosexuality (NARTH), *et al.*

F to M
A Female to Male transsexual is a person whose biological gender is female while the gender identity is male.

Fag, Faggot
Pejorative expression for a male homosexual, generally confined to North America.

Faithfulness, Faithful
In the context of human sexuality, F. means abiding by one's marriage vows

to the exclusion of any other sexual relationship. Amongst those who act on same-sex attraction, and where same-sex marriage is not an option, F. generally means remaining in a committed relationship with a partner. For some in the LGBT community, however, a relationship can be considered F. even when sexual acts occur with others, because the issue to hand is emotional faithfulness. See *monogamy* and *open relationship*.

Gay
A man who is attracted, emotionally and sexually, to other men. Preferred term amongst many homosexual men.

Gay Community
Used to refer to those of either biological gender who experience, and accept, the physical expression of, same-sex attraction, and publicly affirm it on a communal level.

Gender/biological gender
Biologically, the condition of being male or female, sometimes referred to as 'birth-assigned gender'. Males have a so-called Y chromosome, paired with a single X chromosome, while females have two X chromosomes, resulting in correspondingly different physical, mental and emotional characteristics. In sociology, human gender is regarded as a complex of culturally conditioned attitudes and behaviours overlaid on a given biological condition. The term 'gender' is frequently used as equivalent to 'sex'.

Gender Expression
The way in which people communicate their personal sense of gender to others through their appearance and behaviour.

Gender Identity
The gender someone feels him- or herself to be, as distinct from his or her biological gender.

Gerontosexuality
A preference for sexual relationships primarily or exclusively with an elderly partner. Some consider this a sexual orientation or preference.

Heterosexual
A person who is attracted, emotionally and sexually, to the opposite sex.

Homophobia
Pejorative term which may be applied to people who exhibit an entire range of negative attitudes to same-sex attraction, and also to those who experience and act upon it. The view that same-sex sexual behaviour is sinful is considered homophobic in certain realms.

Homosexual

A person who is attracted, emotionally and sexually, to those of the same biological gender. Originally a medical term, it is considered pejorative by some people.

Inclusion

The term inclusion refers to the acceptance, particularly into the Church, of those who both experience and express same-sex attraction. This generally involves recognizing, and formally blessing, partnerships based on such attraction. A commonly used term to emphasize acceptance of same-sex practice is 'full inclusion'. See *openness*.

Intergenerational Love

Used to describe what some regard as consensual, legitimate and loving sexual relationships between adults and legal minors. The North American Man/Boy Love Association (NAMBLA), in the past, and other socially 'progressive' groups presently, oppose the legal imposition of an 'age of consent' to sexual relations. Some regard this as a sexual preference or sexual orientation. (Also man/boy love, boy-lovers, girl-lovers.)

Intentional Family

A relationship, not based on traditional heterosexual marriage or biological parenthood, in which two or more partners choose to live together and operate as a family unit. This may include children from past heterosexual relationships, or children produced by collaborative reproductive techniques, such as artificial insemination etc. The phrase 'Love makes a family' is sometimes used in relation to such alternative families. Children 'created' this way are deliberately stripped of one set of genetic origins, with all that this implies, physically and psychologically, both in the present and in the future.

Intersexed

Biological condition of being born with ambiguous sexual characteristics, such as genitalia. Should be used in preference to the term 'hermaphrodite', which refers to organisms which can function biologically as both male and female. Intersexed people may or may not identify themselves as transgender or transsexual.

Lesbigay

Largely North American term for the 'lesbian, bisexual and gay community'.

Lesbian

A woman who is attracted, emotionally and sexually, to other women. Preferred term amongst many homosexual women. See *gay community*.

LGBT
Abbreviation for Lesbian, Gay, Bisexual and Transgender, as in 'LGBT people, community, inclusion, issues, etc'. Other variations include Intersexed (I), Queer (Q), Questioning (Q) and Straight but supportive of LGBT people (S).

M to F
A Male to Female transsexual is a person whose biological gender is male while the gender identity is female.

Marriage
A legally-recognized relationship between two people, usually of the opposite biological gender, which in most cultures is formally expected to be lifelong, though it may be terminated by divorce. There has also been an implicit assumption of sexual exclusivity, though often the double standard of morality has meant that women were expected to be sexually faithful to their husbands but their husbands were not equally expected to be sexually faithful to their wives. Finally, there has been an implicit assumption that for many if not most married people, the bodily union of the wife and husband will result in children at some point. In increasing numbers of Western countries today, marriages or civil partnerships or unions are legally available to individuals of the same biological gender.

Monogamy
Literally, the practice of being married to only one person, traditionally for life. (See also *marriage*.) With the advent of widespread divorce, the term 'serial M.' has been used to describe the practice of marriage to a succession of spouses. Amongst those who act on same-sex attraction, M. refers to having only one partner in a committed relationship. However, some in the LGBT community regard relationships as monogamous even when sexual acts occur with others, because for them they are emotionally monogamous. See *faithfulness* and *open relationship*.

Necrophilia
The desire to engage in sexual acts with dead bodies. Many claim this is a sexual orientation or preference.

Openness
Individuals and organizations who accept the physical expression of same-sex attraction often describe themselves as 'open'. This term may also, however, refer simply to the acceptance of insights and practices from Christian or religious traditions other than one's own.

Open Relationship
Relationship in which partners knowingly engage in sexual acts with other

people outside the relationship. This is not, therefore, regarded as a lack of faithfulness.

Outing
The act of deliberately making public the fact that someone experiences same-sex attraction or engages in same-sex acts, despite the unwillingness of the person that this should be made known.

Partner/ship
An informal or formal relationship between two people (or more, now), of the same or opposite gender. Partnerships may be exclusive (sexually monogamous) or not. Civil Partnerships contain elements of commitment and definite legal status for the 'partners'. See *marriage*.

Polyamoury (US Polyamory), abbr. Poly
Literally meaning 'many loves', a polyamorous relationship openly involves more than two people. Some think in terms of 'ethical non-monogamy'. Such relationships may be heterosexual, bisexual or gay. Some regard this as a sexual preference, others regard it as a sexual orientation.

Polygamy
Being married to more than one person. Where a man has more than one wife, this is technically polygyny. Having more than one husband is polyandry.

Queer
Historically considered pejorative, now often used by LGBT people as a preferred self-identifying expression and a term of reference for ideas, ideologies, cultural manifestations, etc which challenge the assumption of heterosexual 'normality' and 'normativity'. (Also Queer theology.)

Reparative Therapy (also Conversion Therapy, Re-orientation Therapy)
Therapies aimed at re-orientating those with same-sex attraction. Strongly opposed by those who believe that sexual orientation is unchangeable. See *ex-gay/post-gay*.

Same-sex Attraction (SSA)
Being sexually attracted to, and erotically aroused by, people of the same gender, often, but not always, with a corresponding emotional attachment.

Secondary Virginity
A positive embracing of sexual abstinence after being sexually active. 'A commitment to secondary virginity is often made with the goal of remaining abstinent until committed to a life-long monogamous relationship, such as marriage'. (www.medinstitute.org)

Sexual Orientation

Shorthand expression for the condition of being attracted towards, and sexually aroused by, those of the opposite gender (heterosexual S. O.), the same gender (homosexual S. O.) or both genders, sometimes simultaneously, sometimes sequentially (bisexual S. O.) There are also those whose S. O. is regarded by themselves as indeterminate or uncertain. The questions as to whether and how S. O. is determined are matters of dispute.   See *gerontosexuality, intergenerational love, necrophilia* and *polyamoury.*

Sexual Preference

The same concept as sexual orientation, but with the implication that an individual's S. P. may alter.

Sexually Transmitted Infections

Any disease transmitted through sexual activity. Historically, there have been two main STIs which could be acquired through sexual intercourse, syphilis and gonorrhoea; today, there are over two dozen. Some can be effectively treated with antibiotics, some have developed immunity to previously effective antibiotic treatment, while still others have no known cure.   Proper condom usage gives protection from some but by no means all of these STIs.

Sodomy

Archaic expression for the act of anal intercourse, usually between males and supposedly engaged in by the inhabitants of the biblical towns of Sodom and Gomorrah. In law it is sometimes used to cover all forms and expressions of homosexuality. The term is now generally regarded as pejorative, as is 'buggery'.

Straight

Slang or colloquial expression for heterosexual.

Traditional family

A household based around a pair of married biological parents and their offspring. Other close relatives may also be included in a traditional family. See *nuclear family.*

Transgender

An umbrella term including transsexuals, cross-dressers, and people who identify as neither male nor female. For transgender people, their biological gender and their gender identity do not match, and they may seek to make their gender expression match their gender identity. Can also be the preferred term for those who feel that their gender identity differs from their biological gender, but who do not wish to pursue any form of transition. See *gender.*

Transition

The process by which people who identify themselves as transgender, or who are biologically transsexual, change their gender expression. In some cases, this may involve hormone therapy, living as the opposite gender for an extended period of time, or Sex Reassignment Surgery (SRS). In some countries a person may also legally change his or her name and registered biological gender.

Transsexual

People who do not feel that their biological gender matches their gender identity. Transsexuals may or may not choose to alter their bodies hormonally or surgically. Some transsexuals may also regard themselves as transgender.

Transvestite

Someone who is a cross-dresser. Sometimes considered a pejorative term.

John Richardson was ordained in 1973 after gaining a degree in Biology and Psychology and then studying at St John's College, Nottingham.

Following six years working in Birmingham, including two as priest-in-charge of an inner-city parish, he became chaplain to what was then the North East London Polytechnic, later the University of East London. After another two years in parish work in the East End, he became Associate Minister in the United Benefice of Henham, Elsenham and Ugley. He also spent a year, in 1993, studying for a Diploma in Theology at Moore Theological College, Sydney.

Lisa Severine Nolland's doctoral dissertation (University of Bristol) has recently been published as *A Victorian Feminist Christian: Josephine Butler, the Prostitutes and God* (Paternoster) and she currently works as a lay chaplain. She has taught in North America and the UK at primary, secondary and tertiary levels and is website consultant for Anglican Mainstream.net. She lives in Bristol with her husband, John, their teenage daughter, Elisabeth and, until his death, a beautiful Golden Retriever, Shem – and is step-mother to David, whose mother died when he was seven. For more than twenty years she and John have been connected with Trinity College, Bristol, where John is Vice Principal. To help her cope with 2008, she regularly escapes into the realms of the English historical and literary past, *Just William*, architecture and botany. Her claim to fame is that of being related to a *Titanic* steerage survivor, Oscar Hedman, her irascible great-uncle, ironically known as Uncle Happy.

Audience Participation

Dr Lisa Severine Nolland

Many might feel very discouraged – perhaps even quite hopeless – after reading *God, Gays and the Church.* If this applies to you, please think again. We have raised various worrying – even deeply alarming – issues here which we hope will inform and alert, but not demoralize! This final section gives concrete, practical suggestions on what can be done positively in response.

A few preliminary remarks need to be made here in relation to public responses.

1. You have the right and the responsibility to make your contributions to the public square. If you are concerned about the common good your voice counts as much as anyone else's. You are not doing anything other than what is to be expected of citizens from all walks of life. If in doubt, think 'Islam' – these deeply committed folk know that what they believe is right; they are not intimidated by PC pressure and neither should you be.

2. If you make responding 'a big deal', it will simply never happen, given the pressured, stressful, over-busy lives most of us have. This is easily seen as a task too difficult, a task better 'left to the professionals'. We couldn't disagree more! Your response won't move the world, but it will give it a bit of a nudge. And you will feel less victimized, voiceless and disempowered. The comment of CS Lewis (in a quite different context) is appropriate: 'The great thing is to prevent his doing anything ... The more often he feels without acting, the less he will be able ever to act, and, in the long run, the less he will be able to feel'. (*Screwtape Letters*, XIII)

3. Decide what type of response you can manage: i.e. the short, polite (more like a vote) 'This is my view ...', with the addition of a significant reason or two, versus the longer, more sophisticated explanatory response. Depending upon circumstances, both can work.

4. Tone is almost everything! Keep it warm and courteous, but clear and firm. Some who read your response will be on your side already, while some in the middle might be moved a bit. If you are in regular contact with the group you are contacting, be positive about what you can, as well.

Concrete suggestions include:

o   Make sure you are educated and up-to-date, and personally 'sorted', on these matters yourself; you need to have worked out your own views and why you hold them. If there are skeletons in your closet inhibiting your being able to relate to sexual issues, please deal with them! They help no one – including yourself – and ensure your silence and passivity.

o   Parents and grandparents, talk to your children and grandchildren about sex, even about (what seems to you to be) truly horrific far-too-graphic sexual matters. If you do not, they will find out elsewhere. They need to hear about these matters from you first: what is out there, what your views are, and why you hold them. Your opinion actually counts for far more than you might think.

o   Encourage your pastor/vicar/minister, youth worker, etc. to take a strong, loving, informed lead from the pulpit, or in the youth group etc.

o   Find out what is being taught in your child's (or grandchild's) school in terms of sex, values and family life.

o   If you find helpful, informative 'stuff', share it with those who might know less but be on your side. Informal support is invaluable: cultivate a circle of friends who are similarly concerned, and willing to work and pray together.

o   When you read about alarming developments – or see content on television or film or wherever – deal first with the emotions elicited by the 'news' and then with the material in question. The two must be separated. Otherwise, you simply vent emotionally but fail to help the cause. Indeed, it is likely to be counterproductive, for whoever is dealing with your response has to handle your emotions – which will likely produce a defensive reaction in return – as well as the content of your concern. After you have dealt with the feelings, review your current resources (time, energy, etc.) and decide on what is the most manageable and profitable response.

o   Receive regular e/mailings or keep up to date via CARE, Christian Institute, Lawyers' Christian Fellowship, Christian Concern for our Nation, Evangelical Alliance, etc. (UK) or Alliance for Marriage, Breakpoint/Charles Colson, Catholic Resource Centre, Focus on the Family, iMAPP, LifeSiteNews, etc. (North America), to be aware of the latest cultural developments.

- Try to maintain a generous, positive attitude towards those with whom you disagree. Moreover, understand that many might support you but have other 'Causes' closer to their heart. For some the pressures and choices of life mean they will never be able to do much though they would like to. Still others would help but do not because there is a subconscious horror of the concrete, the practical, or a belief that unless they agree with everything they cannot do anything. Such is life. Find those with whom it does work, and work with them. And do try to avoid the 'uneasy intensity' (CS Lewis again) which is so off-putting to those outside.

- Believe that God knows all about it and is in control of this too!

- Pray!

Annex[1]

General Synod debates on Wednesday, 28 February 2007: Motions and Amendments

On the morning of Wednesday, 28 February 2007 this was the Private Member's Motion put forward by the Revd Mary Gilbert, of the diocese of Lichfield:

> I beg to move:
>
> 'That this Synod acknowledge the diversity of opinion about homosexuality within the Church of England and that these divergent opinions come from honest and legitimate attempts to read the Scriptures with integrity, understand the nature of homosexual orientation, and respect the patterns of holy living to which lesbian and gay Christians aspire; and, bearing in mind this diversity,
>
> (a) agree that a homosexual orientation in itself is no bar to a faithful Christian life;
>
> (b) invite parish and cathedral congregations to welcome and affirm lesbian and gay Christians, lay and ordained, valuing their contributions at every level of the Church; and
>
> (c) urge every parish to ensure a climate of sufficient acceptance and safety to enable the experience of lesbian and gay people to be heard, as successive Lambeth Conferences in 1978 (resolution 10), 1988 (resolution 64), and 1998 (resolution 1.10) have requested.'

The House of Bishops, some weeks before the February Synod, had put down a major amendment to this motion, and this had been circulated to all members. After the Revd Mary Gilbert had opened the debate and several speakers had followed, the Bishops' amendment was put forward by the Bishop of Gloucester, the Rt Revd Michael Perham:

> I beg to move as an amendment:
>
> '*Leave out* all words after "this Synod" and *insert* the words:
>
> "(a) commend continuing efforts to prevent the diversity of opinion

---

[1] See above, *The Stage is Set* p. 4

about human sexuality creating further division and impaired fellowship within the Church of England and the Anglican Communion;

(b) recognize that such efforts would not be advanced by doing anything that could be perceived as the Church of England qualifying its commitment to the entirety of the relevant Lambeth Conference Resolutions (1978: 10; 1988: 64; 1998: 1.10); and

(c) affirm that homosexual orientation in itself is no bar to a faithful Christian life or to full participation in lay and ordained ministry in the Church.".'

This amendment from the bishops was challenged by a further amendment, put forward by Mr John Ward, of the diocese of London:

I beg to move as an amendment to the amendment:

'(i) After paragraph (b) *insert* as a new paragraph

"(c) welcome the opportunities offered by these Lambeth resolutions, including for the Church of England to engage in an open, full and godly dialogue about human sexuality;"

and re-letter the remaining paragraph accordingly; and

(ii) at the end of paragraph (d) (as re-lettered) *insert* the words "and acknowledge the importance of lesbian and gay members of the Church of England participating in the listening process as full members of the Church".'

This amendment was carried. So too was the House of Bishops' amendment, as amended by this one.

In the afternoon, the second Private Member's Motion was on the topic of Civil Partnerships. It was put forward by the Revd Paul Perkin, of the diocese of Southwark, and his Motion attracted **110** signatures, which represents the support of **23.5%** of the total membership of General Synod. It read as follows:

I beg to move:

'That this Synod, deeply concerned that

(a) in an understandable desire to remedy injustice and remove unjust discrimination, the Government's Civil Partnership Act undermines the distinctiveness and fundamental importance to society of the relationship of marriage;

(b) The House of Bishops' Pastoral Statement, while reiterating the Church's basic teaching on marriage, has produced a recipe for confusion by not stating clearly that civil partnerships entered into under the CP Act would be inconsistent with Christian teaching;

(c) the House of Bishops' Pastoral Statement has given to bishops the task of ensuring that clergy who enter into these partnerships adhere to Church teaching in the area of sexuality without giving the bishops the clear means to do so;

(d) by declaring that laypeople who enter into such partnerships should not be asked about the nature of their relationship, in the context of preparation for baptism and confirmation, as well as for the purposes of receiving Holy Communion, the Bishops' Pastoral Statement has compromised pastoral discipline at the local level;

declare its support for bishops, clergy and other ministers who continue to minister the godly discipline required by the Scriptures and the Canons and request the House of Bishops to set up a study of the ways in which that discipline is being applied and the implications thereof for future pastoral guidance and bring a report to Synod by the July 2007 group of sessions.'

This motion too was amended, well in advance, by the House of Bishops. Their major amendment was put forward by the Bishop of Liverpool, the Rt Revd James Jones:

I beg to move as an amendment:

'*Leave out* all words after "this Synod" and *insert* the words:

"(a) acknowledge the diversity of views within the Church of England on whether Parliament might better have addressed the injustices affecting persons of the same sex wishing to share a common life had it done so in a way that avoided creating a legal framework with many similarities to marriage;

(b) recognize the House of Bishops' Pastoral Statement as a balanced and sensitive attempt faithfully to apply the Church's teaching to civil partnerships; and

(c) note the intention of the House to keep the matter under review."'

Later on, this amendment from the Bishops was challenged by an amendment from the Revd Paul Collier, of the diocese of Southwark:

I beg to move as an amendment to the amendment:

'*Leave out* paragraphs (b) and (c) and *insert*:

"(b) note the intention of the House to keep their Pastoral Statement under review".'

This amendment succeeded, as did the Bishops' amendment, as amended by this one.

In both debates, the original motion was completely overtaken, against the wishes of the proposer, by an amendment from the House of Bishops. But in both cases this amendment was altered by a significant amendment from a member of Synod.